Material Handling Equipment Operation

Richard Skiba

Copyright © 2024 by Richard Skiba

All rights reserved.

No portion of this book may be reproduced in any form without written permission from the publisher or author, except as permitted by copyright law.

This publication is designed to provide accurate and authoritative information in regard to the subject matter covered. While the publisher and author have used their best efforts in preparing this book, they make no representations or warranties with respect to the accuracy or completeness of the contents of this book and specifically disclaim any implied warranties of merchantability or fitness for a particular purpose. No warranty may be created or extended by sales representatives or written sales materials. The advice and strategies contained herein may not be suitable for your situation. You should consult with a professional when appropriate. Neither the publisher nor the author shall be liable for any loss of profit or any other commercial damages, including but not limited to special, incidental, consequential, personal, or other damages.

Skiba, Richard (author)

Material Handling Equipment Operations

ISBN 978-1-76350-130-0 (paperback) 978-1-76350-131-7 (eBook) 978-1-76350-132-4 (Hardcover)

Non-fiction

Contents

Preface	1
1. Introduction	3
2. Forklifts	15
3. Order Pickers	81
4. Telehandlers	128
5. Elevating Work Platforms	227
6. Reach Stackers	295
7. Truck Trailer Side Loader	354
8. Pushback Tugger Truck	385
References	420
Index	422

Preface

This book covers a selective range of material handling equipment, specifically forklifts, order pickers, telehandlers. elevating work platforms, reach stackers, truck trailer side loaders and pushback tugger trucks. For each of these, the uses, key components, operating principles, preparation for operations, operational practices, safe operation and finalising operations is covered.

The material handling equipment information provided within this book is intended to be general in nature and may not encompass all aspects of its operation. It is important to note that each item of plant or equipment has its own specific characteristics and operational requirements that may vary. Material handling equipment operators are strongly advised to consult the manufacturer's guides and manuals prior to the operation of any crane to ensure compliance with safety standards and operational procedures.

Furthermore, it is crucial to acknowledge that operations and terminology can differ across jurisdictions. Material handling equipment operators should be aware that regulations and guidelines pertaining to equipment usage may vary depending on the location. Therefore, it is essential for crane operators to familiarize themselves with the applicable laws, regulations, and standards in their respective jurisdictions.

Additionally, material handling equipment operators are urged to review workplace policies and procedures before operating any crane.

Workplace-specific protocols may exist to address unique hazards and safety considerations, which must be adhered to for safe crane operation.

Moreover, it is important to recognize that in many jurisdictions, operational licensing requirements apply. Material handling equipment operators are responsible for ensuring that they meet all jurisdictional legislative requirements relevant to their sites of practice. This may include obtaining appropriate licenses, certifications, or permits to operate cranes legally and safely within their jurisdiction.

Sample load charts, specifications, interpretations and calculations are used throughout this book for demonstration purposes only and should not be taken to be sued in any other manner. Every equipment model is accompanied by its own distinct load chart and characteristics, which may vary depending on the equipment's configurations and rated capacity and is supplied by the equipment's manufacturer. They are not portable from one model to another, and operators must always ensure they are referring to documentation relevant to the plant they are operating.

While efforts have been made to provide accurate and informative equipment operation information, users are reminded of the need for due diligence and compliance with applicable regulations, manufacturer guidelines, workplace policies, and licensing requirements to ensure safe and lawful crane operations.

Chapter One

Introduction

Material Handling Equipment (MHE) constitutes a versatile array of machinery and tools utilized across manufacturing, distribution, warehousing, and logistics processes to facilitate the movement, storage, protection, and control of materials and products. This equipment forms an integral component of industrial and commercial settings, ensuring the smooth flow of materials within various operations. MHE encompasses a diverse range of machinery and tools, including forklifts, conveyors, cranes, pallet jacks, hoists, elevating work platforms, reach stackers, and order pickers, among others. Each type of equipment serves specific purposes and is tailored to handle distinct materials and loads efficiently.

The primary functions of material handling equipment revolve around lifting, transporting, positioning, sorting, storing, and safeguarding materials and products. As an example, forklifts are commonly employed for lifting and transporting heavy loads, conveyors facilitate the movement of materials along fixed paths, while pallet jacks are utilized for loading and unloading palletised goods. Efficient material handling is pivotal for optimizing productivity, reducing labour costs, minimizing material damage, and ensuring workplace safety.

Proper selection and utilization of material handling equipment streamline operations, improve workflow, and enhance overall efficiency in industrial and warehouse environments. Safety remains a paramount concern in material handling operations, necessitating thorough operator training and adherence to safety protocols to prevent accidents, injuries, and damage to goods. Integration with inventory management software, warehouse management systems (WMS), and enterprise resource planning (ERP) systems enables seamless coordination and control of material flow throughout the supply chain. Material handling equipment plays an indispensable role in modern manufacturing, distribution, and logistics operations, contributing significantly to increased efficiency, productivity, and safety in handling materials and products.

A forklift, also known as a lift truck, fork truck, or forklift truck and as shown in Figure 1, is a powered industrial truck used to lift, move, and stack materials. It typically features two forks at the front that can be raised and lowered for lifting and carrying loads. Forklifts are widely used in warehouses, distribution centres, manufacturing facilities, and construction sites to handle a variety of materials, including palletised goods, crates, boxes, and other heavy items.

Forklifts come in various sizes and configurations, ranging from small electric-powered models for indoor use to larger diesel-powered or propane-powered models for outdoor and heavy-duty applications. They are equipped with different types of tyres suitable for different surfaces, such as solid rubber tyres for indoor use and pneumatic tyres for outdoor use.

Figure 1: Yale forklift. Artaxerxes, CC BY-SA 3.0, via Wikimedia Commons.

Operators control forklifts using a steering wheel and pedals to manoeuvre the vehicle and lift and lower loads. They are trained to operate forklifts safely, adhering to specific procedures and safety protocols to prevent accidents, injuries, and damage to goods. Forklifts are essential equipment in material handling operations, offering efficiency and versatility in lifting and transporting materials within industrial and commercial environments.

An order picker, also known as a stock picker or order selector, is a type of forklift designed specifically for use in warehouses and distribution centres to fulfill orders and retrieve items from storage shelves or racks. Unlike traditional forklifts that lift and carry loads on pallets, order pickers feature a platform or cage that lifts the operator vertically to reach items stored at various heights.

Order pickers are typically used in facilities with high-density storage systems, where items are stored on multiple levels of shelving or racking. The operator stands on the platform, which can be raised and lowered hydraulically, allowing them to access items on different shelves without the need for a separate ladder or elevated platform.

Operators use order pickers to navigate through aisles and select specific items from storage locations based on customer orders or inventory requirements. This process is known as order picking or order selection. Order pickers are equipped with controls for steering, lifting, and lowering the platform, as well as safety features such as guardrails and harnesses to protect the operator while working at heights.

Figure 2: Order Picker being used in a warehouse. National Archives at College Park - Still Pictures, Public domain, via Wikimedia Commons.

Order pickers play a crucial role in warehouse operations, helping to increase efficiency and accuracy in order fulfillment processes. They enable operators to quickly and safely access items stored at various heights, allowing for more efficient picking and packing of orders and improving overall productivity in the warehouse.

A telehandler, see Figure 3, also known as a telescopic handler or a telescopic forklift, is a versatile piece of material handling equipment commonly used in construction, agriculture, and industrial settings. It features a telescopic boom or arm that can extend forward and upward, with attachments such as forks, buckets, or platforms at the end.

Figure 3: Telehandler 3 tonne. ERab123, CC BY-SA 4.0, via Wikimedia Commons,

Telehandlers are designed to lift, move, and place heavy loads or materials in areas that are difficult to reach with conventional forklifts or cranes. They offer greater reach and flexibility compared to traditional forklifts, making them suitable for a wide range of applications.

These machines are equipped with hydraulic systems that control the extension and retraction of the boom, as well as the lifting and lowering of the attached load. Some telehandlers also have features like 360-degree rotation of the boom and outriggers for added stability when lifting heavy loads at height.

In construction, telehandlers are often used for tasks such as lifting and positioning building materials like pallets of bricks or bags of cement, transporting materials across uneven terrain, and working at height to place loads on rooftops or upper floors of buildings. In agriculture, they are utilized for tasks such as loading and stacking hay bales, moving feed or equipment, and operating various attachments for handling crops.

Overall, telehandlers are valued for their versatility, manoeuvrability, and ability to perform a wide range of tasks in diverse environments, making them essential equipment in many industries.

An elevating work platform (EWP), also known as an aerial work platform (AWP) or a mobile elevated work platform (MEWP), is a mechanical device used to provide temporary access to elevated areas for work purposes. EWPs are commonly used in construction, maintenance, repair, installation, and cleaning tasks where workers need to reach heights that are beyond the reach of ladders or scaffolding.

These platforms typically consist of a work platform or basket that is mounted on a mechanical arm or boom, which can be raised, lowered, and maneuvered to the desired height. The platform may be supported by hydraulic, pneumatic, or mechanical systems, allowing it to be elevated vertically or extended horizontally.

There are various types of elevating work platforms, including:

1. Scissor Lifts: These platforms have a scissor-like mechanism that extends vertically, providing a stable and relatively large work area. Scissor lifts are commonly used for indoor maintenance and construction tasks.

2. Boom Lifts: Also known as cherry pickers or telescopic booms, these platforms feature an extendable boom that can reach up and over obstacles, allowing workers to access elevated areas at

varying heights and distances. See Figure 4 for an example.

3. Vertical Mast Lifts: These platforms have a single vertical mast that raises the work platform vertically. They are suitable for tasks that require access to tight or confined spaces, such as warehouses or narrow aisles.

4. Personnel Lifts: These compact lifts are designed for vertical access to elevated areas and are often used for tasks like changing light fixtures, painting, or ceiling repairs.

Elevating work platforms are equipped with safety features such as guardrails, harness attachment points, emergency lowering systems, and stability controls to ensure the safety of operators and workers. Proper training and certification are typically required for individuals operating EWPs to prevent accidents and ensure safe use.

Figure 4: Window cleaner on Haulotte HA15IP EWP. Dmitry Ivanov., CC BY-SA 4.0, via Wikimedia Commons.

A reach stacker, as shown in Figure 5, is a specialized type of material handling equipment used in ports, shipping terminals, and container yards for lifting, moving, and stacking ISO standard shipping containers. These heavy-duty vehicles are designed to handle containers of various sizes and weights with efficiency and precision.

Figure 5: Reach stacker of CVS Ferrari in Haders West Railway Station. - Ori Baratz, CC BY-SA 4.0, via Wikimedia Commons.

The main components of a reach stacker include a lifting frame, telescopic boom, spreader attachment, and a chassis with wheels for mobility. The telescopic boom can extend and retract, allowing the reach stacker to lift containers from ground level or from atop other containers, reaching heights sufficient for stacking or loading onto trucks, railcars, or ships.

Reach stackers are highly versatile and can handle containers in various configurations, including single, double, or triple stacks. They are equipped with sophisticated hydraulic systems for precise control of lifting, lowering, and positioning of containers. Some reach stackers also feature rotating cabs, allowing operators to have a better view of the work area and improve manoeuvrability.

These vehicles play a crucial role in container logistics, facilitating the efficient movement of containers between different modes of transportation and storage facilities. They help optimize container handling operations, reduce turnaround times, and improve productivity in ports and terminals.

Safety is a paramount consideration when operating reach stackers due to the heavy loads and potential risks involved. Operators must undergo specialized training and certification to ensure safe and proficient operation of these machines. Additionally, reach stackers are equipped with safety features such as overload protection, stability control systems, and alarms to prevent accidents and ensure the well-being of workers and equipment.

A truck trailer side loader, also known as a sidelift or sidelifter, is a specialized type of trailer used for transporting and loading ISO shipping containers. Unlike traditional trailers that require external lifting equipment like cranes or forklifts to load and unload containers, a side loader has built-in hydraulic lifting mechanisms that allow it to lift containers on and off the trailer without additional equipment.

Figure 6: Truck with trailer with side loader and container. 111 Emergency from New Zealand, CC BY 2.0, via Wikimedia Commons.

The truck trailer side loader consists of several key components essential for its operation. Firstly, the chassis provides the structural framework of the trailer, constructed from steel to withstand the weight of loaded containers. Secondly, the hydraulic lifting mechanism, powered by hydraulic cylinders, pumps, and controls, facilitates vertical movement of containers onto or off the trailer. Telescopic arms extend horizontally from the trailer's sides to engage with containers, their hydraulic adjustments accommodating various container sizes. Twist locks secure containers to the arms during transportation. A control panel, situated near the operator's cab, houses controls for hydraulic functions and twist lock engagement. Finally, the operator's cab contains steering controls, hydraulic levers, and monitoring gauges, allowing for safe and efficient operation of the side loader.

Truck trailer side loaders are commonly used in intermodal freight transportation and logistics operations, where they offer significant advantages in terms of speed, flexibility, and efficiency compared to traditional loading methods. They are particularly useful in areas where access to cranes or forklifts is limited or where rapid container handling is required.

A pushback tugger truck, commonly known as a pushback tractor, is a specialized vehicle used at airports for manoeuvring aircraft on the ground. It is primarily employed for pushing back aircraft from the terminal gate to the taxiway, as well as for repositioning aircraft within the apron area.

Figure 7: Pushback tractor. Photograph by Radosław Drożdżewski (User:Zwiadowca21), CC BY-SA 4.0, via Wikimedia Commons.

A pushback tugger truck, essential for manoeuvring aircraft on the ground at airports, comprises several key components. These include the chassis, providing structural support for the vehicle and designed to endure the stresses of pushing heavy aircraft. Powered by a robust engine, typically diesel, it delivers the necessary torque for moving large commercial planes. The transmission system facilitates smooth acceleration and deceleration, with options ranging from automatic to manual transmissions. A towing hitch at the front enables connection to aircraft for towing via towbars or towbarless systems. The operator's cab houses steering controls, pedals, and monitoring instruments for vehicle performance, while some models feature hydraulic systems aiding in steering, braking, and providing additional power for heavy pushes. Additionally, towing equipment varies based on aircraft type, accommodating different towing methods such as towbars or towbarless systems.

Chapter Two

Forklifts

Forklift trucks are essential for transporting and stacking materials efficiently within various industrial and warehouse settings. They typically feature a short wheelbase and a vertical mast, facilitating the vertical movement of loads. Forklift trucks come in two main types: counterbalanced and non-counterbalanced.

Figure 8: Komatsu Counterbalanced Forklift. George Armstrong, Public domain, via Wikimedia Commons.

Counterbalanced forklift trucks, see Figure 9, utilize the front wheel axle as a fulcrum, akin to a lever. The load is counterbalanced on one side by the weight of the machine on the other side. This design allows all the weight behind the point of balance to act as a counterweight, ensuring stability during lifting and stacking operations.

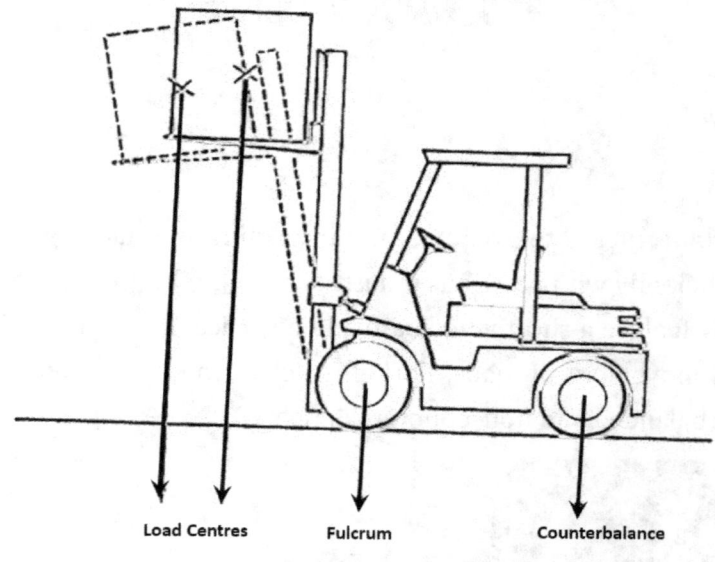

Figure 9: *Counterbalance Forklift Truck.*

On the other hand, non-counterbalanced forklift trucks see Figure 10, such as 'reach' or 'straddle' trucks, have the centre of the load positioned behind the fulcrum point. These trucks are adept at reaching out to deposit loads or straddling stacks for load deposition. It's crucial to note that they should not carry loads unless the reach is retracted. Non-counterbalanced forklifts are particularly useful for specific load stacking tasks and offer greater versatility than their counterbalanced counterparts, especially in warehouse environments where manoeuvrability and precise load placement are paramount.

MATERIAL HANDLING EQUIPMENT OPERATION

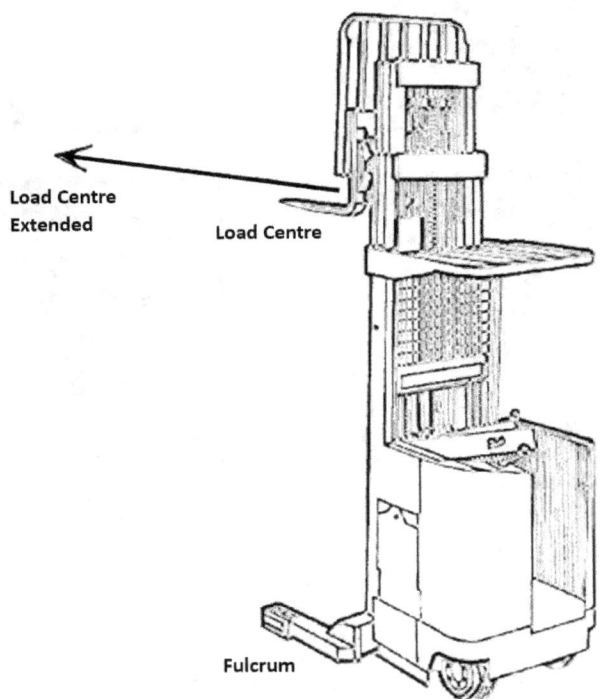

Figure 10: Non-counterbalanced Forklift Truck.

Forklifts are designed with a 3-point suspension system, even in four-wheel counterweighted forklifts, where the rear wheels are centrally attached to the main body, allowing for lateral movement that affects stability (Sanders, 2008). The combination of a high centre of gravity and a narrow wheelbase further contributes to their lateral instability (Sanders, 2008).

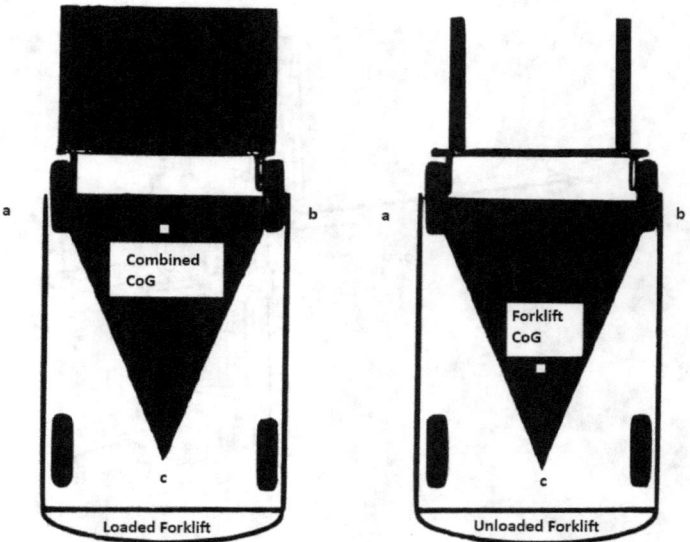

Figure 11: Stability Triangle with loaded and unloaded forklift.

Forklifts have 3-point suspension formed from the front drive axle (a and b) and the steering axle point at the rear of the base (c). As such, the centre of gravity (CoG) changes between a loaded and unloaded forklift as shown in Figure 11 and Figure 12.

Center of gravity (CG) is the point at which the entire weight of an object can be considered to act, causing the object to behave as if all its mass were concentrated at that single point. In simpler terms, it's the point around which an object's mass is evenly distributed in all directions.

In the context of forklifts, understanding the centre of gravity is crucial for safe operation. Forklifts are designed to lift and carry heavy loads, and the distribution of weight plays a significant role in their stability and manoeuvrability. Here's how the centre of gravity relates to forklifts:

1. Stability: The stability of a forklift depends on the position of its centre of gravity relative to its wheelbase. Ideally, the centre of

MATERIAL HANDLING EQUIPMENT OPERATION

gravity should remain within the triangle formed by the forklift's three points of contact with the ground: the two front wheels and the rear steering axle. If the centre of gravity shifts outside this triangle, especially towards the rear or sides, the forklift becomes unstable and prone to tipping over.

2. Load Handling: When lifting a load with a forklift, the centre of gravity of the combined forklift and load system changes. Forklift operators must ensure that the load is properly balanced and centred on the forks to maintain stability. If the load is unevenly distributed or too heavy, it can cause the centre of gravity to shift, increasing the risk of tipping.

3. Cornering and Manoeuvring: During turns and manoeuvres, forklift operators must be mindful of the shifting centre of gravity. Sharp turns or sudden changes in direction can cause the forklift's centre of gravity to shift, potentially leading to instability. Operators should avoid abrupt movements and maintain a slow, controlled speed to minimize the risk of tipping.

4. Overhead Clearance: Forklifts often operate in areas with limited overhead clearance, such as warehouses and loading docks. Operators must be aware of the forklift's mast height and the location of the load relative to the centre of gravity to avoid collisions with overhead obstacles. Raising the mast too high or carrying a load that extends beyond the forklift's stability limits can compromise safety.

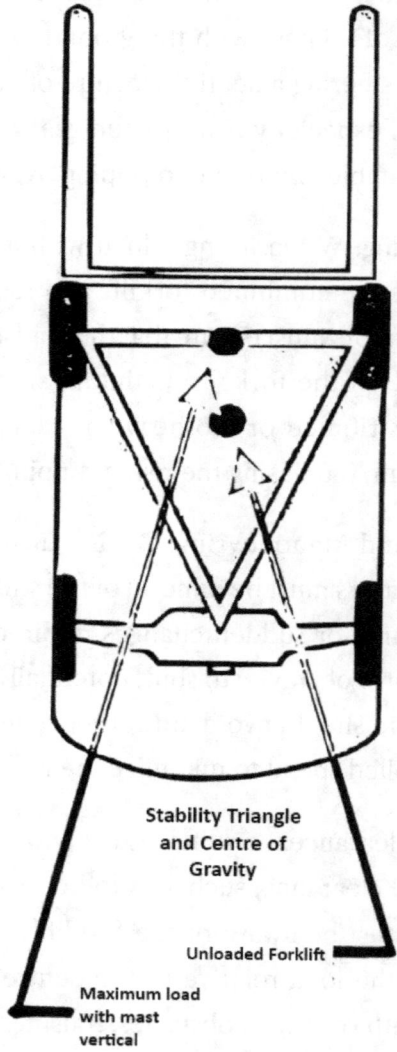

Figure 12: Stability triangle centre of gravity.

Forklift Components

Forklifts consist of numerous components and mechanisms essential for their proper functioning. Familiarizing oneself with the terminology and structure of these parts is crucial for clear communication with colleagues during work tasks. Below are some key elements and components that constitute the anatomy of a forklift truck. The key components are shown in Figure 13.

Figure 13: Forklift components. Back image - Davest3r08, CC BY-SA 4.0, via Wikimedia Commons.

The mast of a forklift serves as the vertical support structure responsible for raising and lowering loads. Positioned typically towards the front of the forklift, the mast lies within the operator's line of vision, allowing for efficient operation. Forklift masts are equipped with various sections, such as duplex, triplex, or quad configurations, enabling the elevation or descent of the forklift carriage along with the forks. Understanding the features and terminology associated with forklift masts, including lift height, free lift height, extended height, and lowered height, is essential when selecting a forklift tailored to specific operational requirements (Logisnext, 2024).

The lift cylinder of a forklift is responsible for powering the vertical movement of the mast, enabling the raising or lowering of the forklift carriage and forks. Operating hydraulically, the lift cylinder functions as a single-acting hydraulic cylinder, exerting force in one direction. Similarly, the tilt cylinder controls the tilt movement of the carriage and adjusts the angle of the forks relative to the ground. The forklift carriage assembly, positioned in front of the mast, serves as a platform for mounting objects controlled by the mast, including the forks and load backrest. Forks, also known as tynes, are the components directly engaging with loads for transport, available in various sizes and shapes to accommodate diverse applications (Logisnext, 2024).

Additionally, the load backrest, attached to the carriage, provides a surface to support loads and prevents them from slipping backward during lifting and travel. It also safeguards the mast components from damage. The counterweight, installed onto the forklift, helps offset the weight being lifted, ensuring stability during lifting and traveling operations. Serving as the power source, forklifts can be powered by engines or batteries, depending on the type. Tire types, including cushion and pneumatic tyres, vary based on operational requirements, with different tire layouts catering to indoor or outdoor environments. The operator cab, whether open or enclosed, houses the controls and features necessary for forklift operation, while the overhead guard enhances safety by protecting operators from falling objects (Logisnext, 2024). Understanding the anatomy of a forklift is crucial for safe and efficient operation in various industrial settings.

Forklift designs vary, and not every forklift configuration will include all the features discussed above.

Forklifts offer a range of customizable options, including fuel type, capacity, lift height, and mast options, among others. When considering purchasing a forklift, it's crucial to consult experienced professionals who can guide you in making the best decision based on your business's materials handling requirements.

The following outlines the various fuel types available for forklifts, delineating their purposes and advantages across different applications.

Understanding these fundamentals will aid in selecting the optimal forklift for your business's materials handling needs.

Electric Forklifts: Battery Electric Forklift

Electric-powered forklifts are predominantly utilized for indoor materials handling, especially on flat, concrete surfaces. One significant advantage of battery electric forklifts is their eco-friendliness, as they do not produce harmful emissions from burning fossil fuels. They are cost-effective to operate and operate quietly, reducing noise pollution in the workplace. Recent advancements in technology have substantially improved the performance of forklift batteries, allowing for longer operating hours, typically covering an 8-9 hour shift. Although the initial cost of electric materials handling equipment may appear higher, the long-term savings on maintenance and charging make it the most cost-effective fuel option.

Figure 14: Crown 35SCTT Electric forklift (36 Volt). Rjluna2, CC BY-SA 4.0, via Wikimedia Commons.

LPG and Petrol Forklifts: Dual Fuel Engine Forklift

LPG and Petrol-powered forklifts, also known as internal combustion forklifts, are better suited to heavier handling tasks and outdoor environments. Modern models feature fuel-efficient technology and lower emission rates compared to older versions. These forklifts can operate for extended periods and can be conveniently refuelled when necessary, unlike electric forklifts that require charging cycles between uses. LPG and Petrol-powered forklifts often come with dual fuel capabilities, allowing owners to switch between fuel types as needed. LPG is particularly popular due to its easy availability and quick replacement process. However, if onsite refuelling stations are unavailable, LPG may be the preferred fuel option. When opting for a forklift with dual fuel capabilities, it's essential to inspect and service both fuel delivery systems regularly to maintain engine performance.

Figure 15: LPG fuelled forklift. TaurusEmerald, CC BY-SA 4.0 , via Wikimedia Commons.

Diesel Forklifts: Powerful Diesel Engine Forklift

Diesel engines offer greater power output, making them ideal for larger forklifts and outdoor, rough terrain, and heavy handling applications. Although diesel forklifts incur higher fuel and maintenance costs in the long run, they are well-suited for industrial applications with rigorous handling requirements.

Figure 16: A forklift with diesel engine. Plenumchamber, Public domain, via Wikimedia Commons.

LPG, Petrol and Diesel Forklifts: Forklifts powered by fossil fuels can be employed for indoor and container handling applications, provided that the indoor areas are well-ventilated. Operators and onsite personnel should be equipped with appropriate personal protective equipment to mitigate risks associated with inhaling hazardous emissions and industrial noise. Regular servicing and daily inspections of fluid levels are crucial for minimizing ongoing maintenance costs and ensuring optimal forklift performance over its lifespan. Adhering to manufacturers' specifications for servicing prevents damage to major components and enhances overall forklift performance.

Working Load

The working load of a forklift refers to the maximum weight that the forklift can safely lift and transport under normal operating conditions. Understanding and adhering to the working load limits of a forklift is crucial for ensuring safety in the workplace and preventing accidents, injuries, and damage to property.

Each forklift model is designed with a specific working load capacity, which is determined by factors such as the design of the forklift, the structural strength of its components, and the stability of its operation. Exceeding the working load capacity of a forklift can lead to instability, tipping, or structural failure, posing serious risks to operators and bystanders.

To determine the working load capacity of a forklift, operators should refer to the manufacturer's specifications, which are typically displayed on a rating plate or capacity plate affixed to the forklift. This information includes the maximum load capacity at various load centres, lift heights, and fork configurations. It is essential to consult this information before operating the forklift and to ensure that loads do not exceed these specified limits.

Factors that can affect the working load capacity of a forklift include the position of the load on the forks, the height to which the load is lifted, and the stability of the ground surface. Operators should also consider environmental conditions such as wind, slope, and obstacles that may impact the safe operation of the forklift.

In addition to knowing the working load capacity of the forklift, operators should also be trained in proper load handling techniques, including how to safely position, secure, and transport loads. Regular maintenance and inspections of the forklift, including its lifting mechanisms and structural components, are essential for ensuring continued safe operation and preventing overloading issues.

By understanding and adhering to the working load limits of a forklift, operators can help maintain a safe working environment and prevent accidents and injuries associated with overloaded or improperly handled loads.

A forklift's load capacity refers to the maximum weight it can safely carry at a specified load centre. If the load is not positioned precisely at the designated centre, the forklift's capacity will be reduced accordingly.

The load capacity data plate provides information about the load each forklift can safely handle under various conditions, including different mast angles or when equipped with attachments. This plate typically includes details such as the load capacity, lift height, load centre distance, brand, and model number. Additionally, it may indicate:

- Any reduction in lifting capacity when a mast is attached.

- Specific down ratings for identified attachments listed on the capacity plate.

As an example of a load plate, Figure 17 shows the load plate for a Clark CY100PD, shown as Figure 18.

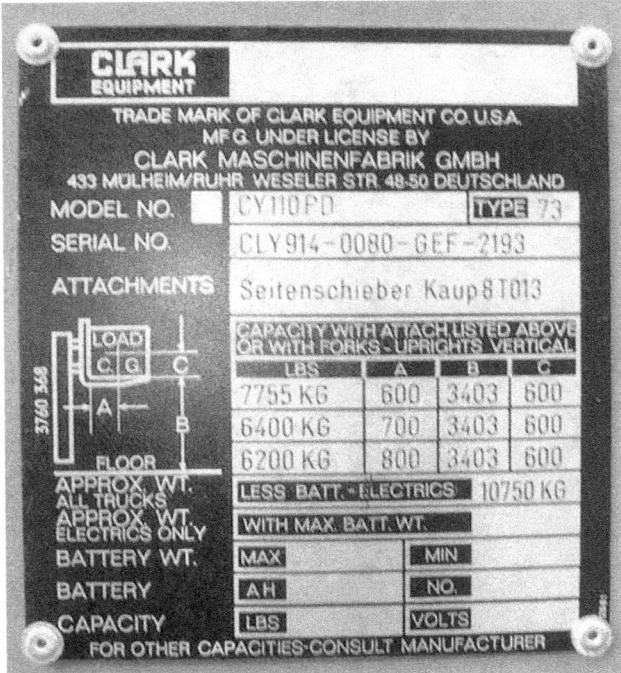

Figure 17: Load capacity data plate for Clark CY100PD. Norbert Schnitzler, CC BY-SA 3.0, via Wikimedia Commons.

Figure 18: German Clark forklift CY100PD. Norbert Schnitzler, CC BY-SA 3.0, via Wikimedia Commons.

The Load capacity data plate shown in Figure 17 indicates that the forklift has a load centre of 600mm and maximum lift height of 3403 mm. The load centre refers to the horizontal distance from the face of the forks to the centre of gravity of the load being carried. It is a crucial factor in determining the stability and safe handling of loads by a forklift.

MATERIAL HANDLING EQUIPMENT OPERATION 31

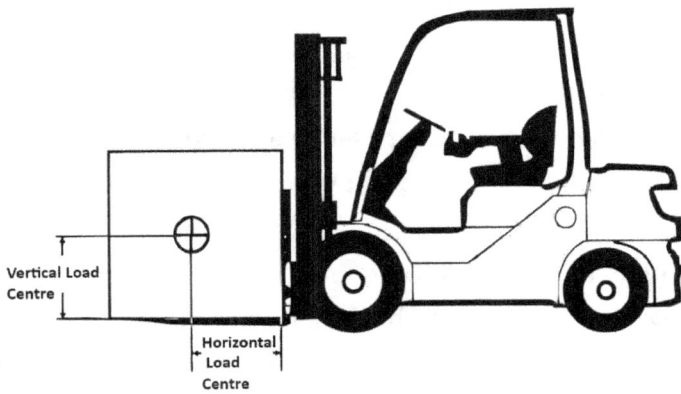

Figure 19: Vertical and horizontal load centres.

The load centre is typically measured from the front face of the forks to the centre of the load being lifted. For standard loads, this distance is often standardized, such as 24 inches (600 mm) or 48 inches (1200 mm). However, it can vary depending on the dimensions and weight distribution of the load. Figure 20 shows another example data plate, also with a load centre of 600mm.

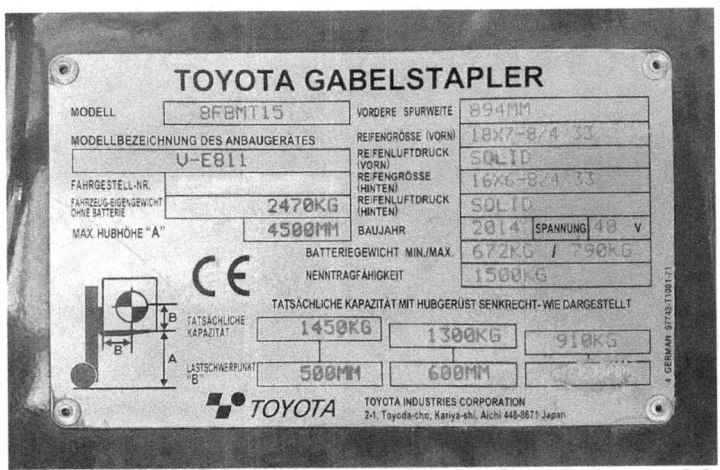

Figure 20: Toyota Gabelstapler data plate. D-Kuru, CC BY-SA 4.0 , via Wikimedia Commons.

Understanding the load centre is essential because it directly affects the forklift's stability and lifting capacity. When a load is positioned farther from the forklift's mast, it creates a greater moment or leverage, which can make the forklift less stable and reduce its lifting capacity. Conversely, positioning the load closer to the mast decreases the leverage and enhances stability.

When attachments are added to a forklift, it can alter the dynamic and operational characteristics of the vehicle. It's crucial for attachments to have both rated and de-rated capacities. Operators should have access to information regarding the de-rated capacity of the forklift when attachments are utilized.

The load-carrying capacity of a forklift is significantly influenced by the lift height or maximum fork height. Forklifts with taller masts may have a higher carrying capacity at lower lift heights compared to maximum lift heights. Therefore, some forklifts with tall masts may feature a dual capacity rating, allowing operators to handle heavier loads at lower heights.

Insufficient understanding of a forklift's load capacity poses serious risks to operators and those around them. Forklift operators should be knowledgeable about:

- How a load's weight, shape, and size affect the forklift.

- The correct method for positioning a load.

- The distinction between the forklift's model number and its load capacity plate.

Stability

Lateral instability, in the context of forklifts, refers to the tendency of a forklift to tip over sideways due to an imbalance in the distribution of weight. Forklifts are designed with a narrow wheelbase relative to their height, which can make them susceptible to tipping if they are not operated with care, especially when carrying heavy loads or navigating uneven terrain.

Several factors can contribute to lateral instability in forklifts:

1. Uneven Weight Distribution: If the load being carried by the forklift is not properly centred or is disproportionately heavy on one side, it can cause the forklift to lean to one side, increasing the risk of tipping over.

2. High Center of Gravity: Forklifts typically have a high centre of gravity due to their elevated masts and loads being carried at height. This high centre of gravity makes them more prone to tipping over sideways, especially when turning or negotiating slopes.

3. Cornering at High Speeds: Making sharp turns or cornering at high speeds can destabilize a forklift, particularly if the operator does not reduce speed or counterbalance the centrifugal force generated during the turn. This can lead to lateral instability and potential tipping.

4. Uneven or Sloped Terrain: Operating a forklift on uneven or sloped terrain can exacerbate lateral instability. The incline of the terrain can shift the centre of gravity of the forklift and its load, increasing the risk of tipping over sideways.

5. Sudden Stops or Acceleration: Abrupt stops or rapid acceleration can disrupt the balance of a forklift, especially if it is carrying a heavy load. The inertia generated by sudden changes in motion can cause the forklift to lean to one side, leading to lateral instability.

To mitigate the risk of lateral instability and tipping, forklift operators should undergo proper training on safe operating procedures.

They should also ensure that loads are properly secured and evenly distributed on the forks, avoid excessive speeds and sharp turns, and be cautious when operating on uneven terrain. Regular maintenance of forklifts, including checking tire pressure and ensuring proper functioning of stability systems, can also help prevent lateral instability accidents.

Take note of the following factors that can influence lateral instability:

- Making sharp turns at high speeds

- Driving across uneven terrain

- Load distribution that is not balanced

- Operating with a flat or under-inflated tire

- Excessive speed while driving

- Traveling with the load raised

- Applying excessive braking force during turns

- Misalignment of the side shift function

- Lifting a load with only one fork arm

- Moving sideways on a sloped surface

- Pulling a load sideways using a jib attachment.

In a forklift, the front wheels serve as a pivot point, with the forks on one side and the machine body on the other. If the weight on the fork ends outweighs the counterweight, it can lead to longitudinal instability, causing the forks to tip upward.

Longitudinal instability, in the context of a forklift, refers to the tendency of the forklift to tip forward or backward due to an imbalance in the distribution of weight along its length. This imbalance can occur when the weight of the load being lifted by the forks exceeds the counterweight of the forklift, causing the front or rear end of the forklift to lift off the ground.

When longitudinal instability occurs, it poses a significant safety risk as it can lead to the forklift tipping over, potentially causing injury to the operator and damage to property. Factors that can contribute to longitudinal instability include carrying heavy loads, improper load distribution, and operating on uneven terrain.

To mitigate the risk of longitudinal instability, forklift operators must adhere to safe operating practices, such as ensuring proper load distribution, avoiding excessive speeds, and not lifting loads beyond the rated capacity of the forklift. Additionally, regular maintenance and inspections of the forklift's components, such as its tyres, brakes, and hydraulic systems, are essential to prevent instability-related accidents.

Operators need to be mindful of the following factors that can contribute to longitudinal instability:

- Exceeding the forklift's load capacity

- Applying abrupt or severe braking

- Improperly adjusting the mast tilt, particularly when carrying loads at elevated heights

- Failing to position the load securely against the heel of the fork arms

- Shifting the load's centre of gravity forward

- Pulling a load towards the forklift's front using a jib attachment

- Lifting a load with a tilted-forward mast when using a jib

- Handling oversized loads

- Installing slipper forks
- Operating the forklift with the reach extended.

Planning for Work

To ensure proper task execution and safety protocols, several steps should be followed:

Firstly, task requirements must be extracted from work orders or equivalent documents and verified with relevant personnel involved. This involves a thorough review of the provided instructions and consultation with supervisors or colleagues to ensure alignment and clarity regarding the scope of work.

Next, adherence to workplace procedures for site inspections is crucial. Familiarization with these protocols is essential, followed by a comprehensive assessment of the work area to identify any potential hazards or limitations that could impact forklift operations. Detailed documentation of findings, including identified hazards, is imperative for further action.

Subsequently, evaluating the suitability of the operating surface for forklift truck usage is paramount. This involves assessing surface conditions such as terrain and gradients to determine compliance with safety requirements. Any issues detected must be promptly addressed to mitigate risks to forklift operation.

Moreover, determining the compatibility of the forklift truck and its attachments with the intended load requirements is essential. This entails referencing manufacturer specifications to ascertain working load limits and evaluating the weight and dimensions of the load(s) to be handled. Compliance with specified limits ensures safe handling of loads.

Additionally, identifying and managing appropriate paths for forklift operation within the work area is vital. This involves mapping out safe pathways, managing traffic flow, and effectively communicating designated routes to forklift operators and other personnel.

Furthermore, identifying and reporting hazard and risk control measures to relevant personnel is critical. This requires a proactive approach to identifying potential hazards associated with forklift operations, assessing associated risks, and promptly reporting findings to supervisors for mitigation.

Ensuring the implementation of a traffic management plan in accordance with workplace procedures is also essential. This involves reviewing and confirming adherence to established traffic management protocols, including designated routes, signage, and communication protocols.

Moreover, identifying appropriate communication procedures with relevant individuals is imperative for ensuring effective coordination and safety. This involves determining communication needs, selecting suitable methods, and clearly communicating procedures to all involved parties.

Finally, confirming coverage of work/task requirements for the relevant work area is essential for task completion and compliance. This entails reviewing identified requirements, confirming task completion, and documenting any deviations or outstanding tasks for record-keeping and future reference.

Every workplace poses potential risks that could lead to dangerous situations. Therefore, operators must conduct thorough inspections of the workplace to identify and mitigate any hazards before commencing forklift operations. In some cases, obtaining a work permit may be necessary to ensure safety compliance.

Key factors to be mindful of include:
- Direction of traffic flow

- Blind spots and corners
- Cross traffic in blind alleyways
- Inclines or slopes
- Ceiling clearance, including low-hanging pipes
- Doorway clearances
- Characteristics of the load (flammable, fragile, unstable, hot)
- High temperatures, especially in areas where LP gas is used
- Condition of road surfaces
- Emissions from the forklift
- Presence of electric overhead wires

It's crucial for other workers and pedestrians to understand the importance of keeping a safe distance from forklift operations, especially during loading, stacking, or when loads are elevated. Any unsafe practices observed should be promptly reported to management. Safety measures such as signage, barriers, and the use of horns and warning lights should be employed to alert personnel about forklift activities, particularly when operating in public areas.

Employers bear the responsibility of providing safe workplaces for all employees and visitors. All parties involved in the workplace must ensure that forklifts are operated safely. Designing separate zones for pedestrians and forklifts in new workplaces can further enhance safety measures.

MATERIAL HANDLING EQUIPMENT OPERATION

Figure 21: Extra care is required where pedestrians are not separated from the travel path. Governo do Estado de São Paulo, CC BY 2.0, via Wikimedia Commons.

Before operating a forklift, a thorough assessment of the workplace and environmental conditions should be conducted to identify and address any potential risks of injury or damage to equipment or loads. While the provided checklist serves as a useful guide, it should be customized to suit individual forklifts and their operating environments. Utilizing the checklist can help ensure safe and efficient forklift operations, minimize injuries, and rectify any unsafe practices.

If you are involved in the storage or handling of flammable dangerous goods, it is essential to adhere to the following guidelines:

- Review Material Safety Data Sheets (MSDS) and package labelling to identify the hazardous properties of each flammable dangerous good.

- Classify areas within the workplace where flammable liquids, gases, or solids are stored or handled as hazardous areas according to relevant standards, for example AS/NZS 60079.10.1:2009 Explosive atmospheres – Classification of areas – Explosive gas atmospheres (IEC 60079-10-1, Ed.1.0(2008) MOD).

- Mark each hazardous area with appropriate markings, warning lights, and signs.

- Keep ignition sources separated from hazardous areas by an appropriate distance or physical barriers.

- Provide comprehensive training and supervision to workers regarding the risk of ignition sources and methods for preventing fire or explosion.

- Avoid using spark ignition forklift trucks (including petrol and LP gas-powered) in any hazardous area.

- Refrain from using any forklift trucks in areas where flammable atmospheres exist continually (zone 0 area), ensuring these areas are free from sources contributing to the flammable atmosphere before forklift entry.

- Strictly adhere to hot work permits at all times, including measures such as monitoring flammable vapor and gas, inspecting the area and forklift before entry, ensuring adequate ventilation, and shutting down processes or materials that may contribute to a flammable atmosphere.

- Utilize forklift trucks compliant with relevant standards, such as AS 2359.12-1996 or non-spark ignition engines in zone 1 areas, implementing an appropriate hot work permit system.

- Use modified forklift trucks or non-spark ignition engine forklifts with an effective hot work permit system in zone 2 areas where flammable atmospheres may occur for short periods.

- Employ forklift trucks specifically designed for use in explosive or flammable areas, ensuring compliance with relevant Australian Standards.

- Provide thorough training to all employees on eliminating risks associated with handling flammable atmospheres and materials, as well as potential ignition sources.

- Enforce a strict 'no smoking' policy in refuelling or battery charging areas.

- Avoid using naked flames when checking levels of battery cells.

- Handle and store liquid fuel and LP gas in accordance with relevant Australian Standards.

- Ensure adequate ventilation in workplaces using LP gas, petrol, or diesel-powered forklift trucks.

- Refuel, park, and store LP gas-powered forklift trucks in well-ventilated areas away from combustible material and sources of heat or ignition, ensuring the LP gas cylinder is turned off when not in use.

- Replace LP gas cylinders following procedures compliant with relevant Australian Standards.

- Recharge and change batteries following correct procedures and in accordance with relevant standards, ensuring the park brake is applied and vent caps are functional.

- Prevent the build-up of flammable gases during battery charging by keeping the battery cover open.

- Use appropriate tools and keep metal objects away from battery cells during battery changing or charging.

- Avoid using liquids with a flashpoint below 61 degrees Celsius for cleaning forklift trucks.

- Adhere to recommendations from flameproofing companies regarding the inspection and maintenance of flameproofing features for flameproofed forklifts.

- Establish and maintain procedures for diesel forklifts with flameproofing, ensuring the spark arrestor tank on the exhaust line is attended to as recommended by the flameproofing company.

Areas where flammable liquids are stored or used are typically designated as having a "hazardous atmosphere". Before being used in such environments, forklifts must undergo modification or "flame proofing" and have a compliance plate indicating this. Diesel-powered forklifts that are flame proofed feature an exhaust water wash box, which needs to be flushed and refilled at the start of every shift. Battery-powered forklifts with flame proofing should not be connected to the battery charger near areas where flammable liquids are handled in open containers. Petrol and LP gas forklifts are not flame proofed due to their spark ignition system.

Extreme caution is necessary when operating forklift trucks in flammable atmospheres or when handling flammable materials. Safe work practices are crucial during refuelling or battery charging. Potential ignition sources include sparks or flames from the exhaust, engine heat, flashback from vapours drawn into the engine, over-revving, excess speeding, sparks from brake components, sparks from tynes striking concrete, static electricity from tyres, or arcs from electrical equipment.

Using non-flameproof forklift trucks in areas where flammable dangerous goods are handled can pose an immediate risk of fire or explosion. Such forklifts should not be allowed into areas where fuels and other flammable materials are mixed, transferred, or decanted.

It's not typical for forklift trucks to be manufactured as flameproof. Flameproofing is usually done as a specialized engineering activity after the initial manufacturing process. The extent of flameproofing depends on the flammable zones where the machine will operate (Zone 1 or Zone 2, never Zone 0). Not all forklift trucks can be economically flameproofed. Generally, it's cost-effective to flameproof forklift trucks with compression engines (diesel fuel) or electric engines but not those with spark ignition engines (LPG fuel or petrol).

Preparing for Work

In forklift operations, maintaining consultation with workplace personnel is crucial to ensure that the workplan aligns with site requirements and complies with safe work procedures. This involves ongoing communication with relevant individuals to clarify any uncertainties and ensure consistency in task execution.

Assessing weather and environmental conditions is essential to determine their potential impact on forklift truck operations. This assessment follows manufacturer requirements and safe work procedures to ensure safe operation under varying conditions.

Risk control measures for identified hazards are systematically checked for implementation to mitigate potential risks. This process involves verifying that the prescribed measures are in place and effectively addressing identified hazards in accordance with safe work procedures.

Accessing the forklift truck in a safe manner is paramount and must adhere to both manufacturer requirements and workplace procedures. This involves following established protocols to safely enter and exit the forklift, minimizing the risk of accidents or injuries.

Regular checks of the forklift truck logbook are conducted to ensure compliance with manufacturer specifications, regulatory requirements, and safe work procedures. Any discrepancies or issues identified are promptly reported, recorded, and addressed in accordance with established protocols.

Pre-start checks are diligently carried out to assess the condition of the forklift truck before operation. Any damage or defects observed during these checks are reported, recorded, and addressed following safe work procedures and manufacturer requirements to maintain safety standards.

According to OSHA's 29 CFR 1910.178(g)(7), all forklifts must undergo examination at least once daily before being put into service (Vector Solutions, 2023). If a forklift operates continuously, inspections should occur after each shift.

The forklift operator is responsible for conducting two types of inspections:

1. Pre-operational visual inspection with the key off.

2. Operational inspection with the engine running.

Both inspections will be detailed in this section, beginning with the pre-operational inspection.

If the forklift operator identifies the need for repair or servicing during these inspections, the forklift must be immediately taken out of service.

General Pre-Operational Inspection Items

Before starting the forklift, visually inspect the following (Vector Solutions, 2023):

- Oil level

- Water level

- Hydraulic fluid level

- Hydraulic hoses for leaks, cracks, or defects

- Mast chains for cracks, breaks, or defects. Chain tension should be checked using a stick or similar device, never by hand.

- Tyres for condition and pressure, inspecting for cuts and gouges

- Forks, including the top clip retaining pin and heel

- Loaded backrest extension

- Finger guards

- Safety decals and nameplates for proper placement and legibility, ensuring information matches the model and service numbers and attachments

- Operator manual for completeness and legibility

- Operator compartment for debris or grease

- Safety belt and all other safety devices for proper functioning

Pre-Operational Inspections for Electric Forklifts

For electric-powered forklifts, include these items in the pre-operation inspection in addition to the general list:

- Cables and connectors for frays, exposure, or damage

- Battery restraints

- Electrolyte levels, ensuring the use of proper personal protective equipment

Pre-Operational Inspections for Internal Combustion Forklifts

For forklifts powered by an internal-combustion engine, include these items in the pre-operation inspection in addition to the general list:

- Liquid propane tank, checking mounting, dents, cracks, and fit within the tank profile

- Pressure relief valve alignment

- Hoses, connectors, and tank restraint brackets for leaks or damage, ensuring the use of proper personal protective equipment

Pre-Operational Inspections for Liquid Propane Forklifts

For forklifts powered by liquid propane, include these items in the pre-operation inspection in addition to the general list:

- Engine oil

- Brake reservoir

- Engine coolant

- Air filter

- Belts, hoses, and radiator condition

- Hood latch functionality

Correct setup of the forklift truck, including the attachment of relevant accessories, is essential as per the work plan and relevant manufacturer requirements. This ensures that the forklift is configured appropriately for the intended task, promoting efficient and safe operation.

Instances of injuries occur frequently when individuals attempt to mount the forklift they are about to operate. Common hazards include:

- Hitting one's head on the overhead cage

- Slipping, tripping, and falling, especially if feet slide off the step

Here are some strategies to mitigate these risks:

- Ensure that hands are clean, dry, and empty before mounting the forklift.

MATERIAL HANDLING EQUIPMENT OPERATION

- Wear suitable shoes or boots with non-skid properties.

- Check footwear for grease or any slippery substances.

- Firmly grasp the handhold for stability. Avoid using the steering wheel as support, as it may move and lead to loss of balance.

- Exercise caution with footing, proceed slowly, and be deliberate in actions.

- Ascend into the forklift cautiously without jumping.

Figure 22: Grasp the handhold for stability entering the forklift.

Adherence to these simple safety practices is essential. Further, when disembarking from a forklift, always verify that the parking brake is engaged, the forks are lowered, and the controls are neutralized.

Figure 23: *Seatbelt must be worn. Navy Medicine from Washington, DC, USA, Public domain, via Wikimedia Commons.*

Visibility is crucial. Avoid operating forklifts in poorly lit areas or when visibility is obstructed.

A significant portion of forklift-related injuries arises during mounting or dismounting, often resulting in musculoskeletal back injuries. Reviewing the design of access steps, grab rails, and the positioning of controls and foot pedals can help minimize this prevalent injury.

Forklifts should feature steps with secure footing, anti-slip surfaces, and grab handles to ensure three points of contact while mounting or dismounting. These considerations are vital when procuring a new forklift.

Reducing the frequency of mounting and dismounting can also decrease the incidence of slips, trips, and falls.

Forklift operators commonly suffer from neck and back strains. Neck injuries often occur due to upward gaze during high stacking or looking behind while reversing. Implementing aids to limit neck strain can help mitigate these injuries.

Back strain may result from encountering bumps or driving on uneven surfaces. Workplaces experiencing these injuries should assess and enhance the quality and condition of forklift seats and road surfaces.

Soft-tissue injuries to the neck and back, such as sprains and strains, can lead to long-term health issues. Employers can realize substantial returns on investment by purchasing or leasing ergonomic forklifts, thus preventing these injuries.

Operational checks are routinely performed to verify the proper functioning of the forklift truck during operation. Any identified damage or defects are promptly reported, recorded, and addressed in accordance with manufacturer requirements and safe work procedures to maintain operational integrity.

Hazard and risk control measures are continuously monitored for implementation and communicated to individuals in the work area. This ensures that everyone is aware of the existing hazards and the corresponding control measures in place, promoting a safe working environment in accordance with established procedures.

The following provides a generalised forklift Starting Sequence:

1. Turn the key in the ignition to start the forklift.

2. Ensure the shifter lever, located under the left side of the steering wheel, is in the centre position for neutral.

3. Activate the emergency brake lever on the left side of the machine by pulling it down.

4. Insert the key into the ignition on the right side of the steering

column and turn it forward to start the forklift's engine.

5. Lift the fork up by 2–4 inches (5.1–10.2 cm) using the control levers located to the right of the steering wheel. Adjust the levers according to the forklift manual to raise the fork's tines off the ground.

6. Depress the brake pedal located to the left of the accelerator pedal before releasing the emergency brake. Keep your foot on the brake pedal to prevent the machine from moving.

7. Use the shifter to select the direction of travel. Push the shifter forward for forward motion or pull it back for reverse. Ensure the shifter is in the neutral position when stopped.

8. Press the accelerator pedal, located beneath the steering wheel on the right side, with your right foot to start moving. Begin with a slow speed until you are accustomed to operating the forklift.

9. Utilize the horn, located at the centre of the steering wheel, when passing through busy areas or intersections to alert others.

10. Turn the steering wheel in the desired direction while driving, using the knob on top for better control. Make sharp turns cautiously, especially when the back of the tines approaches corners.

11. When driving in reverse, maintain awareness of your surroundings and use caution, especially when making tight turns due to rear-wheel steering.

MATERIAL HANDLING EQUIPMENT OPERATION 51

Figure 24: Maintaining awareness of surroundings and using caution in reverse. Maria Rachel Melchor, Public domain, via Wikimedia Commons.

The controls of a forklift may vary depending on its model. Prior to operating a forklift, it is essential for operators to acquaint themselves with the controls through a thorough walkthrough of the operator cabin. This ensures that the operator can effectively and safely manoeuvre and control the forklift.

Operators may refer to the forklift owner's manual for clarification on unit controls.

Hand Controls: The initial set of forklift controls are manually operated and are typically situated near the steering wheel column. These controls are responsible for directing the movement of the unit and the forks.

Directional Controls: Similar to driving a car or other heavy machinery, forklifts feature a set of directional controls including a steering wheel, indicators, parking brake, and transmission controls. These controls, when combined, enable the operator to manoeuvre the forklift safely and accurately within a work environment.

Steering Wheel: Positioned at the centre of the operator cabin, the steering wheel allows the operator to turn the wheels left or right to navigate the forklift in the desired direction.

Transmission Controls: Forklifts are equipped with simplified transmission controls - forward, neutral, or reverse. Operators can select either forward or reverse to move the forklift in the chosen direction.

Parking Brake: Similar to a car, forklifts feature a parking brake that, when engaged by the operator, securely holds the unit in place.

Indicators: A crucial safety feature in busy environments, indicators signal to other forklift operators and pedestrians the intended direction of the forklift.

Hydraulic Tyne Controls: Located beside the steering wheel column, the hydraulic tyne controls enable the operator to manipulate the hydraulic movements of the forks. Depending on the forklift model, these controls may consist of lift knobs or fingertip controls.

Forklifts typically have three or four hydraulic controls, including those for raising and lowering the forks, tilting the forks, and adjusting the carriage and forks' side-to-side movement. Some forklifts may also feature a fourth hydraulic control for fine-tuning the width of the forks to accommodate smaller pallets or irregular loads.

Foot Controls: Within the forklift operator cabin, several control pedals are situated on the floor. Leading manufacturers such as Hyster and Yale maintain a standard automotive layout for these pedals across their forklift models.

Accelerator Pedal: This pedal regulates the forklift's acceleration and speed, with pressing or releasing the pedal controlling the speed of travel.

Brake Pedal: Serving as a critical safety feature, applying pressure to the brake pedal activates the brakes, safely reducing the forklift's speed to comply with speed limits or bringing it to a complete stop.

Clutch Pedal: Larger combustion engine forklifts may be equipped with a clutch pedal, allowing operators to adjust acceleration by shifting gears.

Inching Pedal: Often positioned to the left of the steering wheel column, opposite the other pedals, the inching pedal enables operators to make precise movements while providing full power to the hydraulic controls.

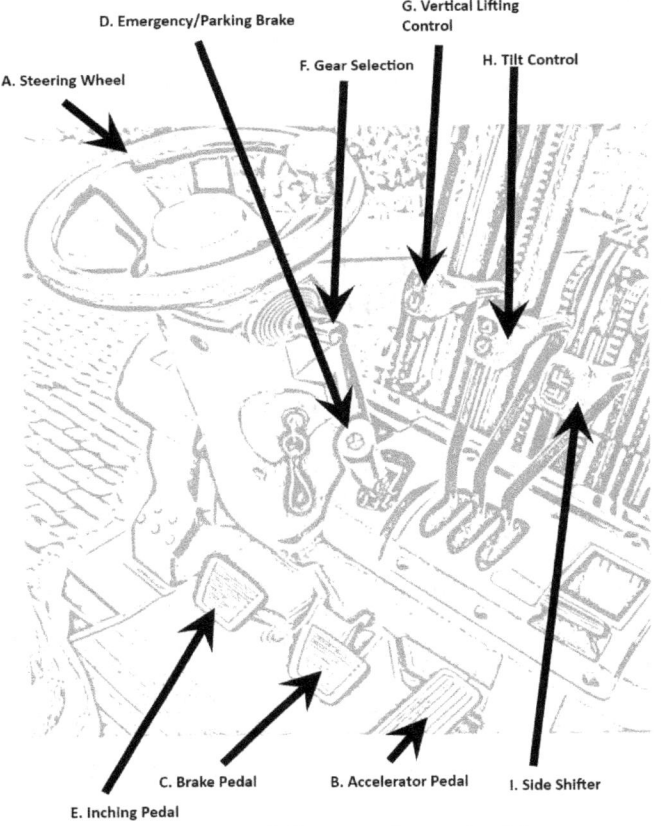

Figure 25: Forklift controls, typical layout.

Most forklifts operate similarly to a standard automatic-transmission car, featuring a key-start ignition, a centrally positioned steering wheel (A), an accelerator pedal on the right (B), and a brake pedal (C) on the left or centre (referring to Figure 25). The emergency/parking brake, depending on the model, may be a larger lever on the left side (D) or a floor pedal.

An inching pedal (E) might also be present on some forklifts, situated on the far left. The inching pedal disengages the transmission without requiring the forklift to be shifted into neutral during a lift, akin to the function of a clutch in a standard-transmission car. This enables the operator to make small adjustments near a load without relying solely on the main brake pedal. However, not all models include an inching pedal, and some operators may opt not to use them.

To shift gears on a forklift, an arm on the left side of the steering wheel (F) is typically used, similar to where a turn indicator would be located in a left-side drive car. Moving the lever upwards shifts the forklift into drive, positioning it in the middle activates neutral, and moving it downward places the forklift into reverse, often accompanied by an audible beeping sound.

Despite having a rear-steering axle with limited manoeuvrability, the steering wheel controls operate in the same manner as those of a standard automobile—turning clockwise steers the forklift right, while turning counterclockwise steers it left.

To operate a forklift's lifting controls, the necessary levers are usually located on the operator's right side in a series of either three or four levers.

- (G) The first lever from the left controls vertical lifting, allowing the operator to pull back to lift the front attachment and push forward to lower it.

- (H) The second lever from the left controls tilt, enabling the operator to tilt the entire attachment assembly backward or forward by pulling back or pushing forward. Some forklifts may have a button on this lever for automatic leveling of the fork attachment.

- (I) The third lever from the left is the side-shifter, allowing horizontal movement of the fork attachment. Pulling it back moves the fork to the right, while pushing it forward moves it to the left.

Operating the Forklift

Many individuals assume that operating a forklift is straightforward, akin to driving a car (Vector Solutions, 2023). However, driving a forklift differs significantly from driving a car, necessitating an understanding of various factors before operating the truck. Forklift trucks should solely be utilized on stable, level surfaces. In instances of unstable terrain, four-wheel drive or rough terrain types should be employed.

Safety Procedures: Implementing a comprehensive set of safety operating procedures for every workplace device is imperative. These procedures should be regularly updated and accessible to all staff through training sessions. Here's what to do:

- Provide comprehensive training and information for operators covering all aspects of forklift truck operation and maintenance. Maintain records of training sessions attended by each operator.

- Wear suitable personal protective equipment (PPE) when necessary, such as during battery changing or charging activities.

- Before commencing each shift, conduct a thorough inspection of the forklift truck and attachments, including lift and tilt systems, brakes, steering, controls, tyres, warning devices, and more.

- Establish safety protocols for fuel handling and storage, as well as battery changing and charging procedures.

- Develop a method for determining the weights of loads being handled.

- Ensure work areas are safe for forklift truck use, implementing measures such as fitting raised edges on loading docks, installing warning signs or barricades, imposing speed limits, providing adequate lighting, and using secure ramps to access work areas.

When Raising the Load: Ensure safe practices when lifting loads by adhering to the following guidelines:

- Keep loads as low as possible at all times.

- Apply the handbrake when raising or lowering the load.

- Use hydraulic controls gently to avoid jerky movements.

- Ensure forks are centred when entering a pallet and avoid tilting the mast backward or forward.

- Avoid allowing forks to protrude through a pallet.

- Ensure the load rests against the heel of the fork arms for proper load centring.

- If the load weight is unevenly distributed, position the heavier end against the heel of the fork arms.

- Confirm the forks are centred on both sides of the mast.

- Adhere to load capacity limits and avoid overloading pallets.

- Prevent unwrapped loads from extending more than a third

MATERIAL HANDLING EQUIPMENT OPERATION

above the load backrest extension to avoid potential hazards.

Visibility Concerns While Operating the Forklift: Maintain unobstructed visibility while operating the forklift to minimize accident risks. Follow these requirements and recommendations:

- Keep a clear view and inspect all directions before commencing operation.

- Utilize spotters, rearview mirrors, and aids to enhance visibility.

- Use headlights in dimly lit areas or during night operations.

- Exercise caution when transitioning between bright and dark areas to avoid temporary visibility disruptions.

- Slow down and sound the horn at cross aisles and blind spots to alert others.

- Install physical barriers and warning tracks in areas prone to limited visibility.

Beginning to Drive the Forklift: Before moving the forklift, ensure a clear path by inspecting the direction of traffic. Sound the horn or utilize a spotter if vision is obstructed. Proceed cautiously, watching for hazardous curves, blind spots, intersections, and pedestrian traffic.

When Tilting the Load:

- Elevate the load clear of the stack before tilting it backwards.

- Always travel with the load tilted backwards and kept close to the ground.

- When placing the load down, ensure to bring it over the stack before tilting it forwards.

- Lower the load with the mast vertical or slightly tilted forward.

Travelling:
- Forklifts are single-person vehicles. Avoid carrying passengers unless equipped with an approved seat and footrest under the overhead guard.

- Only lift people using a Workcover approved work platform and obtain Workcover authorization beforehand.

- Keep left in two-way traffic aisles and reduce speed on wet or greasy surfaces.

- Avoid turning a forklift on a sloping surface to prevent lateral stability issues.

- Drive slowly up and down inclines, adhering to manufacturer specifications for hill operation.

- When reversing, always look behind and ensure the path is clear.

- Check surroundings before driving away and avoid sharp turns at high speed.

- Face the forks downhill when driving on inclines without a load to maintain stability.

- In the event of an overturn, stay seated and brace yourself, avoiding any body parts outside the forklift frame.

- Beware of rear-end swing during turns and maintain a safe distance from edges, pedestrians, or objects.

- Ensure the forklift is refuelled only at designated areas, following safety protocols.

- When ending the shift, park the forklift in the designated area, lower the forks, apply the park brake, turn off the forklift, and

MATERIAL HANDLING EQUIPMENT OPERATION

remove the key, never leaving it running unattended.

General Forklift Operation Tips:

1. Ensure operators are qualified and licensed.

2. Wear appropriate safety workwear to prevent accidents.

3. Conduct routine equipment checks before operation, reporting any faults immediately.

4. Follow proper starting procedures, adjusting seat position and mirrors as needed.

5. Adhere to workplace rules and designated roadways while operating the forklift.

6. Operate at a safe speed, making gradual changes in direction and speed.

7. Avoid hazards such as bumps, slippery surfaces, and loose objects.

8. Ensure the load is stable, secured, and evenly distributed across forks.

9. Maintain clear visibility, using mirrors or spotters if necessary.

10. Use forklifts solely for carrying loads, avoiding unauthorized passengers.

11. Keep clear of the mast and do not walk under loads or machinery.

12. Exercise caution when driving on ramps, moving forward uphill and in reverse downhill.

13. Avoid overloading the forklift, staying within its capacity limits.

14. Use proper refuelling procedures, avoiding open flames or sparks.

15. When ending the shift, park the forklift properly and follow shutdown procedures.

Figure 26: Caution must be taken on ramps and inclines. U.S. Army photo by Sgt. 1st Class Alan B. Owens, Public domain, via Wikimedia Commons.

When operating the forklift at higher speeds, it's crucial to anticipate and take measures to avoid potential hazards, including:

- Tip overs resulting from excessive speed.

- Collisions with pedestrians and obstacles due to lack of attention and insufficient stopping time. In essence, maintain a slower speed and remain vigilant. Additionally, adhere to the following requirements and recommendations:

- Maintain a clear view of the path of travel.

- Operate the forklift at a speed that allows for safe stopping.

- Exercise caution on wet or slippery surfaces by reducing speed.

- If the load obstructs forward visibility, ensure it trails behind.

- Sound the horn and reduce speed at intersections or areas with obstructed views.

- Execute turns smoothly at a safe speed, particularly in confined spaces.

- Ascend or descend grades slowly and consider driving with the load upgrade on steep inclines.

- Avoid running over loose objects and adhere to posted speed limits and warning signs.

Changing the Forklift's Direction of Travel Changing the direction of a forklift poses various hazards, including tip overs, collisions with pedestrians or objects, and potential accidents with other vehicles. To mitigate these risks, follow these requirements and recommendations:

- Always come to a complete stop before changing directions.

- Utilize a horn or warning light to alert pedestrians when reversing.

Steering and Turning the Forklift When steering a forklift, potential dangers include collisions, load falls, and tip overs resulting from sharp turns. To prevent these incidents, adhere to these requirements and recommendations:

- Plan your route ahead and anticipate turns.

- Avoid turning with elevated forks or on grades.

- Reduce speed when turning, especially in confined spaces.

- Exercise caution to account for the wide swing of the forklift's rear end during turns.

- Initiate turns as close as possible to the inside corner to mitigate swing hazards.

Reversing the Forklift Reversing the forklift increases the risk of accidents, including striking pedestrians or objects. Exercise extreme caution when backing up and follow these guidelines:
- Maintain a clear view and look behind when reversing.

- Be mindful of limited visibility and consider using aids like mirrors or spotters.

- Account for noise levels and the possibility of pedestrians wearing hearing protection.

- Leave ample space for pedestrians and avoid grabbing the overhead guard when reversing.

MATERIAL HANDLING EQUIPMENT OPERATION

Figure 27: Reversing to unload. Trondheim Havn from Trondheim, Norway, CC BY-SA 2.0, via Wikimedia Commons.

Operating the Forklift on Grades (Inclines and/or Declines) Operating a forklift on grades presents risks such as tip overs and falling loads. Follow these precautions to mitigate these hazards:

- Drive unloaded forklifts with the forks downgrade.

- Avoid driving loaded forklifts with the load downgrade.

- Drive loaded forklifts forward with the load upgrade when ascending ramps.

- Drive loaded forklifts in reverse with the load upgrade when descending ramps.

- Refrain from turning the forklift while on a grade.

When halting a forklift, initiate braking gradually when preparing to come to a stop.

Handling Loads

The primary objective of operating a forklift is to lift and relocate loads, making it essential to understand proper load handling techniques when driving a forklift. This section will explore various tips and considerations for safely managing loads with a forklift, covering aspects such as preparation, approach, mast positioning, lifting and lowering procedures, high-tier handling, and handling loads in truck trailers and railroad cars.

Before engaging with a load, be mindful of the following:

- Off-centre loads, which may lead to forklift tipping or load instability

- Avoiding overloading the forklift, as it can result in tipping or load displacement

- Checking for any damaged loads

- Ensuring that loads are properly secured and not loose

Furthermore, it is crucial to adhere to the following requirements and recommended practices:

- Secure the load adequately to maintain stability and secure arrangement

- Prioritize wrapping or banding damaged merchandise before transport

- Whenever possible, centre the load for optimal balance

- Exercise caution when handling off-centre loads that cannot be centred

- When dealing with uncentered loads, position the heaviest part closest to the front wheels of the forklift

MATERIAL HANDLING EQUIPMENT OPERATION

- Familiarize yourself with the load capacity of the forklift and avoid exceeding its limits

- Recognize that the forklift's load capacity assumes centred loads; any deviation may impact capacity and pose risks

- Utilize the load extension backrest to enhance load stability and security

It is imperative for operators to prioritize safety precautions and familiarize themselves with different types of loads and forklifts to prevent potential accidents. Neglecting to do so could result in severe consequences, underscoring the importance of thorough training and awareness.

When manoeuvring a forklift on an incline, specific precautions must be observed, including tilting the load back and raising it only as necessary to clear the road surface. Additionally, operators must adhere to the forklift's rated capacity, ensuring that loads do not exceed its specified limits to prevent hazards.

Load carrying presents inherent risks, given the weight and nature of forklifts. Even when traveling at low speeds, forklifts pose a danger, with increased risks when fully loaded and driven at higher speeds. Operators bear the responsibility of ensuring that each load is carried, lowered, and set down in accordance with manufacturer guidelines and company protocols.

The forklift's capacity, indicated by load capacity data plates, serves as a crucial reference point for operators, outlining the maximum weight it can safely lift at a specified load centre. Overloading must be avoided at all costs, as it can lead to damage to the forklift and pose safety hazards to operators and pedestrians.

Furthermore, the shape and size of a load influence the lifting process, necessitating careful consideration to maintain stability. Raising a load compromises the forklift's stability, especially when tilting forwards or backwards, emphasizing the need for caution during operation.

Loading procedures for trucks and large vans require meticulous attention to detail to prevent accidents. Alternately loading pallets on both sides of a truck prevents imbalance and potential overturning. Similarly, loading pantechnicons (large vans) necessitates confirming factors such as mast height clearance, ventilation, weight support, secure bridge plate placement, chocking van wheels, and ensuring the driver's absence from the cabin during loading operations. Additionally, keeping the load low minimizes risks during loading procedures.

Accidents can occur when a forklift operator approaches a load too quickly or turns sharply while approaching it.

To prevent incidents during load approach, adhere to these requirements and recommendations:

- Approach the load slowly and cautiously

- Stop 8-12 inches (20-30 centimetres) in front of the load

- Ensure the forklift is positioned squarely in front of the load

- Confirm that the forks are at the correct height for lifting

- Set the direction control to neutral

- Avoid raising or lowering the forks unless the forklift is stationary and the brake is engaged

- Prior to lifting, ensure there is adequate overhead clearance as visibility may be obstructed after the load is elevated

- Use the inching pedal to slowly manoeuvre the load to the stack

Figure 28: Correct approach to load. Aristidek5maya, CC BY-SA 4.0, via Wikimedia Commons.

The mast, located at the front of the forklift, is crucial for lifting and lowering loads.

Exercise caution to prevent tip overs and load drops while adjusting the mast:

- Use caution when tilting loads with the mast

- Avoid tilting the mast forward with elevated forks unless picking up or putting down a load

- When stacking materials, tilt the mast backward only enough to stabilize the load

- For loads nearing the truck's maximum capacity, tilt the mast back and position the heaviest part of the load against the carriage

- Exercise caution when tilting the mast forward to position the load onto the stack

- Never travel with the load tilted forward, as it increases instability

Figure 29: Mast tilted forward to align to pallet to pick up the load. Aristidek5maya, CC BY-SA 4.0, via Wikimedia Commons.

When positioning the forks to lift a load, be aware of potential hazards such as tip overs, load drops, and collisions.

To minimize these risks, adhere to these requirements and recommendations:

- Ensure forks are level before inserting them into a pallet

- Insert forks under the load sufficiently, with at least two-thirds of the fork length under the load

- Avoid protruding forks through closely stacked pallets

MATERIAL HANDLING EQUIPMENT OPERATION

- Center the load's weight between the forks

- Adjust forks to distribute weight evenly, either manually or with a fork positioner

- Tilt the mast back slightly to stabilize the load after lifting

- Exercise extreme caution when lifting off-centre loads, as they increase the risk of tip overs

After properly positioning the forks, proceed with lifting the load, being mindful of potential hazards such as insufficient clearance, falling loads, and stuck loads.

To mitigate these risks, follow these requirements and recommendations:

- Check for overhead clearance before lifting

- Lift the load approximately 4 inches above the lower stack

- Tilt the mast back slightly to ensure the load rests against the backrest extension

- Ensure the load is not caught on anything

- Return the lift control lever to neutral gradually

After transporting the load, prepare to lower and unload it, being mindful of potential hazards such as falling loads and collisions with objects.

Performing high tiering, which involves stacking materials multiple tiers high using forklifts, introduces specific risks that must be addressed.

These hazards include:

- Overloading the stack

- Risk of tip over

To mitigate these risks, adhere to the following requirements and recommendations:

- Prioritize placing heavier loads at the bottom of the stack and lighter loads at the top.

- Ensure that the load remains below the capacity of the reach truck when the mast is fully extended.

- Exercise caution when extending the reach mechanism forward while depositing a load on the top tier, proceeding slowly and attentively.

- Be mindful when tilting a load forward or backward during high tiering operations.

Forklifts should be taken out of service promptly if any of the following issues arise:

- Mechanical breakdown

- Leakage

- Overheating

- Fire

Adhere to these requirements and recommendations for removing forklifts from service. If a forklift operator identifies any of the following signs, it's imperative to cease operation, park the forklift safely, and seek assistance:

- The forklift is deemed unsafe for operation due to any reason

- Any defects are detected during operation

- Hazardous sparks or flames emanate from the exhaust system of the forklift

- Any component of the forklift exceeds the normal operating temperature

- A fuel system leak is detected

Forklift Attachments

Attachments can significantly impact the stability and Safe Working Load of a forklift, underscoring the importance of using approved jib attachments.

When employing an attachment, adhere to the following guidelines:

- Refrain from rotating the load while in motion if a load revolve mechanism is installed.

- Exercise caution, recognizing that jib attachments tend to be less stable than forks due to their higher centre of gravity.

- Operate the forklift as if it were partially loaded, even when the jib attachment is empty.

- Keep the jib as low as possible and maintain the mast in a vertical or backward-tilted position.

- Avoid lifting loads with a forward-tilted mast when using a jib attachment.

- Do not tilt the mast forward when the jib is loaded.

- Maintain the load at a low height.

- Travel at reduced speeds and execute turns slowly.

- Ensure that jib attachments are correctly secured with the locking bolt engaged.

- Inspect slings before using them for lifting operations.

- Align the hook directly over the load before lifting to ensure stability.

- Display the Safe Working Load on all jib attachments above the lifting points where a lifting hook is attached.

- Confirm that hooks can move at least 15 degrees in all directions and swivel freely.

- Refrain from rotating loads on attachments while the forklift is in motion.

- Be mindful that slipper forks, often used, can alter the load centre.

- Always ensure that the forklift is approved to use attachments. Safe Working Loads for approved attachments will be indicated on the data plate.

Forklift attachments are integral to various workplace tasks, offering benefits such as decreased load-moving time, reduced manpower, fewer employee hours spent operating forklifts, decreased workforce size, lower fuel consumption, and minimized stock damage. However, proper training for operating attachments is essential for operators, complementing their existing forklift operation skills.

When using attachments, it's crucial to recognize that they affect the forklift's load capacity and centre of gravity, diminishing its stability. Thus, operators should drive as if the forklift were partially loaded even before picking up any load. Traveling at slow speeds and making gentle turns is advisable. Additionally, ensure that the attachment is listed on the data plate to ascertain its compatibility with the truck and load type.

Before utilizing an attachment on a forklift, conduct thorough checks:

- Verify that the attachment is suitable for the forklift and load type.

MATERIAL HANDLING EQUIPMENT OPERATION

- Ensure proper attachment to the forklift with an appropriate locking device.

- Confirm that the forklift's data plate permits the use of the attachment.

Figure 30: Range of forklift attachments.

Selecting the appropriate attachment for your specific application can significantly enhance the productivity of your logistics operations. But with numerous configurations available, choosing the right one can be daunting. Today, we'll discuss some of the most common attachments and their benefits to help you make an informed decision.

SIDESHIFTERS (SS): Side Shifters are among the most commonly used attachments today, often coming standard with forklifts. They enable operators to shift the forks (tynes) laterally, making small adjustments without manoeuvring the entire forklift. This two-way hydraulic attachment provides precise side-to-side movement, enhancing stacking accuracy and reducing the need for precise truck positioning.

Benefits:

- Accurate fork positioning without extensive truck manoeuvres.

- Reduced fuel consumption and truck wear.

- Faster loading or unloading times.

- Minimized pallet damage.

FORK POSITIONERS (Fpos): Fork Positioners are another prevalent attachment, allowing hydraulic adjustment of forklift tynes' spacing. This facilitates the handling of pallets of varying sizes and irregular objects, enabling operators to align forks with pallets more accurately and efficiently.

Benefits:
- Accurate fork positioning without manual adjustments.

- Reduced manual labour for fork positioning.

- Decreased fuel consumption and truck wear.

- Reduced pallet damage.

- Improved load handling efficiency.

PAPER ROLL CLAMPS (PRC): Paper Roll Clamps are designed for handling various-sized paper rolls, commonly used in the paper industry. Equipped with automatic pressure controls, these clamps ensure proper pressure allocation without damaging the paper roll. The curved arm design enables efficient handling, including 360° rotation.

Benefits:
- Increased handling efficiency with 360° rotation.

- Reduced paper damage with automatic clamp pressure and diverse clamp pads.

- Tailored specifically for the paper industry.

PUSH/PULL OR SLIP SHEETER (Ppull): Push/Pull attachments are ideal for handling slip-sheet-stacked loads, eliminating the need for

MATERIAL HANDLING EQUIPMENT OPERATION

pallets. They push to unload and pull to load using slip sheets, reducing maintenance costs, storage space, and stock damage.

Benefits:

- Quick installation and removal without fork removal.

- Easy handling of goods with slip sheets. Benefits of Slip Sheets:

- Reduced packaging weight and increased storage space.

- Low cost compared to pallets.

- Elimination of pallet exchange.

CARTON CLAMP: Carton clamps are designed for handling large rectangular or square-shaped objects without pallets, commonly used in various industries. These clamps securely grip uniform, square slip-sheet loads, saving storage space and reducing handling times.
Benefits:

- Elimination of the need for pallets for rectangular/square objects.

- Reduced pallet purchase and repair costs.

- Lowered shipping costs due to no pallets.

- Increased storage space.

- Specialization in handling rectangle and square objects.

- Reduced handling times for various goods.

SINGLE-DOUBLE PALLET HANDLER: Single-Double Pallet Handlers transport single or two pallets side by side, doubling handling capacity. They reduce loading and unloading times and minimize truck manoeuvres.

Benefits:

- Potentially doubles pallet handling capacity.

- Handles both single and double pallets.

- Decreases loading and unloading times.

- Minimizes truck manoeuvres.

- Reduces fuel consumption and truck wear.

ROTATORS: Rotators facilitate load dumping or inversion, capable of rotating a full 360 degrees for versatile handling options.

Concluding Operations

To execute the shutdown procedures for a forklift truck in accordance with manufacturer requirements and safe work procedures, follow these steps:

1. **Refer to Manufacturer Guidelines**: Consult the manufacturer's manual or guidelines specific to the forklift model being used. These documents typically outline the proper shutdown procedures recommended by the manufacturer.

2. **Prepare for Shutdown**: Ensure the forklift is in a safe location away from pedestrian and vehicle traffic. Lower the forks to the ground and retract any attachments. Park the forklift on a level surface.

3. **Engage Parking Brake**: Activate the parking brake to prevent the forklift from moving unintentionally during shutdown.

4. **Turn Off Engine**: Switch off the engine using the designated controls or ignition switch. Allow the engine to idle for a short period before shutting it down completely to allow for proper

MATERIAL HANDLING EQUIPMENT OPERATION

cooling and lubrication.

5. **Disable Power**: If applicable, disable the power source or remove the key to prevent unauthorized use of the forklift.

6. **Inspect the Area**: Conduct a brief inspection of the immediate area around the forklift to ensure there are no hazards or obstacles that may pose a risk during the next operation.

7. **Secure Forklift**: Implement any additional securing measures as required by safe work procedures or company policies to prevent unauthorized access or use of the forklift.

Parking the forklift is a critical aspect of forklift operation, as a parked forklift can pose hazards to both the operator and others nearby. These hazards include the risk of the forklift being parked incorrectly, leading to potential collisions with people or objects, as well as the possibility of the forklift moving unexpectedly.

To mitigate these risks, it is essential to properly secure the parked forklift. An important consideration is that a forklift is considered unattended if the operator is 25 feet away or further, even if the forklift remains within the operator's view. Additionally, anytime the operator leaves the forklift and it is no longer within their sight, even if it is closer than 25 feet away, it is considered unattended.

When parking a forklift, it is crucial to adhere to specific requirements and recommendations to ensure safety:

- Avoid parking on a grade whenever possible.

- Never park in areas designated as unauthorized.

- Ensure the forklift does not obstruct aisles or exits when parked.

- Select an appropriate parking area, following company guidelines and recommendations.

- Apply the brake gradually when preparing to stop the forklift.

- After coming to a complete stop, tilt the mast forward slightly and lower the load fully.

- Neutralize the forklift controls to prevent unintended movement.

- Engage the parking brake once the forklift is stationary.

- Turn off the ignition to further secure the forklift.

- Exit the forklift without jumping, as detailed in the dismounting procedure.

- If parking on a grade, utilize wheel blocks to prevent the forklift from rolling.

By following these procedures and guidelines, operators can ensure that parked forklifts are securely positioned, reducing the risk of accidents and enhancing overall workplace safety.

Getting off the forklift requires the same level of caution as mounting it does. To avoid potential hazards during dismounting, consider the following measures:

- Ensure your hands are clean, dry, and free of any objects before dismounting the forklift.

- Wear appropriate footwear that provides traction and minimizes the risk of slipping.

- Check your shoes for any grease or other slippery substances that could cause instability.

- Utilize the handhold for support when dismounting rather than relying on the steering wheel, which may move unexpectedly.

- Maintain careful footing throughout the dismounting process, proceeding slowly and deliberately.

- Avoid jumping off the forklift; instead, pull yourself up and out of the vehicle safely.

To secure the forklift truck to prevent unauthorized access or use in accordance with safe work procedures, follow these guidelines:

1. **Engage Parking Brake:** Ensure the parking brake is engaged to prevent the forklift from moving unintentionally.

2. **Remove Key:** If the forklift is equipped with an ignition key, remove the key from the ignition switch to prevent unauthorized starting of the vehicle.

3. **Implement Physical Barriers:** Utilize physical barriers such as chains, gates, or barriers to restrict access to the forklift when it is not in use.

4. **Lock Controls:** If available, lock or secure the controls of the forklift to prevent unauthorized operation.

5. **Store Key Securely:** Store the ignition key in a designated, secure location known only to authorized personnel.

6. **Implement Access Controls:** Implement access controls such as key card readers or passwords to restrict access to the forklift to authorized operators only.

7. **Communicate Policies:** Clearly communicate and enforce policies regarding the use and access of forklifts to all employees to ensure compliance and safety.

Chapter Three

Order Pickers

An order picker is a type of forklift used primarily in warehouse and distribution centre settings for picking individual items or cases from high storage locations such as racks or shelves. Unlike traditional forklifts that lift pallets, an order picker is equipped with a platform or cage that allows an operator to elevate themselves to the desired picking height. This enables the operator to access items at various levels within the storage system, making it easier to fulfill customer orders efficiently. Order pickers are commonly used in e-commerce fulfillment centres, retail distribution warehouses, and other facilities where individual item picking is required.

Figure 31: Order Picker. TMHE's New Order Picker – BT Optio OSE250, Toyota Material Handling Europe, unmodified, CC BY-SA 2.0, via Flickr.

An order picker represents a specialized tool designed to expedite piece picking and handle loads without the need for pallets. Here are essential safety tips to ensure operators maintain safety standards when utilizing this equipment in various settings such as customer order warehouses, storage facilities, manufacturing plants, or retail stockrooms (JLG, 2020):

1. Prioritize completing the required order picker training before operating the machinery. Recognized as a Class II electric motor narrow aisle lift truck by OSHA in the US, proper training ensures compliance with safety guidelines and minimizes the risk of workplace incidents, thus safeguarding your organization against potential penalties and protecting staff from associated hazards.

2. Perform a comprehensive hazard assessment tailored to your

MATERIAL HANDLING EQUIPMENT OPERATION

work environment, identifying and addressing potential risks associated with lift operation. Factors such as navigating through congested aisles, managing loads, avoiding obstacles, and inspecting equipment should be thoroughly considered to implement effective risk mitigation strategies.

3. Utilize fall protection measures by securing oneself with a body harness while working at elevated heights. Additionally, take advantage of built-in safety features such as railings and gates to prevent accidental exits from the platform.

4. Maintain control of the equipment by keeping both hands on the controls during operation, regardless of whether it involves driving, stopping, or lifting. This practice ensures operator safety and enhances manoeuvrability, especially in confined spaces.

5. Adhere to designated traffic lanes and remain vigilant of pedestrians and other moving objects within the workspace. Implementing traffic safety protocols, respecting speed limits, and adhering to right-of-way rules help minimize the risk of accidents in shared spaces.

6. Understand the order picker's load capacity and avoid exceeding the specified weight limits. Consult the machine's manual to determine the maximum load capacity, factoring in the combined weight of the load, operator, and any accompanying tools.

7. Wear appropriate personal protective equipment (PPE) tailored to warehouse environments, including safety goggles, slip-resistant boots, gloves, high-visibility vests, and hard hats. These items offer vital protection against various workplace hazards, ensuring the operator's safety during lift operation.

An order picker, also known as a stock picker and as shown diagrammatically in Figure 32, typically consists of several key components that facilitate its operation and functionality in warehouse environments. Here's an overview of the main parts or components of an order picker:

1. **Mast**: The mast is the vertical structure of the order picker that houses the lifting mechanism. It comprises vertical rails or channels along which the carriage travels, allowing the platform or forks to be raised and lowered to access different heights within the warehouse.

2. **Platform or Forks**: The platform or forks are the load-bearing components of the order picker that hold the items being picked or transported. Depending on the design, the platform may be equipped with safety features such as guardrails or gates to prevent falls.

3. **Controls**: Order pickers are equipped with control panels or consoles that allow the operator to manoeuvre the vehicle, raise and lower the platform or forks, and perform other necessary functions. These controls typically include buttons, switches, levers, or joysticks.

4. **Operator Compartment**: The operator compartment is the area where the operator stands or sits while operating the order picker. It may include a platform, cabin, or standing area with safety features such as a non-slip surface and handrails for stability.

5. **Power Source**: Order pickers are powered by electric motors, either battery-powered or connected to an external power source. The power source provides the energy needed to operate the lifting mechanism, drive system, and other electrical components of the vehicle.

6. **Wheels**: Order pickers are equipped with wheels or casters that allow them to move smoothly and manoeuvre within the warehouse. Some models may have swivel casters for enhanced agility and ease of navigation in tight spaces.

7. **Safety Features**: Modern order pickers are equipped with various safety features to protect both the operator and the surrounding environment. These may include proximity sensors, audible alarms, emergency stop buttons, and visual indicators to warn of potential hazards.

8. **Attachments**: Depending on the specific application, order pickers may be equipped with various attachments or accessories to enhance their functionality. Common attachments include side shifters, fork positioners, carton clamps, and paper roll clamps, among others.

The combination of these components enables order pickers to efficiently and safely handle the picking and transportation of goods within warehouse and distribution centre environments.

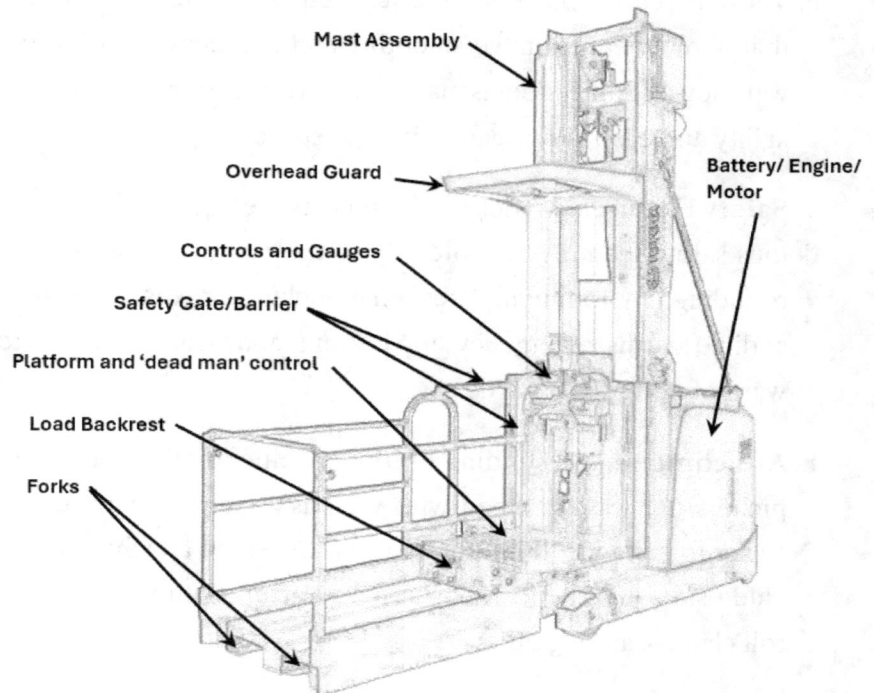

Figure 32: Components of an order picker.

The operational characteristics of an order picker play a vital role in dictating its functionality and performance within the confines of a warehouse or distribution centre. Here's a comprehensive overview of the key operational attributes defining an order picker:

Vertical Lifting Capability stands out as one of the primary operational features defining an order picker. Equipped with vertical masts, these vehicles facilitate operators' access to inventory stored on shelves or racks at various heights. This capability enables operators to efficiently retrieve individual items or entire orders from elevated storage locations.

Manoeuvrability is another critical characteristic of order pickers. Designed to be highly agile, these vehicles can navigate through narrow aisles and tight spaces within the warehouse environment. Such agility is essential for seamless movement between storage locations and accessing inventory across the facility.

Load Capacity denotes the maximum weight an order picker can safely lift and carry. Adhering to the specified load capacity is paramount to prevent overloading, which could compromise both safety and performance. Operators must ensure compliance with these limits during operational activities.

Operator Platform typically features a designated standing area where operators control the vehicle's movements. This platform provides a stable and secure position for operators to access inventory at various heights while ensuring safety during operation.

Controls on order pickers are intuitive and facilitate driving, platform elevation adjustments, and other functions. These controls may include buttons, switches, levers, or joysticks, depending on the specific model and manufacturer, enabling smooth and efficient operation.

Safety Features are integral to order picker design, aiming to protect operators and prevent accidents. Common safety features include guardrails, non-slip surfaces, emergency stop buttons, proximity sensors, and visual indicators, enhancing operational safety within the warehouse environment.

Efficiency is a key objective in order picker design, aiming to streamline picking processes and reduce time and effort required for inventory access. Fast lifting speeds, quick acceleration and deceleration, and ergonomic design contribute to operational efficiency, enhancing productivity within the facility.

Versatility is inherent to order picker functionality, enabling their use in various tasks such as order picking, inventory replenishment, and stock replenishment. Their ability to access elevated storage locations makes them suitable for handling diverse products and materials within the warehouse.

The operator's platform serves as the designated area where the operator stands to manoeuvre the lift truck (also referred to as the operator's station), facilitating order picking tasks typically involving quantities less than a full pallet. Several requirements must be met for the operator's platform (Association Sectorielle Transport Entreposage, 2010):

1. It must incorporate an overhead guard to ensure operator safety.

2. The platform surface should be equipped with a non-slip covering to prevent slips and falls.

3. One or more side guards must be in place, easily deployable to shield the operator from falling hazards during order picking.

Regarding the wood pallet upon which the articles are positioned:
- It should be in sound condition and solely used for merchandise placement.

- A secure hold on the pallet is ensured by a clamp mechanism.

- Movement on the pallet by the operator is discouraged for safety reasons.

Standard wood pallet dimensions typically measure 1220 mm x 1016 mm (48 in x 40 in), with a load centre set at 600 mm (24 in). The pallet clamp is designed to accommodate varying thicknesses of pallet stringers, allowing for versatility in handling different pallet formats. Proper alignment with the gripping device is essential to avoid instability, as inadequate support may result if the pallet is not levelled.

The lift truck's capacity plate provides guidance on load capacity limits. Distributing articles on the pallet according to the manufacturer's guidelines is essential to prevent load destabilization and off-centring, which could diminish the load capacity and compromise safety.

There are generally two types of pallets in common usage: expendable pallets and reusable pallets.

- Expendable pallets, also known as single-use pallets, are designed for a one-time use and are typically considered part of the packaging. These pallets are often crafted from low-grade wood, pressed wood, cardboard, or expanded polystyrene due to their disposable nature.

- It is not advisable to utilize single-use pallets with an order picking truck due to their limited durability and structural integrity.

On the other hand, reusable pallets offer multiple use cycles, distinguishing them from expendable pallets. These pallets are typically sturdier, better constructed, and have a longer lifespan, averaging around five to six years.

Figure 33: Reusable wooden pallet. Dbenbenn, CC BY-SA 3.0, via Wikimedia Commons.

When operating an order picking truck, it is recommended to prioritize the use of reusable pallets. These pallets should meet certain criteria, including being in good condition, robust, and compatible with both the lift truck and the load being transported.

Designed exclusively for order picking purposes, the additional platform is not intended for lifting personnel and can be easily installed or removed without the need to dismantle any part of the hoisting system. Its dimensions can vary depending on specific requirements.

Typically constructed from non-slip metal, the platform features two openings to accommodate the forks of the lift truck for lifting. It is securely locked or permanently affixed to the lift truck to ensure stability during operation.

Compared to a standard wood pallet, the additional platform is heavier and has a load centre positioned farther away, typically at 600 mm (24 in). Consequently, using the platform reduces the lift truck's load capacity by up to 50% (Association Sectorielle Transport Entreposage, 2010).

When employing an additional platform, it is essential to equip the order picking truck with a secondary capacity plate that reflects the reduced load capacities. The load capacity of the platform is determined by the lift truck manufacturer based on a centred distribution of loads on the platform.

The load capacity is determined by various lift height ranges specified on the capacity plate provided by the lift truck manufacturer. As the height of the operator's station increases, the load capacity decreases accordingly. Consequently, the load capacity could inadvertently be exceeded solely by raising the operator's station, even without adding any additional articles.

Without a height indicator for the operator's station, it becomes challenging for the operator to adhere to the prescribed load capacities.

Order picking on the additional platform typically begins with the operator placing items at the far end of the platform and gradually moving towards their operating station. However, this approach may

MATERIAL HANDLING EQUIPMENT OPERATION

result in uneven distribution of weight on the platform, leading to potential underestimation of the actual load weight. Consequently, it often becomes challenging, and sometimes impossible, for the lift truck operator to adhere to the capacity indicated on the additional platform's capacity plate provided by the lift truck manufacturer.

Additionally, the operator must account for their own weight when navigating on the additional platform. The cumulative effect of off-centre loads (referred to as the "lever effect"), combined with the lift height of the operator's station and the operator's weight on the additional platform, contributes to an underestimation of the load's impact on the lift truck's stability, even when the total weight remains below the specified capacity limit.

Various factors, including the total off-centre loads, lift height, and the operator's weight on the additional platform, interact to underestimate the load effect, potentially exceeding the maximum specified load capacities. For operators working at considerable heights, the consequences of a lift truck overturning due to instability resulting from this underestimated load effect could be severe. Hence, it is imperative for the operator to meticulously manage the total weight on the additional platform under such conditions.

Guidance

There are three primary methodologies for steering and guiding order pickers:

1. Operator-Controlled Guidance: This conventional approach relies on operators to manually navigate order pickers within the warehouse. Operators typically use control panels or joysticks to manoeuvre the unit forward, backward, and side-to-side. This method is commonly employed in smaller warehouses or where layouts are straightforward. However, its reliance on operator control may increase the likelihood of accidents and

equipment damage due to the greater freedom granted to operators.

2. Roller Guidance: Roller guidance employs sensors, cameras, and advanced technologies to automate the navigation of order pickers within larger or more complex warehouse environments. Rollers mounted on the order picker's frame interact with guards positioned along the aisle's sides, guiding the unit along a predefined path without requiring manual steering. This system resembles a train-and-track setup and offers advantages such as reduced equipment damage, lower injury risks, and enhanced warehouse productivity.

3. RFID or Wire Guidance: Order picker wire guidance integrates radio frequency identification (RFID) technology, wherein the order picker is equipped with an RFID detector and a wire is embedded beneath the warehouse floor. As the order picker traverses over the RFID wire, it receives signals that enable the onboard navigation system to adjust its route autonomously, avoiding obstacles and hazards. This approach shares the benefits of roller guidance without necessitating modifications to the order picker or the installation of aisle bumpers. However, wire guidance entails significant initial expenses and operational disruptions during installation, which involves skilled personnel cutting notches in the floor, burying the wire, and sealing it with epoxy. Nonetheless, these inconveniences represent a one-time investment unless future route modifications or expansions are required.

Working at Height

Given that order pickers are engineered for operations at elevated heights, it is imperative to comprehend the additional safety protocols that come into play. There are various crucial safety measures to be mindful of while operating order pickers within a warehouse setting (Hinz, 2013).

Operations Beyond 1 Meter from Ground Level: When working at heights exceeding 1 meter, it is essential to lower the machine to 600mm or below before proceeding forward or reversing to the next location. This precaution is crucial as the stability of the load at elevation might be compromised during movement. Following this, the machine should come to a complete stop before being raised to the desired working height again. All order pickers are equipped with limit switches to prevent movement at heights, and tampering with these switches should be strictly avoided.

Figure 34: Working at height with an order picker.

Safe Travel Height: Before making a turn or exiting an aisle, the order picker must be lowered to a safe travel height, which is clear of the ground but below axle height. This measure ensures that the order picker remains stable and does not risk tipping over during manoeuvres.

Harness Utilisation: Operators must wear a harness at all times when operating an order picker, and when in motion, the platform's handrail must be closed. This practice significantly reduces the risk of falls from the order picker.

MATERIAL HANDLING EQUIPMENT OPERATION 95

Figure 35: Wearing a harness at height.

Traffic Management: Effective traffic management plays a pivotal role in ensuring safety while operating an order picker. Creating awareness among individuals about operational areas is the simplest way to mitigate risks. This can be achieved through methods such as posting signs, erecting barriers, or deploying a flag person to regulate traffic flow.

Identification of Potential Hazards: Maintaining vigilance regarding potential hazards within the work area is of utmost importance. Careful consideration should be given to determine the safest path for moving loads and operating the order picker to prevent accidents, injuries to personnel, and damage to machinery, equipment, and inventory. Key factors to watch out for in the work area include the presence of hazards, designated stopping points, areas requiring reduced speed, horn signalling points, the need for reversing, adequacy of ventilation and lighting, available manoeuvring space, appropriate ground surface conditions, and clearance requirements.

Load Effect Indicator

There is a device designed to provide the operator with information regarding the total weight on the additional platform. It takes into account both the lift height and the lever effect, which encompasses the total off-centre loads. When the operator reaches a lift height where the load capacity approaches or exceeds the maximum permitted limit, they are alerted through both audible and visual signals. This device is specifically compatible with the order picking truck and offers real-time updates to the operator regarding changes in the total load on the additional platform during order picking. It considers factors such as the lever effect resulting from the arrangement of articles on the additional platform, the varying lift height ranges, and the operator's own weight when they step onto the additional platform.

Planning for Order Picking Operations

For order picking operations, planning for work includes:
1. Identify Task Requirements:

    - Review work orders or equivalent documents to identify task requirements.

    - Confirm task requirements with relevant personnel.

- Conduct a site inspection according to workplace procedures to ensure alignment with task requirements.

2. Confirm Work Coverage:

   - Verify that all work is confirmed to ensure coverage of task requirements for the relevant work area.

   - Ensure adherence to workplace procedures during the confirmation process.

3. Select Order Picking Forklift Truck:

   - Use relevant methodology to select the appropriate order picking forklift truck.

   - Consider factors such as load type and weight characteristics, workplace conditions, manufacturer specifications, and workplace procedures.

4. Assess Working Area:

   - Inspect the working area to identify potential hazards and obstacles.

   - Determine appropriate paths for operating the order picking forklift truck and moving within the work area.

   - Ensure compliance with workplace procedures during the assessment process.

5. Confirm Traffic Management Plan Implementation:

   - Verify the implementation of the traffic management plan for the work area.

   - Understand and adhere to the traffic management plan in

accordance with workplace procedures.

6. Identify Communication Procedures:

- Determine appropriate communication procedures for co-ordinating order picking operations.

- Test communication methods with relevant personnel to ensure effectiveness.

7. Assess Operating Surface Quality:

- Evaluate the quality and suitability of the work area operating surface for operational use.

- Follow workplace procedures to assess the condition of the operating surface.

To begin with, when preparing for order picker use, the first step is to identify the task requirements. This involves reviewing work orders or any equivalent documents that outline the specific tasks to be completed. By thoroughly examining these documents, operators can gain a clear understanding of what needs to be accomplished during the order picking process. Additionally, it's crucial to confirm these task requirements with relevant personnel, such as supervisors or team leaders, to ensure clarity and alignment.

After confirming the task requirements, the next step is to conduct a site inspection in accordance with workplace procedures. This inspection serves to verify that the work environment is suitable and aligned with the identified task requirements. During the site inspection, operators assess factors such as the layout of storage areas, accessibility of inventory, and any potential hazards or obstacles that may impact the order picking process. By conducting this inspection, operators can ensure that the work area is properly prepared and conducive to safe and efficient order picker operation.

Following the identification of task requirements, the next step in preparing for order picker use is to confirm work coverage. This involves verifying that all necessary tasks for the relevant work area have been acknowledged and accounted for. Operators must ensure that no aspect of the assigned work is overlooked or omitted, as each task contributes to the overall efficiency and productivity of the operation.

During the confirmation process, it is essential to adhere strictly to workplace procedures. This ensures that all necessary steps are taken to confirm work coverage accurately and effectively. Operators should follow established protocols and guidelines to prevent errors or oversights that could potentially lead to delays or operational inefficiencies. By maintaining adherence to workplace procedures, operators can uphold the integrity and reliability of the order picking process.

When selecting an order picking forklift truck, operators must employ a systematic approach to ensure the appropriate vehicle is chosen for the task at hand. This involves utilizing relevant methodology tailored to the specific requirements of the operation. Factors such as the type and weight characteristics of the load, as well as the prevailing workplace conditions, must be carefully considered during the selection process.

Operators should take into account the manufacturer specifications of each available forklift truck model to determine which one best suits the intended task. This includes assessing factors such as lifting capacity, manoeuvrability, and operational features to ensure compatibility with the demands of the job. Additionally, adherence to workplace procedures is essential to guarantee that the selected forklift truck meets all necessary safety and operational standards.

By carefully evaluating these factors and employing a methodical approach to selection, operators can choose the most suitable order picking forklift truck for the task at hand. This ensures optimal performance, efficiency, and safety throughout the order picking process, contributing to the overall success of warehouse operations.

Before commencing order picking operations, it is imperative to conduct a thorough assessment of the working area to ensure a safe and efficient environment for the task at hand. This begins with a comprehensive inspection to identify any potential hazards or obstacles that may pose risks to both personnel and equipment. Hazards such as uneven surfaces, obstructions, or confined spaces must be noted and addressed accordingly to mitigate potential accidents or incidents.

Following the hazard identification process, operators must determine appropriate paths for operating the order picking forklift truck and navigating within the work area. This involves planning routes that optimize efficiency while minimizing the risk of collisions or interference with other personnel or equipment. Factors such as aisle width, visibility, and clearance must be carefully considered when selecting operational paths to ensure smooth and uninterrupted workflow.

Throughout the assessment process, strict adherence to workplace procedures is paramount to ensure compliance with safety regulations and operational guidelines. This includes following established protocols for hazard identification, route planning, and risk mitigation strategies. By adhering to these procedures, operators can maintain a safe working environment and minimize the likelihood of accidents or injuries during order picking operations.

General Guidelines (Association Sectorielle Transport Entreposage, 2010):

- Verify that the order picking truck is equipped with a second capacity plate, accounting for the weight of the additional platform.

- Provide training to operators on interpreting capacity plates on both the lift truck and various additional platforms.

- Supervise the implementation of fall protection measures, including the mandatory use of safety harnesses.

- When pedestrians are in the vicinity, secure the work area of the order picking truck with stanchions.

- Ensure travel occurs on debris-free ground to maintain safe operation.

- Only initiate a turn when the operator's station is lowered to minimize risks.

- Consistently adhere to maximum permitted load capacities, as sudden braking or changes in direction can lead to load off-centring or fork lift truck overturning.

- Prevent pallets or merchandise from extending excessively over the edge of pallet racks, hindering upward and downward movements.

- Verify that the design of the additional platform includes safeguards against falls, such as guardrails on open sides. Avoid placing articles on guardrails unless designed for that purpose.

Assessing the working area before initiating order picking activities is essential to identify and mitigate potential hazards, plan appropriate operational paths, and ensure compliance with workplace procedures. By conducting a thorough assessment and adhering to established protocols, operators can create a safe and efficient environment conducive to successful order picking operations.

Once the working area has been assessed and potential hazards identified, it is crucial to confirm the implementation of the traffic management plan to ensure the safety of all personnel and equipment within the facility. This involves verifying that the established traffic management plan is in place and being effectively implemented to regulate the movement of vehicles and pedestrians in the work area.

Operators must have a clear understanding of the traffic management plan and adhere to its guidelines in accordance with workplace procedures. This includes following designated traffic routes, obeying speed limits, and yielding to other vehicles or pedestrians as specified in the plan. By adhering to these protocols, operators can help maintain a safe and orderly flow of traffic within the facility, reducing the risk of accidents or collisions.

Furthermore, operators should remain vigilant and proactive in identifying any deviations or issues with the traffic management plan and promptly report them to the appropriate personnel for resolution. Regular communication and cooperation among team members are essential to ensure the effective implementation of the plan and address any potential safety concerns that may arise during order picking operations.

Effective communication is vital for coordinating order picking operations and ensuring the safety and efficiency of the workflow. To begin, it is essential to determine appropriate communication procedures that facilitate clear and concise communication among personnel involved in order picking tasks. This may include using handheld radios, intercom systems, or other communication devices, depending on the size and layout of the work area.

Once the communication procedures have been established, it is crucial to test the effectiveness of these methods by conducting communication drills or simulations with relevant personnel. This allows operators to familiarize themselves with the communication devices and protocols and ensures that everyone understands how to communicate effectively during order picking operations.

During the testing phase, operators should verify that communication channels are clear and free from interference, and that messages can be transmitted and received accurately and promptly. Any issues or concerns regarding communication should be addressed and resolved before proceeding with actual order picking tasks to minimize the risk of miscommunication or errors during operations.

In addition to formal communication procedures, operators should also be encouraged to maintain open lines of communication with their team members and supervisors through verbal exchanges and visual cues. This allows for real-time collaboration and problem-solving, enhances situational awareness, and promotes a culture of safety and teamwork within the workplace.

Assessing the quality and suitability of the operating surface is crucial before initiating order picking operations with an order picker. This involves evaluating the condition of the work area operating surface to ensure it meets the necessary standards for safe and efficient use. Operators should follow workplace procedures designed to assess the condition of the operating surface, which may include visual inspections and physical assessments.

During the evaluation process, operators should look for any potential hazards or irregularities on the operating surface that could pose safety risks or impact the performance of the order picker. This may include cracks, potholes, debris, or slippery patches that could affect traction or stability during operation. Any issues identified should be promptly addressed or reported to supervisors for resolution.

Additionally, operators should consider factors such as the surface material, slope, and load-bearing capacity to determine the suitability of the operating surface for order picking tasks. Surfaces should be flat, level, and capable of supporting the weight of the order picker and its load without risk of sinking or shifting. If the operating surface does not meet these criteria, operators may need to take corrective action or seek alternative operating locations to ensure safe and efficient operations.

By assessing the quality and suitability of the operating surface before commencing order picking activities, operators can mitigate the risk of accidents, injuries, and equipment damage. This proactive approach helps to create a safer working environment and ensures that order picking operations can be conducted smoothly and effectively.

Preparing for Order Picking Operations

To prepare for and ensure safe and efficient order picking operations, the following steps should be undertaken:

- Maintain Consultation with Workplace Personnel: Continuous communication with relevant personnel is essential to ensure alignment of the work plan with site requirements. This ongoing consultation helps clarify any uncertainties and ensures consistency with workplace procedures.

- Assess Environmental Conditions: Evaluate the conditions of the work area to identify any factors that could impact the positioning of the order picking forklift truck. Adhering to safe work procedures during this assessment helps mitigate risks associated with environmental hazards.

- Check Implementation of Risk Control Measures: Verify that risk control measures for identified hazards are effectively implemented according to safe work procedures. This ensures that potential risks are minimized, maintaining a safe working environment for all personnel.

- Access the Forklift Truck Safely: Access the order picking forklift truck following manufacturer specifications and safe work procedures. Adherence to proper access protocols is crucial for preventing accidents and injuries during operation.

- Inspect the Forklift Truck Logbook: Review the order picking forklift truck logbook to ensure accuracy, completion, and necessary rectifications. Adherence to manufacturer requirements and safe work procedures maintains the reliability and safety of the equipment.

- Perform Pre-Start Checks: Conduct thorough pre-start checks on the order picking forklift truck to identify any damage or defects. Report and record any issues found, taking appropriate action according to safe work procedures and manufacturer specifications.

- Visually Check Safety Equipment: Prior to operation, visually inspect safety equipment for working at height to ensure it is in good condition. Report any damage or defects, record findings, and take necessary action in accordance with safe work procedures.

- Start the Forklift Truck: Initiate the order picking forklift truck following manufacturer specifications and safe work procedures, listening for any abnormal noises. Identifying unusual sounds can help detect potential mechanical issues requiring attention.

- Conduct Operational Checks: Perform operational checks on all safety devices and mechanisms of the order picking forklift truck. Report any damage or defects, record observations, and take appropriate action as per manufacturer specifications and safe work procedures.

Before commencing operations, it is important that the operator (EP Equipment, 2019):

- Understands the maximum lifting capacity of the machine, typically indicated on the metal data plate affixed to the chassis. If this information is not readily available, inform your supervisor.

- Thoroughly examines all operator documentation, including manuals, as they may contain essential details specific to your equipment that are not immediately apparent.

- Inspects for any disconnected, worn, or damaged parts. Promptly report any identified issues to your supervisor.

- Acquaints themselves with the safety features of the machine, such as the reversing switch or auto-braking system.

- Maintains a firm grip on the controls and ensure proper body balance before operating the machine.

Work Organization Guidelines (Association Sectorielle Transport Entreposage, 2010):

- Determine the weight of articles before the operator begins picking.

- Arrange articles in the pallet rack with lighter items at the top and heavier items at the bottom.

- Coordinate article picking considering their combined weight on the additional platform and their placement in the pallet rack.

- Monitor the operator's control over the total load on the additional platform, ensuring it never surpasses the maximum capacity specified on the capacity plate. Two key principles are at play:

- As order picking advances, the total weight on the additional platform increases.

- With the operator's station at greater heights, the lift truck's load capacity diminishes.

Performing pre-start checks on an order picker is essential to ensure its safe and effective operation. Here's a step-by-step guide on how to conduct these checks:

1. **Visual Inspection:**

   - Begin by visually inspecting the order picker from all angles. Look for any visible signs of damage, such as cracks, dents, or leaks.

   - Examine the structure, including the mast, forks, and chassis, for any abnormalities or wear and tear.

   - Check for loose or missing bolts, nuts, or fasteners that could affect the stability or operation of the order picker.

2. **Functional Testing:**

   - Test all key functions of the order picker, including lifting, lowering, steering, and braking mechanisms.

   - Operate the controls to ensure smooth and responsive performance.

   - Listen for any unusual noises or vibrations that may indicate mechanical issues.

3. **Safety Features:**

   - Verify that all safety features, such as emergency stop buttons, horns, and lights, are functioning correctly.

   - Test the safety interlock systems to ensure they engage and disengage properly.

- Check the condition of safety harnesses or restraints, ensuring they are secure and undamaged.

4. **Battery and Power Source:**

   - If the order picker is electric-powered, check the battery or power source for adequate charge and any signs of damage.
   - Inspect the battery terminals for corrosion and ensure they are securely connected.
   - If the order picker is powered by an internal combustion engine, check the fuel level, oil level, and coolant level as per manufacturer specifications.

5. **Documentation Review:**

   - Review the order picker's logbook and maintenance records to ensure all required inspections and maintenance tasks have been completed.
   - Verify that any previous issues or defects have been addressed and documented properly.

6. **Record Keeping:**

   - Record the results of the pre-start checks in the order picker's logbook or maintenance records.
   - Document any issues or defects identified during the inspection process, including their location and severity.

7. **Reporting and Action:**

   - Report any damage, defects, or safety concerns identified during the pre-start checks to the appropriate personnel,

MATERIAL HANDLING EQUIPMENT OPERATION

such as a supervisor or maintenance technician.

- Follow established procedures for reporting and addressing issues, which may include tagging the order picker as out of service until repairs are completed.

- Take appropriate action to address any identified issues in accordance with safe work procedures and manufacturer specifications.

By conducting thorough pre-start checks and promptly addressing any issues, operators can ensure the safety, reliability, and performance of the order picker before use. These checks help prevent accidents, minimize downtime, and maintain compliance with safety regulations and operational standards.

The visual inspection should encompass (but not be limited to):

- Checking the battery and its connectors (if utilizing a lead-acid battery, ensuring proper maintenance is essential).

- Verifying the presence of all guards and covers.

- Checking the hydraulic fluid level to ensure adequacy.

- Inspecting the wheels, lift chains, and hoses for any signs of damage or wear.

- Confirming the presence and legibility of all warning lights, decals, and relevant documents. Inspecting the condition of the harness and tether.

- Checking for any other unusual occurrences or abnormalities.

The operational inspection should encompass (but not be limited to):

- Ensuring the lift and lower functions operate correctly.

- Checking the effectiveness of the brakes.

- Verifying that the deadman pedal functions as intended.

- Ensuring the proper operation of the speed control, steering, horn, emergency power button, and all other switches and alarms.

Performing the daily inspection is not only a requirement by OSHA but also a prudent safety measure. It aids in identifying any minor issues before they escalate into more significant (and costlier) problems.

Similar to conventional electric forklifts, order pickers also necessitate regular maintenance to ensure optimal performance and safety. Due to having fewer moving parts compared to internal combustion lift trucks, order pickers generally require less maintenance. As part of a preventative maintenance service, forklift technicians typically conduct the following tasks:

- Inspecting and lubricating lift chains to ensure smooth operation.

- Checking hydraulic hoses for signs of wear, cracks, or damage to prevent potential hydraulic issues.

- Inspecting brakes for wear and assessing their effectiveness in stopping the vehicle safely.

- Changing the hydraulic fluid and filter(s) to maintain proper hydraulic system functionality.

- Inspecting all safety guards, including the overhead guard, as well as safety equipment such as lights, alarms, and fire extinguishers, while ensuring the presence and legibility of all decals and nameplates.

- Replacing wearable parts such as switches, brushes, contactor tips, bearings, etc., to maintain operational efficiency.

- Inspecting the forks for signs of wear and damage to ensure safe material handling.

- Ensuring all manuals and necessary documents are present for reference and compliance purposes.

It's essential to emphasize that only qualified and authorized personnel should conduct maintenance and inspections on industrial lift trucks. If assistance is needed in maintaining your order picker or fleet of order pickers, please reach out to us today. You can also find more information about our forklift maintenance services and their associated benefits.

Operating an Order Picker

While various models of order pickers populate the market, their fundamental operational principles remain consistent. Typically, electric-powered, these machines are equipped with either 24-, 36-, or 48-volt batteries, an electric motor, and various hydraulic pumps. Featuring a centralized drive wheel and a set of non-powered casters either in the front or rear, their design may position the electronic control board and battery predominantly at the front end, depending on the specific model.

For efficient and safe order picking operations, it's crucial to adhere to the following guidelines:

1. Implementing Hazard Prevention/Control Measures:

    - Identify potential hazards in the work area and implement control measures to mitigate risks.

    - Communicate these measures effectively to all personnel working in the area, ensuring awareness and compliance with safe work procedures.

2. Assessing Weight and Positioning of Load:

- Evaluate the weight and positioning of loads on the platform to ensure they comply with the specifications outlined on the order picking forklift truck's data plate.

- Adhere to manufacturer specifications and safe work procedures when assessing and adjusting the load to maintain stability and prevent accidents.

3. Operating the Forklift Truck Safely:

- Operate the order picking forklift truck in accordance with manufacturer specifications and established safe work procedures.

- Ensure proper training and certification for operators to handle the equipment safely and efficiently.

4. Monitoring Path and Load Stability:

- Constantly monitor the path of the forklift truck and the stability of the load when moving, lowering, and placing items.

- Adhere to safe work procedures to avoid hazards and ensure the stability of materials throughout the picking process.

5. Transporting Loads Using Relevant Movements:

- Utilize all relevant order picking forklift truck movements in accordance with safe work procedures to transport loads efficiently and safely.

- Follow established protocols for lifting, lowering, and maneuvering the truck to minimize the risk of accidents or injuries.

6. Responding to Unplanned and Unsafe Situations:

   - Be prepared to respond promptly to any unplanned or unsafe situations that may arise during order picking operations.
   - Follow safe work procedures to address and resolve issues effectively while prioritizing the safety of personnel and materials.

7. Working Safely at Heights:

   - When working at heights, ensure that fall arrest/restraint equipment is used safely and efficiently according to safe work procedures.
   - Provide appropriate training and equipment to personnel working at heights to minimize the risk of falls or accidents.

8. Parking and Isolating the Forklift Truck:

   - Park and isolate the order picking forklift truck appropriately in accordance with manufacturer specifications and safe work procedures.
   - Securely immobilize the vehicle and follow established protocols for shutting down and isolating the equipment to prevent unauthorized use and ensure safety when not in operation.

Operating an order picker forklift is generally straightforward. Key controls include:

1. Deadman Pedal:

- Positioned at the bottom, the deadman pedal requires the operator's pressure to activate the order picker. Without depressing this pedal, the machine remains inactive.

2. Joystick:

- Utilized by wrist movements, the joystick facilitates forward or backward motion of the order picker.

3. Steering Wheel:

- Used to manoeuvre the order picker, particularly in models where tire visibility or orientation determination via the steering wheel is challenging. Some models feature a digital direction indicator to aid in trajectory visualization.

4. Platform Controls:

- Located near or on the joystick, these controls manage platform elevation, allowing operators to adjust it as needed for picking tasks.

5. Pallet Claw:

- Found in many modern order picker models, the pallet claw, operated by a foot lever, grips the pallet stringers to prevent them from sliding off the forks.

MATERIAL HANDLING EQUIPMENT OPERATION

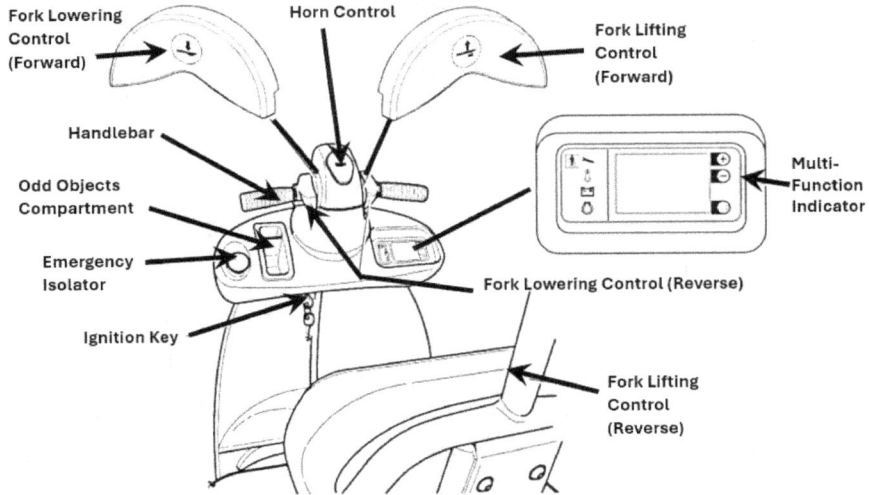

Figure 36: Sample order picker controls.

Additionally, certain order picker forklifts incorporate roller systems at the base, facilitating battery loading. Once loaded onto handling carts, batteries can be effortlessly slid into place on the rollers and secured with heavy-duty metal plates. Once in position, the battery is connected to the order picker's chassis using an SB connector. Businesses such as warehouses, distribution centres, retailers, and fulfillment centres stand to benefit from the use of order picker forklifts, given their practicality in handling daily physical tasks.

Most standard-size order pickers typically have a maximum load capacity (weight limit) ranging from 1,500 lbs. to 3,000 lbs. (680 kg to 1,360 kg). Smaller order pickers, such as the CLARK OSQ192, have weight lifting capacities around 600 lbs. (272 kg), while larger units can handle loads of up to 3,000 lbs. (1,360 kg) (Conger, 2024).

Ensure to refer to the data tag for the specific load capacity of your order picker. Additionally, provide training to your workers on weight limits and ensure they do not exceed the rated load capacity of the order pickers.

Not every order picker will reach the same height. Mid-level order pickers typically reach heights ranging from 15 to 25 feet (4.6 to 7.6 meters), while high-level pickers can extend up to heights between 20 and 35 feet (6.1 to 10.7 meters). It is essential to select order pickers capable of reaching the tallest shelves in your warehouse. This information can be found on the order picker's data plate (Conger, 2024).

Starting Sequence for an Order Picker:

1. Preparation: a. Ensure the order picker is parked in a designated area away from pedestrian and vehicle traffic. b. Turn off all accessories, lights, and power sources. c. Apply the parking brake and ensure the vehicle is securely in place. d. Perform a visual inspection of the order picker, checking for any signs of damage or abnormalities.

2. Safety Check: a. Verify that all safety guards, covers, and protective devices are in place and functioning correctly. b. Check the seatbelt and ensure it is securely fastened. c. Inspect the operator platform for stability and ensure there are no obstructions. d. Confirm that the deadman pedal is functional and responsive.

3. Power-Up Sequence: a. Turn the ignition key to the "on" position while simultaneously depressing the deadman pedal. b. Observe the instrument panel for any warning lights or indicators. Address any issues indicated before proceeding. c. Listen for any unusual sounds or vibrations that may indicate mechanical issues.

4. Operational Checks: a. Test the functionality of the lift and lower functions by raising and lowering the platform slightly. b. Check the steering response by turning the steering wheel left and right. c. Test the horn and ensure it emits a clear and audible sound. d. Engage the forward and reverse gears and confirm smooth acceleration and braking. e. Verify the operation of any

additional features or accessories specific to the order picker model.

5. Final Preparations: a. Adjust the mirrors and seat position for optimal visibility and comfort. b. Confirm that all necessary equipment and tools are secured on the order picker. c. Briefly review the planned tasks and routes for the shift with relevant personnel.

6. Ready for Operation: a. Once all checks are complete, release the parking brake. b. Gradually accelerate and begin manoeuvring the order picker to the designated work area. c. Maintain awareness of surroundings and adhere to safe operating practices throughout the shift.

By following this starting sequence, operators can ensure that the order picker is properly prepared for safe and efficient operation in the warehouse or distribution centre environment.

Effects of Load Centre, Centre of Gravity and Leverage on Order Pickers

The Effects of Load Centre, Centre of Gravity, and Leverage on Order Pickers are crucial factors that impact the stability, lifting capacity, and safe operation of these vehicles.

Load Center: The load centre, often referred to as the load centre distance, is a critical measurement used in forklift and order picker operations. It represents the distance from the face of the forks to the centre of gravity of the load being lifted. It is typically expressed in inches or millimetres and plays a crucial role in determining the safe lifting capacity of a forklift or order picker. When the load is centred and evenly distributed on the forks, the load centre is at its standard position. However, if the load is unevenly distributed or extends beyond the standard load centre, it can affect the stability and lifting capacity of the equipment.

Center of Gravity: The centre of gravity (COG) refers to the point at which the entire weight of an object is concentrated. In the context of order pickers, it is essential to understand the COG of both the load being lifted and the equipment itself. When lifting a load with an order picker, the goal is to keep the combined centre of gravity of the load and the equipment within a stable range to prevent tipping or instability. Operators must consider the position of the load, the height of the lift, and any additional platforms or attachments when assessing the COG. Proper load placement and distribution are crucial for maintaining stability and preventing accidents.

Leverage: Leverage, in the context of order pickers, refers to the mechanical advantage gained by using the lifting mechanism to raise and lower loads. It involves the application of force at a certain distance from a pivot point, such as the fulcrum of a lifting mechanism. The leverage exerted by an order picker depends on factors such as the length of the forks, the lifting height, and the load centre distance. Understanding leverage is important for operators to effectively control the lifting and lowering of loads, as well as to maintain stability and balance during operation. Improper use of leverage can lead to overloading, tipping, or other safety hazards. Therefore, operators must be trained to operate order pickers safely and efficiently while considering the principles of leverage.

The effects of these concepts on an order picker include:

1. Load Centre:
    - Load centre distance determines the distance from the face of the forks to the centre of gravity of the load being lifted.
    - Effects:
        - As the load centre distance increases, the load's leverage

on the forks increases, potentially reducing the lifting capacity of the order picker.

- Longer load centre distances shift the centre of gravity further from the forks, making the order picker less stable.

- Operators must ensure that loads are properly centred and evenly distributed on the forks to maintain stability and prevent tipping.

2. Centre of Gravity (COG):

    - Centre of gravity refers to the point at which the entire weight of an object is concentrated.

    - Effects:

        - The position of the load's centre of gravity significantly influences the stability of the order picker.

        - If the combined centre of gravity of the load and the equipment extends beyond the stable range, it can cause the order picker to tip over.

        - Operators must carefully assess the COG of both the load and the equipment, considering factors such as load placement, height of lift, and any additional attachments.

3. Leverage:

    - Leverage involves the mechanical advantage gained by using the lifting mechanism of the order picker.

    - Effects:

        - Proper understanding and control of leverage are essential for safely lifting and lowering loads.

- Improper use of leverage can lead to overloading, tipping, or loss of control of the order picker.

- Operators must consider the length of the forks, lifting height, load centre distance, and load weight when applying leverage to ensure safe and efficient operation.

- Training on leverage principles is critical for operators to prevent accidents and maintain stability during order picking operations.

As such, stability plays a crucial role in ensuring the safe operation of order picking forklifts. Various factors influence the stability of an order picker, including the centre of gravity (CG) and the load centre distance.

The centre of gravity (CG) represents the point around which an object is balanced in all directions. In the case of an order picker, which consists of moving parts, the CG shifts as the mast tilts forward or backward and as the upright moves up or down. When a load is picked up, the combined CG of the order picker and the load must remain within the stability triangle, defined by the area between the front wheels and the pivot of the steering axle, for the truck to remain stable. If the CG shifts beyond this triangle, the truck becomes susceptible to tipping forward or turning on its side.

Factors such as the size, weight, shape, and position of the load, as well as the height to which it is elevated, tire pressure, and dynamic forces during movement, impact the centre of gravity and stability of the loaded truck. Dynamic forces, such as acceleration, braking, operating on uneven surfaces, or turning, can also affect stability.

Even when unloaded, an order picking forklift must be operated with caution as it can tip over more easily than a loaded truck, particularly if the centre of gravity shifts due to factors like picking up a load at the tip of the forks or movements of the forklift itself.

The load centre distance, which refers to the distance from the loading platform's vertical face to the centre of gravity of the load, also affects the forklift's capacity. As the load centre distance increases, the forklift's capacity decreases. If the load is not positioned properly against the edge of the operator's platform, both the rated capacity and stability of the order picker may be compromised.

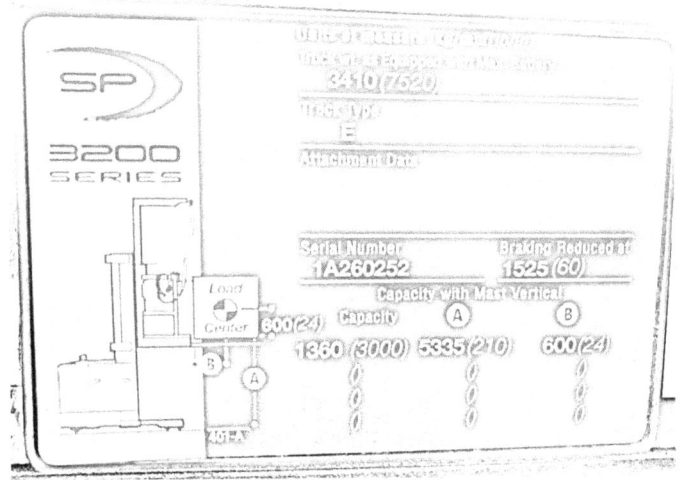

Figure 37: Sample data plate.

It is essential to refer to the load chart or data plate of the specific order picker being used to determine its rated capacity. The rated capacity indicates the maximum load that the order picker can safely carry at a given load height and load centre distance, ensuring safe and efficient operation.

Handling Loads

When handling loads with the forklift, it's crucial to adhere to specific guidelines to ensure safety and prevent damage to the equipment:

- Avoid carrying the load on only one fork arm, as this can compromise the stability of the order picker and potentially damage the forklift.

- Before reversing the order picker, ensure that warning devices are functioning correctly and always check over both shoulders.

- When possible, face the direction of travel and ensure that all warning devices are operational to alert nearby personnel.

- When traveling with a load, ensure that the order picker is not raised more than 600mm from the ground, as exceeding this height can compromise stability. Do not tamper with safety features designed to prevent travel while raised.

- Lower the load as close to the ground as possible for stability while traveling. Sound the horn before lowering or traveling while raised.

- If the load obstructs visibility, drive forward if feasible, ensure the pathway is clear, and use warning devices such as a horn and flashing lights. Consider repacking the load if necessary and enlist someone to assist with guidance.

- Be mindful of rear-end swing and maintain a safe operating speed based on factors such as load size, weather conditions, ground/floor conditions, and the presence of personnel and other equipment.

- Continuously monitor load movement to ensure the safety of personnel in the area and the stability of both the load and the order picker.

- Avoid traveling on slopes, ramps, or inclines, as order picking forklifts are prone to overturning on such surfaces. Stick to hard, level surfaces while traveling.

- When loading onto a truck from a loading dock, ensure secured dock plates or bridge plates are in place. Never turn into another rack while the platform is elevated; lower the platform first.

- Be aware of environmental conditions such as slippery surfaces, soggy ground, heavy winds, and sun glare, and take appropriate precautions such as wearing appropriate PPE and adjusting driving behaviour accordingly.

- In the event of contact with power lines, warn others to stay away, attempt to break contact with the power lines, and follow safety procedures for exiting the forklift. Report the incident to supervisors, the power company, and safety regulators, and refrain from using the forklift until it has been checked and cleared for service.

When placing a load with an order picking forklift truck, follow these steps:

1. Approach the destination of the load gradually and cautiously.

2. Lower the load gently to the desired position.

3. If equipped, release the pallet locking device.

4. Reverse the order picker to remove the forks, ensuring they do not scrape against the pallet.

When replenishing stock onto racking or shelves, it's essential to consider the following:

- Ensure that the racking or shelves can support the weight of the load.

- Stack the loads on a stable and level surface.

- Place heavier items at the bottom of the stack.

- Avoid stacking stock to heights that may compromise stability.

In the event of an Order Picker Malfunction, swift action is imperative to mitigate potential risks and ensure the safety of personnel and equipment. If there is a sudden drop of the platform or suspicion of issues with the brakes, steering, or hydraulic system, immediate precautions must be taken. Firstly, lower the load being carried and promptly turn off the order picker to prevent any further complications.

Upon encountering such a malfunction, conduct a thorough inspection of the order picking forklift to identify any visible signs of damage or wear. Pay particular attention to hydraulic lines, checking for any splits or bulges that could indicate a hydraulic system issue. It's essential to address these potential problems promptly to prevent any escalation of the situation.

Subsequently, report the detected fault to an authorized individual within the organization. This ensures that appropriate action can be taken to rectify the issue and prevent any further operation of the malfunctioning equipment. When operating an order picker, any malfunction or defect in critical components such as the engine, brakes, steering, or other equipment poses significant risks. These risks may include potential accidents, injury to individuals, instability of the equipment, and the inability to complete essential order picking tasks. Therefore, timely reporting and resolution of faults are crucial to maintaining a safe working environment and ensuring operational efficiency.

Concluding Order Picker Operations

To ensure the safe shutdown of an order picking forklift truck, it is essential to follow manufacturer specifications and adhere to safe work procedures. Here's how to accomplish this:

1. **Shutting Down the Forklift Truck:**

MATERIAL HANDLING EQUIPMENT OPERATION

- Park the order picking forklift truck on a level surface away from any hazards or obstacles.

- Engage the parking brake to prevent any unintended movement of the vehicle.

- Turn off the engine or power source of the forklift truck as per the manufacturer's instructions.

- Follow any specific shutdown procedures outlined in the operator's manual provided by the manufacturer.

- Ensure all controls are returned to their neutral or off position.

- Lower the forks or platform to the ground, if applicable, to stabilize the truck.

- Wait for any moving parts to come to a complete stop before exiting the vehicle.

2. **Securing the Forklift Truck:**

    - Once the forklift truck is shut down, secure it to prevent unauthorized access or use.

    - Remove the key from the ignition and keep it in a designated secure location.

    - If available, activate any anti-theft devices or immobilizers installed on the vehicle.

    - Ensure the forklift truck is parked in a designated area or storage location as per workplace procedures.

    - If required by legislative obligations or workplace policies, install additional security measures such as wheel locks or chains.

- Communicate the status of the forklift truck to other personnel to indicate that it is not available for use.

Once you have completed using the forklift, it's essential to conduct a thorough check to ensure it is prepared for the next operator. Here's what you need to do:

1. If applicable, attach batteries to a charger. During the charging process, batteries emit explosive gases that must be vented from the work area to prevent potential explosions. It's crucial to charge batteries in a well-ventilated space, away from any naked flames, as hydrogen gas can accumulate and ignite during charging.

2. Avoid smoking near a charging battery, as cigarette fumes could ignite, leading to an explosion or fire.

3. When connecting or disconnecting an electric battery from the transformer (power source) and/or the forklift truck:

    - Turn off the power before making any connections or disconnections.

    - Inspect all connections to ensure they are secure.

    - Turn on the power only after reconnection is complete.

    - Ensure that no one accesses the order picker while the battery is charging.

4. Check the batteries to ensure they are adequately filled with water, as required.

5. Conduct operational checks once the battery is reconnected to

the forklift truck before operating the vehicle.

If you encounter any faults or issues while operating the forklift:
1. Immediately cease any operations and remove the keys from the ignition.

2. Tag the forklift with a danger tag to prevent anyone from using it.

3. Record the problem in the forklift's logbook or on the inspection checklist, providing detailed information.

4. Report the fault to an authorized individual or supervisor.

Minor repairs to the forklift may be undertaken by competent and authorized personnel.

Chapter Four

Telehandlers

Telehandlers, also known as telescopic handlers, boom lifts, reach forklifts, or teleporters, are extensively utilized in agriculture and civil industries to transport loads to areas inaccessible by conventional forklifts. Modern telehandlers, as shown in Figure 38, are versatile hybrid units combining the load-lifting capabilities of a forklift with the lifting range of a crane. Equipped with a telescopic boom, they can accommodate various attachments, facilitating a wide array of tasks with a simple quick hitch design enabling swift and secure attachment changes as required.

Figure 38: JCB 531-70 Telehandler. Bob Adams from Amanzimtoti, South Africa, CC BY-SA 2.0, via Wikimedia Commons.

Their functionality varies, serving as telescopic forklifts, cranes for lifting suspended loads, or elevating work platforms through specialized attachments, each configuration adhering to distinct design standards. Operator proficiency also varies based on the telehandler's configuration.

Typically featuring a side-mounted cab with the boom positioned to the right, visibility from the cab may be hindered by structural elements, posing challenges during reversing or lifting large loads. Improper operation can lead to tipping, contact with power lines, load slippage, or attachment detachment, resulting in injuries or fatalities, emphasizing the paramount importance of promoting safe practices.

Key aspects of telehandlers include their versatility in accommodating various attachments, extended reach and height capabilities, diverse applications across industries such as agriculture, construction, and warehousing, along with inherent limitations necessitating adherence to load charts and operator training. Furthermore, many telehandlers feature four-wheel steering, enhancing manoeuvrability in confined spaces, underscoring the critical significance of safe operation due to the associated risks with lifting heavy loads to considerable heights.

Telehandlers serve as invaluable multi-functional equipment, fulfilling roles of forklifts, cranes, and more, catering to the diverse needs of various industries.

Telehandlers predominantly function as tools for lifting and placing objects but find extensive application across diverse industries. In agriculture, they handle tasks such as moving hay, while in construction, they contribute to earthmoving, excavation, and transporting heavy loads to elevated locations. Additionally, telehandlers are instrumental in tasks like soil ploughing, heavy debris clearance, and accessing elevated areas with general materials.

Telehandlers represent a fusion of crane and forklift functionalities, offering the flexibility to be equipped with diverse attachments like winches, muck grabs, or buckets. Additionally, they can be outfitted with platforms, effectively transforming into boom lifts.

Their exceptional mobility enables easy transportation to various locations and sites due to their adaptability. With three steering modes available (4-wheel drive, crab steering, and front wheel), coupled with robust construction for traversing rough terrain, telehandlers excel in on-site operations at quarries, agricultural settings, and construction sites.

Different telehandler types offer unique benefits. For instance, rotational telehandlers possess the ability to rotate around the chassis, enhancing flexibility even while stationary.

Despite varying lifting capacities dictated by machine specifications, telehandlers can hoist loads weighing up to 45 tonnes. However, their lifting capability diminishes as the load's distance from the centre increases with boom extension. To counter this, front stabilizers can extend lifting capacity, often complemented by built-in computers issuing warnings when nearing weight limits.

Furthermore, telehandlers contribute to enhanced safety by substituting manual lifting on worksites, simplifying complex moving tasks. Ensuring maximum onsite safety necessitates trained and qualified operators, with careful path preparation to execute tasks devoid of risks.

Telehandlers Deliver:

1. Heavy Lifting: Telehandlers excel at lifting heavy loads, adhering to lift capacity and height specifications, including both palletised and non-palletised goods when appropriately equipped. Unlike forklifts limited to linear movements, telehandlers offer diagonal manoeuvrability, facilitating the handling of loads inaccessible to standard forklifts.

Their enhanced manoeuvrability allows access to tight spaces and odd angles through extendable booms, making them ideal for confined spaces. Deployable stabilizers provide added stability and safety during heavy lifting.

1. Versatility: The telescopic boom is integral to the telehandler's adaptability, accommodating a wide range of attachments securely via quick hitch mechanisms. Various attachments, such as forklift carriages, crane jibs, scoop and bucket attachments, and work cages or platforms, expand telehandler functionalities, potentially yielding significant cost savings by obviating the need for additional equipment like cranes or elevating work platforms.

2. On and Off-Road Capabilities: Equipped with four-wheel drive, telehandlers traverse both on and off-road terrains with ease. Robust tyres support heavy loads while navigating rugged construction sites, agricultural areas, or mining environments. Additionally, road registration facilitates safe transportation of

loads between job sites or from delivery trucks.

3. Enhanced Safety: Telehandlers minimize manual lifting tasks, reducing the risk of employee injuries due to unsafe or repetitive manual handling. Maximum onsite safety necessitates operation by fully trained and qualified operators, adhering to specified lifting capacities and heights to mitigate risks of injury, equipment damage, or workplace fatalities.

The primary classifications of telehandlers are Fixed Boom (or non-slewing) Telehandlers and Rotating Telehandlers (or slewing).

Fixed Boom Telehandlers Fixed boom telehandlers, the original telehandler variant, feature a stationary cab and a forward-pointing telescopic boom. While these models offer a more limited range of motion, they excel in handling heavier loads due to manufacturers consolidating counterweight technology within the telehandler's structure. Despite their restricted movement, fixed boom telehandlers efficiently transport pallets, packages, and loose materials within work sites or industrial yards. Unlike forklifts, telehandlers provide broader carrying and transportation capabilities, coupled with superior lifting reach and height.

The primary advantage of fixed boom telehandlers lies in their heavy-duty capabilities. These models are the preferred choice for transporting equipment or materials across rugged terrain and long distances. Fixed boom telehandlers typically exhibit greater stability with heavy loads and boast a longer boom, making them invaluable assets for major projects characterized by expansive spaces and substantial tasks.

In contrast, rotating telehandlers, as shown in Figure 39, represent a newer model, emerging in the late 1900s, and swiftly gaining popularity. Unlike fixed boom telehandlers, rotating telehandlers feature a cab and boom capable of 360-degree rotation while maintaining a stationary body. This configuration significantly expands the telescopic boom's range of motion, rendering them highly suitable for projects necessitating manoeuvrability in tight spaces.

Rotating telehandlers are not primarily intended for heavy lifting but excel as dynamic movers among telehandler variants. Despite this, they still offer impressive standard lift and carrying capacities compared to forklifts and similar machinery. Whether engaged in major construction projects or industrial yard operations, rotating telehandlers are well-equipped to meet project demands efficiently.

Figure 39: Rotating telehandler. Asurnipal, CC BY-SA 4.0, via Wikimedia Commons.

Advantages of Rotating Telehandlers The unique advantage of rotating telehandlers lies in their ability to navigate tight spaces effortlessly. With a cab and boom capable of 360-degree rotation, these telehandlers enable seamless pallet pickup and placement without the need for extensive manoeuvring of the telehandler's body. This feature proves especially beneficial in confined areas where frequent manoeuvring would result in time wastage. While rotating telehandlers may not match the lifting capacity and height of their fixed boom counterparts, they still offer remarkable capabilities.

In addition to the two distinct types, telescopic handlers are available in various configurations, each offering different lifting capacities (Paul, 2022).

Compact Models: Compact telehandlers are suitable for lifting moderately weighted loads to moderate heights. Typically, super-compact telescopic handlers can lift a maximum weight of 2.5 tonnes to a height of approximately 6 meters, while compact telehandlers have a lifting capacity of up to 4 tonnes to heights of around 10 meters. Figure 40 shows a compact telehandler. The maximum lift height for the telehandler in Figure 40 is 18.04 feet (5500 millimetres) with a maximum forward reach of 10.5 feet (3200 millimetres). At maximum reach, it can handle loads of up to 2645 pounds (1200 kilograms), while at maximum height, the maximum load capacity is 5952 pounds (2700 kilograms). The telehandler's overall maximum lift capacity is also 5952 pounds (2700 kilograms).

MATERIAL HANDLING EQUIPMENT OPERATION 135

Figure 40: Manitou MLT 627 turbo telehandler fitted with a Strimech bulk handling bucket. BulldozerD11, CC BY-SA 3.0, via Wikimedia Commons.

Standard Lift: Standard telehandlers generally have a lifting capacity ranging from 2 to 6 tonnes, capable of lifting loads to heights between 6 and 11 meters.

High Lift: For tasks requiring lifting at considerable heights, high lift telescopic handlers are available. These models can handle weights of 3 to 6 tonnes and lift them to heights exceeding 17 meters, with certain JCB telehandler booms extending to 20 meters.

Heavy Load: Projects involving exceptionally heavy loads necessitate heavy load telehandlers. These telehandlers can manage loads weighing up to approximately 7.5 tonnes.

The various steering options available for telehandlers, as shown in Figure 41, enhance their manoeuvrability, regardless of whether you choose the fixed or rotating model. Telehandlers offer distinct steering types, a unique feature exclusive to this machinery. These steering options include:

1. Front-wheel steering: In this mode, only the front wheels pivot, providing optimal safety, particularly when the telehandler is utilized on roads.

2. Four-wheel steering: This steering configuration involves the rotation of both front and rear wheels in opposite directions, resulting in the tightest turning radius. However, it is suitable exclusively for off-road applications.

3. Crab steering: In this mode, all four wheels swivel in the same direction, enabling lateral movement. Crab steering proves invaluable in confined spaces, eliminating the need for traditional turning manoeuvres.

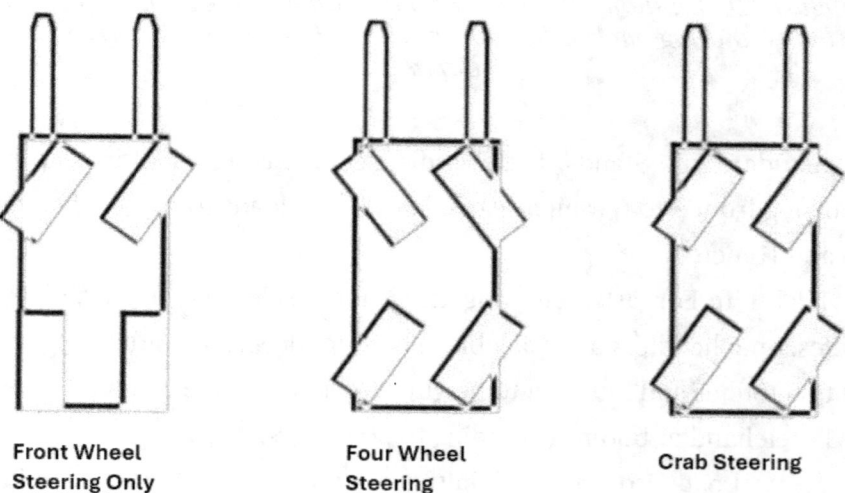

Figure 41: Telehandler steering modes.

Before selecting a telehandler to suit your requirements, several considerations should be taken into account. These include the machine's capacity, both in terms of load weight and lifting height, ensuring it aligns with your operational demands. Additionally, the reach capability, turning radius for manoeuvrability, stability ensured by the boom

MATERIAL HANDLING EQUIPMENT OPERATION

pivot pin, and tire suitability for various terrains are essential factors to evaluate. Moreover, examining steering mechanisms and the availability of compatible accessories further enhances the telehandler's suitability for specific tasks and environments.

Main Components of a Telehandler include:

1. Chassis:

    - The chassis serves as the foundation of the telehandler, providing structural support and housing other components. It is typically constructed from sturdy materials to withstand heavy loads and rough terrain.

2. Boom:

    - The boom is a crucial component of the telehandler, consisting of telescopic sections that extend and retract to adjust the reach and height of the machine. It is usually equipped with attachments for lifting and carrying various loads.

3. Cab:

    - The cab houses the operator and essential controls for operating the telehandler. It is designed to provide comfort and visibility to the operator during use, often featuring ergonomic seating, controls, and visibility aids.

4. Engine:

    - The engine powers the telehandler, providing the necessary energy to operate hydraulic systems, drive mechanisms, and other components. It is typically a diesel or gasoline engine, chosen for its durability and torque characteristics.

5. Hydraulic System:

- The hydraulic system controls the movement of the boom, attachments, and other hydraulic functions of the telehandler. It consists of hydraulic pumps, cylinders, valves, and hoses, operated by the operator through control levers or joysticks.

6. Counterweight:

    - Counterweights are added to the telehandler to improve stability and balance, especially when lifting heavy loads. They are strategically positioned on the chassis to offset the weight of the load being lifted.

7. Tyres:

    - Tyres provide traction and support for the telehandler, allowing it to move across various terrains safely. Telehandlers may feature different types of tyres depending on the application, including pneumatic, solid, or foam-filled tyres.

8. Steering System:

    - The steering system allows the operator to control the direction of the telehandler's movement. It may include options such as front-wheel steering, four-wheel steering, or crab steering, providing flexibility and manoeuvrability in different operating environments.

9. Attachments:

    - Attachments are tools or accessories mounted on the end of the boom to perform specific tasks. Common attachments include forks for lifting pallets, buckets for carrying materials, and jibs for lifting suspended loads.

Each component of a telehandler plays a vital role in its overall functionality and performance. The chassis provides stability and support, while the boom enables lifting and reaching capabilities. The cab ensures operator comfort and control, while the engine and hydraulic system power the machine's operations. Counterweights and steering systems enhance stability and manoeuvrability, while tyres provide traction and support. Finally, attachments expand the telehandler's versatility, allowing it to perform a wide range of tasks across different industries and applications. Overall, these components work together to make telehandlers efficient and versatile machines for material handling and lifting operations.

Figure 42: Typical components on a fixed boom telehandler. Back Image - Jean Housen, CC BY-SA 3.0, via Wikimedia Commons.

Figure 42 shows the main typical components on a non-slewing or fixed boom telehandler and Figure 43 does the same for a rotating, or slewing, telehandler.

Figure 43: Typical components on a rotating telehandler. Back Image - Lionel Allorge, CC BY-SA 3.0, via Wikimedia Commons,

Two of the primary risks associated with operating telehandlers involve lateral stability and visibility. Lateral stability becomes a concern when lifting loads, as the machine's centre of gravity shifts upwards, particularly evident on sloped terrain where the risk of tipping increases. This risk escalates further when driving with a raised load or when handling suspended loads, potentially leading to instability. Additionally, visibility issues arise when the boom is elevated or when carrying large loads, heightening the risk of accidents involving pedestrians and the telehandler (Construction Plant-hire Association, 2015).

To mitigate these risks, telehandlers are often equipped with visibility aids, and operators are urged to maintain vigilance and conduct thorough visual checks before manoeuvring. While supervisors are tasked with ensuring adequate segregation and supporting operators in enforcing safety measures, ultimately, it is the operator's responsibility to ensure safe operation by actively monitoring their surroundings and seeking assistance if visibility is compromised. Segregation of pedes-

MATERIAL HANDLING EQUIPMENT OPERATION

trians from moving vehicles should always be prioritized, with visibility aids serving as supplementary measures. Furthermore, special attention should be given to maintaining visibility of the load, especially with high-reaching telehandlers where judging distance at height can be challenging (Construction Plant-hire Association, 2015).

The centre of gravity (COG) and load centres play critical roles in the stability and operation of telehandlers.

1. Center of Gravity (COG):

    - The centre of gravity refers to the point within an object or system where the force of gravity can be considered to act. In the case of telehandlers, the COG is affected by various factors, including the weight distribution of the machine and any loads it is carrying.

    - When a load is lifted by the telehandler's boom, the center of gravity of the entire system shifts. As the load is raised, the COG rises accordingly. This shift in COG can affect the stability of the telehandler, especially if the machine is operating on uneven terrain or with an elevated load.

    - If the telehandler is on a slope while lifting a load, the COG may move towards the tipping line, increasing the risk of overturning. Operators must be aware of these dynamics and take precautions to maintain stability, such as avoiding operating on steep slopes or ensuring proper counterweighting.

2. Load Centres:

    - Load centres refer to the point on a load where the weight is concentrated. Different attachments and loads can have varying load centres, affecting the telehandler's stability and lifting capabilities.

- When a load is not evenly distributed or is off-centre, it can create imbalance and increase the risk of tipping or instability, particularly when the load is raised to significant heights.

- Operators must consider the load centres when selecting and attaching loads to the telehandler. They should ensure that loads are properly secured and evenly distributed to maintain stability and prevent accidents.

Overall, understanding the effects of the centre of gravity and load centres is crucial for safe telehandler operation. Operators should be trained to assess and manage these factors to minimize risks and ensure safe and efficient lifting operations.

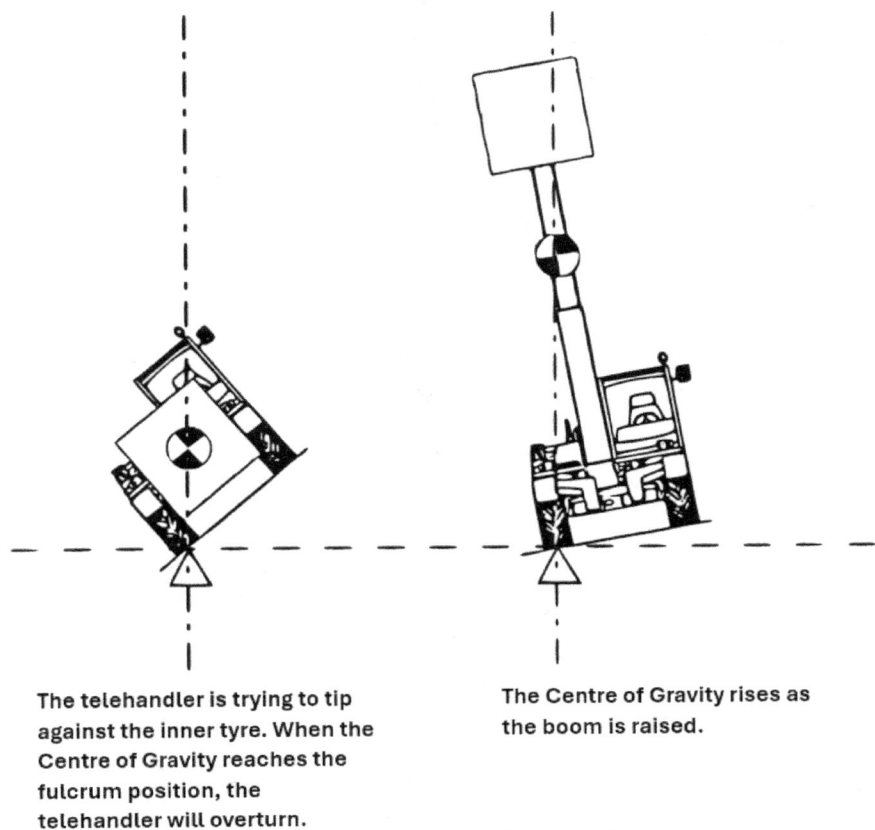

Figure 44: Telehandler lateral stability.

Understanding the design specifications, intended usage, and limitations of telehandlers is crucial for safe operations. Any use outside of these prescribed areas introduces additional hazards that operators must be vigilant of. Telehandlers are typically designed according to European Standard BS EN1459, which specifies conditions such as stationary lifting on flat, compacted ground or traveling with forks (Construction Plant-hire Association, 2015). Deviating from these conditions, such as using telehandlers on slopes or with non-fork attachments, requires a reassessment of risks. Stability tests conducted during design and development involve placing telehandlers on tilted platforms to evaluate stability, revealing that stability decreases significantly with raised booms or loads. Unlike machines with outriggers, telehandlers feature freely oscillating rear axles, forming a triangular tipping line and reducing lateral stability, especially when the boom is raised. Furthermore, stability tests are typically performed with a standard load of 1-meter cubes, so using larger or irregularly shaped loads poses additional risks that must be evaluated. To ensure stability, telehandlers should only be operated on firm ground, lift vertically or utilize frame leveling features, apply brakes when stationary during lifts, and be operated by trained and certified personnel.

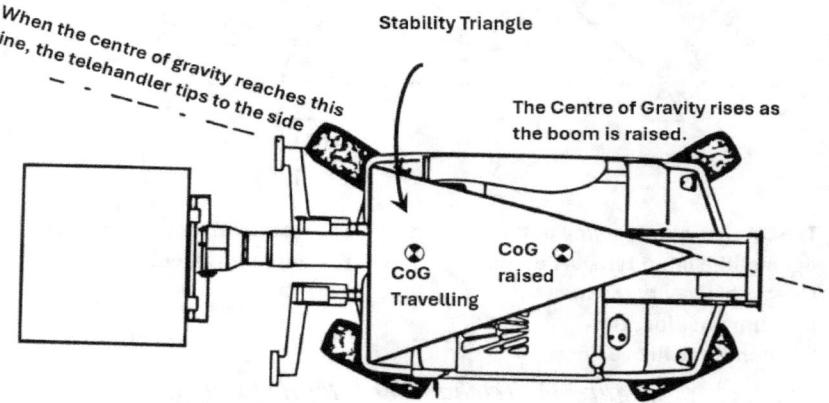

Due to the typical freely oscillating rear axle of a telehandler, its balance inherently leans towards the stability triangle. As the boom rises, not only does the centre of gravity rise, but it also shifts rearward. Consequently, the telehandler experiences a rapid decline in lateral stability while enhancing stability in the forward direction as the boom elevates.

Figure 45: Typical Stability Triangle for Fixed Boom Telehandlers.

Telehandler stability can be significantly affected while traveling due to several factors:

    1. Speed: Traveling at high speeds can increase the risk of instability, especially when navigating uneven terrain or sharp turns. Higher speeds can lead to sudden shifts in weight distribution and decrease the telehandler's ability to maintain balance.

2. Terrain: The type and condition of the terrain can greatly impact stability while traveling. Uneven surfaces, slopes, and obstacles can cause the telehandler to tilt or become unbalanced, especially if the wheels lose traction.

3. Load Position: The position of the load being carried can also affect stability while traveling. If the load is not properly secured or is positioned too high or too far forward, it can shift during travel, destabilizing the telehandler.

4. Center of Gravity: The centre of gravity of the telehandler and its load plays a crucial role in stability while traveling. Any changes in the distribution of weight, such as uneven loading or raising the boom, can impact stability.

5. Turning: Making turns while traveling can introduce additional stresses on the telehandler's stability. Sharp turns or sudden manoeuvres can cause the telehandler to lean to one side, increasing the risk of tipping over.

Traveling with a telehandler requires careful consideration of speed, terrain, load position, and turning manoeuvres to maintain stability and prevent accidents. Operators must be trained to assess these factors and adjust their driving techniques accordingly to ensure safe operation.

The various factors that contribute to the instability of a telehandler during operation:

1. Dynamic Motion: Any movement of the telehandler introduces instability due to the shifting of its weight distribution. Whether it's driving forward, backward, or turning, the telehandler's centre of gravity is constantly in flux, making it prone to tipping over if not carefully controlled.

2. Steering and Centrifugal Force: When the telehandler attempts

to steer, it generates centrifugal force, which pushes outward from the centre of rotation. This force adds to the lateral instability of the telehandler, particularly during sharp turns or manoeuvres.

3. Steering Wheels: Even steering the wheels while the telehandler is stationary can lead to instability. Manipulating the steering mechanism causes shifts in weight distribution, potentially leading to overturning if not done cautiously.

4. Suspended Load: When lifting a load with the telehandler's boom, the load may swing back and forth. This swinging motion further shifts the centre of gravity of the telehandler, increasing the risk of instability, especially if the load is heavy or improperly secured.

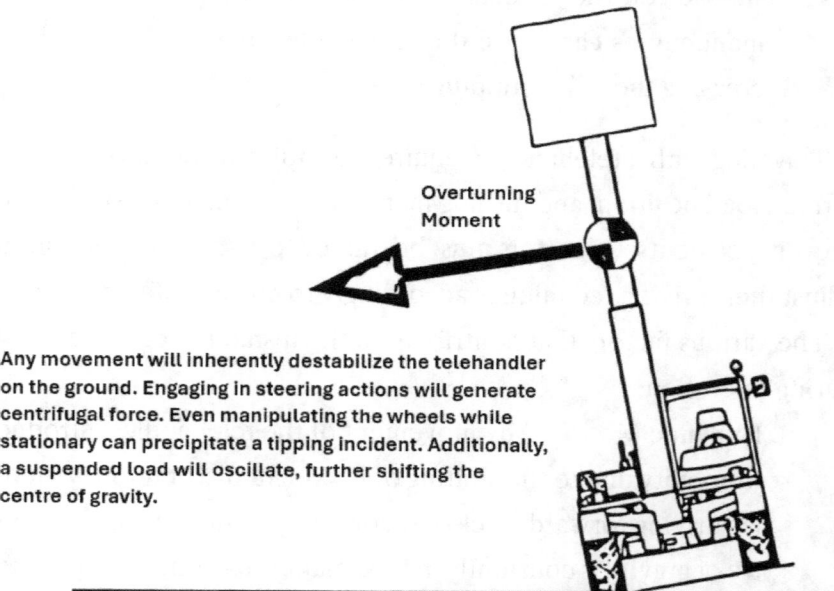

Figure 46: Telehandler dynamic stability.

Tyres also play an important role in maintaining stability and load-carrying capacity in telehandlers. Several tyre-related issues can compromise these aspects, such as incorrect tyre pressure, discrepancies in tire diameter within the same axle due to uneven wear, improper ply rating, utilization of tyres not meeting performance standards, tyres with identical nominal sizes but differing physical dimensions, and inadequate tyre repairs. Each of these factors can have a significant impact on the overall stability and performance of the telehandler, emphasizing the importance of proper tyre maintenance and selection for safe operation.

Rated Capacity and Load Charts

The rated capacity of a telehandler refers to the maximum weight that the telehandler itself is designed to lift and carry safely under specified conditions. This capacity is determined by the manufacturer and is typically stated in the telehandler's specifications. It takes into account factors such as the telehandler's structural integrity, stability, and hydraulic system capabilities.

It's essential to note that the rated capacity (RC) of a telehandler will decrease as the boom extends or raises. This decrease occurs due to several factors related to the boom length:

1. Lever Arm Effect: The longer the boom, the greater the lever arm created between the load and the telehandler's centre of gravity. This increased leverage applies more torque or moment to the telehandler, making it harder to maintain stability and balance. Consequently, the RC may be reduced to compensate for this heightened leverage.

2. Structural Integrity: Longer booms place additional stress and strain on the telehandler's structural components, including the boom itself, hydraulic system, and chassis. Manufacturers must ensure that the telehandler can withstand these added forces

while maintaining safety and stability. If the boom length exceeds the telehandler's structural limits, the RC may be decreased to prevent structural failure.

3. Hydraulic Performance: Longer booms demand more hydraulic power to lift and manoeuvre loads effectively. The telehandler's hydraulic system must deliver sufficient force and control throughout the entire range of motion of the boom. If the hydraulic system is not adequately sized or configured for the longer boom, it may limit the telehandler's RC.

4. Stability: Longer booms can elevate the telehandler's overall height and centre of gravity, reducing its stability and tipping resistance. Manufacturers may need to adjust the telehandler's RC to account for the increased risk of tipping or overturning associated with longer booms, particularly when lifting heavy loads at extended heights.

Overall, it's crucial for manufacturers to consider these factors and the decrease in RC as the boom extends or raises to ensure safe and effective operation of the telehandler.

Attachment rated capacity refers to the maximum weight that a specific attachment, such as forks, buckets, or jibs, is designed to lift and carry when attached to the telehandler. Each attachment has its own rated capacity, which is also determined by the manufacturer based on factors such as its design, materials, and construction.

Operators must consider both the telehandler's rated capacity (RC) and the attachment's rated capacity when determining the maximum weight that can be safely lifted and carried. While an attachment may be capable of handling a certain weight, it does not guarantee that the telehandler can lift that weight in all positions or configurations.

The telehandler's RC refers to the maximum weight that the telehandler itself is designed to lift and carry safely under specified conditions.

This capacity is determined by factors such as the telehandler's structural integrity, stability, and hydraulic system capabilities.

Similarly, the attachment's RC refers to the maximum weight that the attachment is designed to lift and carry when attached to the telehandler. Each attachment has its own rated capacity, determined by factors such as its design, materials, and construction.

When using an attachment with a telehandler, it's essential to consider both the telehandler's RC and the attachment's RC to ensure that the combined weight does not exceed the safe lifting capacity of the equipment. Failure to do so could result in instability, structural damage, or accidents. Therefore, operators must carefully evaluate both the telehandler's and the attachment's RC to determine the maximum weight that can be safely handled in any given situation or configuration.

Overall actual capacity is the maximum weight that the telehandler can safely lift and carry when equipped with a particular attachment and operating under specific conditions. This capacity is determined by considering both the rated capacity of the telehandler itself and the rated capacity of the attachment being used. The overall actual capacity may be limited by the lower of the two rated capacities, ensuring that the telehandler and attachment are not overloaded and operated within safe limits.

In summary, telehandler rated capacity refers to the maximum weight the telehandler can lift, attachment rated capacity refers to the maximum weight an attachment can lift, and overall actual capacity considers both the telehandler and attachment capacities to determine the maximum weight that can be safely lifted and carried.

Most lift charts are typically based on a unit with forks that have a 24-inch load centre (approximately 600 millimetres). However, longer forks and various attachments can significantly alter these calculations. For further details, consult your user manual or reach out to the manufacturer to inquire about the availability of alternative load charts.

To interpret the load chart effectively, operators must first ascertain several factors:
- The weight and dimensions of the materials.
- The required lift height to access the designated area.
- The telehandler's capacity and lifting capabilities.

Once these factors are determined, operators must position the unit correctly for placement or retrieval. These positions are often indicated on the telehandler load chart by letters ranging from A to H, and sometimes beyond, as in the sample load chart shown as Figure 47. Adhering to this letter range ensures a safe lift or placement for the materials, minimizing the risk of material damage, unit strain, or load dropping.

Each telehandler load chart contains a grid that shows the maximum reach and lift range of the unit. This range reflects the retracted and extended boom positions. Reach is shown on the bottom, lift on the left side, and capacity in the centre of the chart.

MATERIAL HANDLING EQUIPMENT OPERATION 151

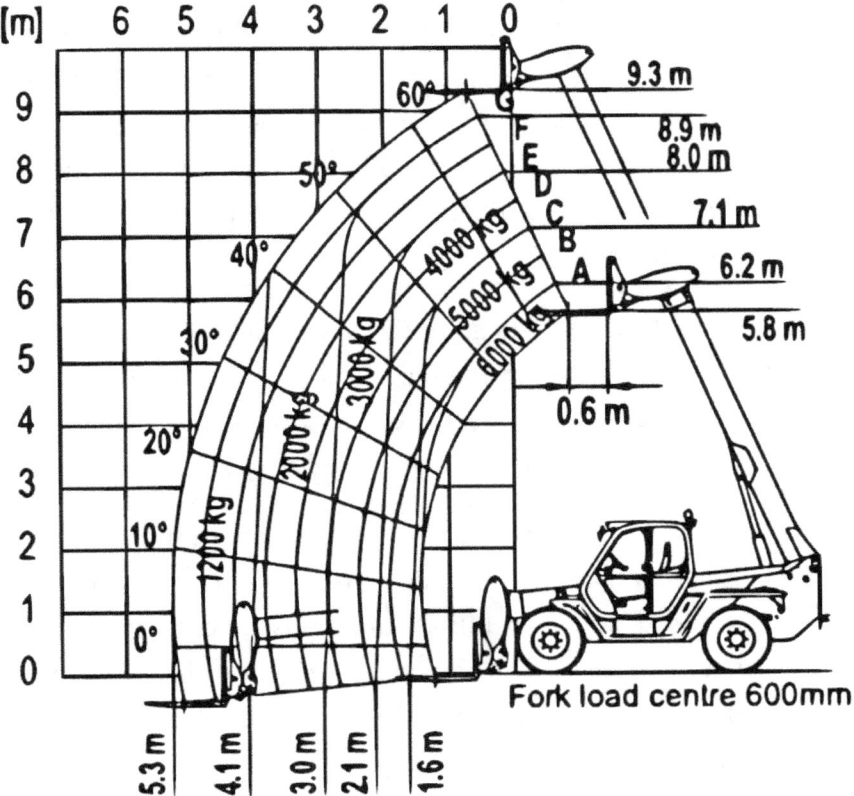

Figure 47: Sample fixed boom telehandler load chart.

To read a load chart for a fixed boom telehandler, follow these steps:
1. Understand Load Chart Basics: Familiarize yourself with the load chart provided by the manufacturer. The load chart typically presents a graph or table showing the telehandler's maximum lifting capacities based on various factors such as boom extension, lift height, and load radius.

2. Identify Key Parameters: Look for key parameters indicated on the load chart, including boom extension (horizontal reach), lift height (vertical reach), load radius (distance from the centre of the telehandler to the centre of the load), and load weight.

3. Locate Load Capacity Zones: The load chart is divided into different zones or regions, each representing a specific combination of boom extension, lift height, and load weight. These zones indicate the telehandler's maximum lifting capacity under those conditions. Typically, load capacities are higher closer to the telehandler and decrease as the boom extends or the lift height increases.

4. Find the Corresponding Values: Determine the specific parameters of your lifting operation, including the desired lift height, boom extension, and load weight. Locate these values on the load chart to identify the corresponding load capacity.

5. Verify Safe Operation: Ensure that the planned lifting operation falls within the specified load capacity zone on the load chart. If the load weight or lifting conditions exceed the maximum capacity indicated on the chart for a given boom extension and lift height, adjustments may be necessary to ensure safe operation.

6. Consider Environmental Factors: Take into account environmental factors such as ground conditions, wind speed, and terrain slope, as these can affect the telehandler's stability and lifting capacity. Adjustments may be required to compensate for these factors and ensure safe operation.

7. Consult User Manual: If you encounter any uncertainty or require further clarification, refer to the telehandler's user manual or contact the manufacturer for assistance. They can provide additional guidance on interpreting the load chart and ensuring safe lifting operations.

MATERIAL HANDLING EQUIPMENT OPERATION

Figure 48 shows a sample load chart for a rotating telehandler. To read a load chart for a rotating telehandler, follow these steps:

1. Familiarize with Load Chart Structure: Start by becoming familiar with the load chart provided by the manufacturer. The load chart typically presents a graph or table showing the telehandler's maximum lifting capacities based on various factors such as boom extension, lift height, load radius, and slewing angle.

2. Identify Key Parameters: Look for key parameters indicated on the load chart, including boom extension (horizontal reach), lift height (vertical reach), load radius (distance from the centre of the telehandler to the centre of the load), and slewing angle (the angle of rotation of the boom).

3. Locate Load Capacity Zones: Similar to fixed boom telehandlers, the load chart for rotating telehandlers is divided into different zones or regions, each representing a specific combination of boom extension, lift height, load radius, and slewing angle. These zones indicate the telehandler's maximum lifting capacity under those conditions.

4. Find the Corresponding Values: Determine the specific parameters of your lifting operation, including the desired lift height, boom extension, load radius, and slewing angle. Locate these values on the load chart to identify the corresponding load capacity.

5. Verify Safe Operation: Ensure that the planned lifting operation falls within the specified load capacity zone on the load chart. If the load weight or lifting conditions exceed the maximum capacity indicated on the chart for a given combination of parameters, adjustments may be necessary to ensure safe operation.

6. **Consider Environmental Factors:** Take into account environmental factors such as ground conditions, wind speed, and terrain slope, as these can affect the telehandler's stability and lifting capacity. Adjustments may be required to compensate for these factors and ensure safe operation.

7. **Consult User Manual:** If you encounter any uncertainty or require further clarification, refer to the telehandler's user manual or contact the manufacturer for assistance. They can provide additional guidance on interpreting the load chart and ensuring safe lifting operations.

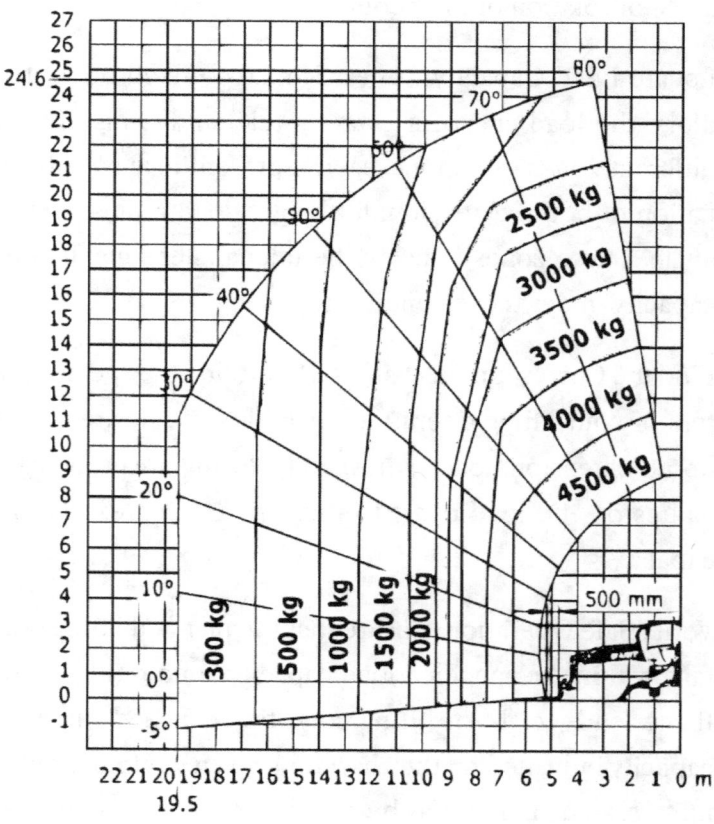

Figure 48: Sample rotating telehandler load chart.

As an example of interpreting a telehandler load chart, using the chart shown as Figure 47, the operator needs to place a 3000kg load at a height of 5 m and a reach of 2.1m. The material is palletised with a load centre of 600mm. Utilizing a fork carriage and a properly selected model, the operator reviews the load capacity chart and determines that the boom angle indicator should read 38 degrees and the boom extension, visible from the side of the boom, will be the black "C" zone. This is represented on the load chart as Figure 49.

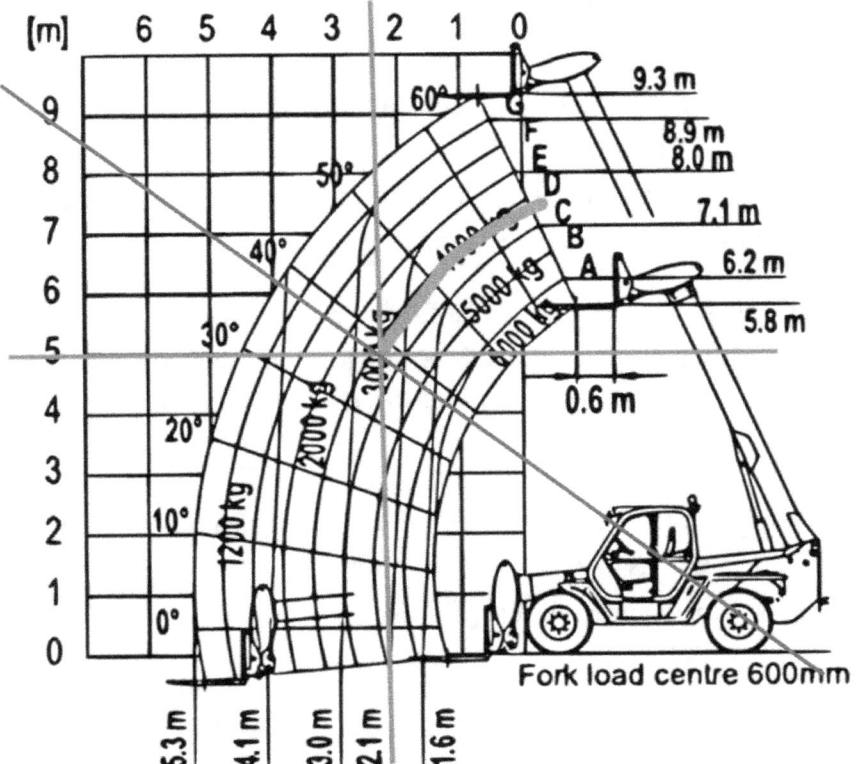

Figure 49: Load chart interpretation for a 3000kg load at a height of 5 metres and a reach of 2.1m.

Planning for Telehandler Operations

Planning for telehandler operations involves several steps to ensure safe and efficient operation:

1. Identifying Tasks: Begin by identifying tasks from work orders or equivalent documents. Confirm these tasks with relevant personnel and conduct a site inspection in accordance with workplace procedures.

2. Inspecting Work Area: Inspect the telehandler work area operating surface and travel path. Assess them for operational use following manufacturer instructions and workplace procedures.

3. Establishing Capacity: Determine the telehandler's Rated Capacity (RC), the attachment's Rated Capacity (RC), and overall Actual Capacity (AC) required for the work/task. Refer to manufacturer specifications, load charts, boom length, boom angle, slope indicators, and workplace procedures.

4. Assessing Path and Area: Assess the operating path and work area for obstructions before moving and placing loads. Follow workplace procedures to ensure safe manoeuvring.

5. Identifying Hazards: Identify hazards and assess risks associated with telehandler operation. Eliminate or implement control measures as necessary, and inform relevant personnel following workplace procedures.

6. Confirming Traffic Management: Confirm understanding and implementation of the traffic management plan, ensuring compliance with workplace procedures.

7. Establishing Communication: Identify appropriate communication methods and procedures. Test communication with associated personnel to ensure effectiveness and adherence to workplace procedures.

8. Confirming Tasks: Confirm all tasks to ensure alignment with requirements for the relevant work area. Verify compliance with workplace procedures.

9. Confirming Equipment: Confirm that the telehandler and attachment(s) selected are appropriate for the activity, considering factors such as load weight, size, and terrain.

Assessing the path and work area for safe telehandler operation involves a systematic evaluation. Firstly, visually inspect the path the telehandler will traverse to identify any obstacles, debris, or uneven terrain that could impede safe operation. Additionally, ensure sufficient clearance for the telehandler and any attached loads, considering overhead obstacles such as tree branches, power lines, or building overhangs.

Next, assess the ground conditions along the operating path, looking for potential hazards such as loose gravel, mud, or uneven surfaces that could affect stability or traction. Identify any potential risks or hazards along the path, such as pedestrian traffic, other vehicles, or confined spaces, and take note of areas where visibility may be limited.

Determine the most appropriate routes for manoeuvring the telehandler, considering factors such as space constraints, turning radius, and accessibility to the work area. Communicate with other personnel in the vicinity to ensure they are aware of the telehandler's movements and coordinate any necessary adjustments to their activities.

Adhere to workplace procedures and safety protocols for navigating the operating path, following designated traffic routes and signage, and avoiding shortcuts or unauthorized areas. If any obstacles or hazards are identified, take appropriate action to address them before proceeding, which may involve removing obstacles, adjusting the route, or implementing additional safety measures.

Visibility of individuals near the telehandler is crucial for accident prevention. Limited visibility, especially when the boom is raised or when carrying large loads, coupled with inadequate segregation, has been recognized as a leading cause of accidents involving pedestrians and telehandlers. To enhance visibility, telehandlers are often equipped with aids. It is the operator's responsibility to ensure these aids are in good working order and properly adjusted. If they are not functioning correctly, the machine should not be used. Supervisors should fully support operators in this regard.

Certain stages of a telehandler's work cycle pose specific visibility challenges. For instance, a suspended load may obstruct the forward view, and the raised boom may obscure the side view. Risk assessments should incorporate the physical dimensions of loads and their impact on visibility, especially when lifting suspended loads. When loading or unloading a truck, the partially raised boom may obstruct the view to the front offside and block the wing mirror's view to the rear offside. It is safest to keep the telehandler stationary and use the telescopic boom instead of the wheels for such operations. Truck drivers should remain in designated safe locations during these operations.

While the PCBU (Person Conducting a Business or Undertaking) is primarily responsible for ensuring adequate segregation, and supervisors must enforce it, operators bear the responsibility of checking for pedestrians before moving, manoeuvring, and traveling. If visibility is compromised, operators should seek assistance or exit the cab to ensure safety.

Regarding the visibility of the load being lifted, the increasing vertical reach of telehandlers, up to 22m at present, poses challenges for operators in keeping the load in full view and judging distances. Planning telehandler operations should account for these challenges, and a signaller should be provided if necessary. Signalling methods, such as hand signals or portable radios, should be considered. Although some telehandlers allow remote control of boom functions, potential disadvantages, such as operator risk and limited view, must be considered.

MATERIAL HANDLING EQUIPMENT OPERATION

Operators should always maintain sight of the telehandler boom and load, except when directed by a signaller with a clear view of the load and its path.

It's imperative that operators and contractors are well-informed about potential site hazards that could impact the safe utilization of telehandlers, as well as any site regulations dictating their permissible use.

Ground conditions must undergo thorough assessment to ensure the safe operation of telehandlers. Site housekeeping is essential to maintain areas where telehandlers are deployed free of debris, as such clutter can significantly impede safe telehandler operation.

Roads, access ways, and entrances should ideally be consolidated and free of potholes to minimize the necessity of traversing uneven or unstable terrain. If off-road operation cannot be avoided, operators should be made aware of hazards that could contribute to overturning risks or other safety concerns.

Operating on inclines, slopes, and gradients necessitates strict adherence to designated speeds and ground conditions to ensure operator control at all times. Traffic routes should ideally be on consolidated ground or temporary roadways offering equivalent safety. Maximum slopes provided are helpful for planners but should not be used in combination.

Ensuring a clear operating path and work area when moving and placing loads with heavy machinery is critical for safety and efficiency. This includes attending pre-start briefings, gathering necessary documentation, conducting visual assessments, identifying overhead obstructions, checking ground stability, assessing human activity, marking identified obstructions, planning a clear path, verifying with spotters or ground personnel, utilizing machinery safety features, continuous assessment, documenting and reporting, and prioritizing safety at all times.

Identifying hazards associated with telehandler operation is crucial for ensuring a safe working environment. This includes:

1. Hazard Identification: Thoroughly assess the telehandler operation area for potential hazards. These may include uneven terrain, overhead obstructions, pedestrian traffic, confined spaces, and equipment malfunctions.

2. Risk Assessment: Once hazards are identified, evaluate the level of risk they pose to personnel, equipment, and the surrounding environment. Consider factors such as severity, likelihood, and potential consequences.

3. Hazard Elimination: Whenever possible, eliminate hazards entirely to prevent accidents or injuries. This may involve removing obstacles, repairing equipment, or implementing engineering controls to mitigate risks.

4. Implement Control Measures: If hazards cannot be eliminated, implement control measures to reduce the associated risks. This may include implementing administrative controls such as signage, barriers, or work procedures, or providing personal protective equipment (PPE) to personnel.

5. Inform Relevant Personnel: Communicate identified hazards and implemented control measures to all relevant personnel, including operators, supervisors, and other workers in the vicinity. Ensure that everyone understands the risks involved and knows how to operate safely in the presence of these hazards.

6. Follow Workplace Procedures: Adhere to established workplace procedures for hazard identification, risk assessment, and control measure implementation. Document all identified hazards and control measures as per organizational policies.

Identifying hazards related to the task at hand is crucial for ensuring safe telehandler operation. These hazards can vary based on factors such as the work environment, telehandler type, attachments used, load characteristics, travel route, and personnel involved. It's essential to assess potential risks associated with the surrounding area, other ongoing operations nearby, and the need for coordination among different tasks.

When operating a telehandler, it's important to be vigilant of potential dangers and take proactive measures to mitigate risks. Hazards to be mindful of include overturning, electrocution from overhead power lines, contact with workers or bystanders, unsecured loads leading to crushing, inappropriate use or maintenance of handling attachments, unsafe procedures, and unintended machine movement. Ensuring attachments are properly secured, avoiding standing on forks or pallets, and preventing attachments from being used as makeshift work platforms are critical safety practices.

Several typical risks are commonly associated with telehandler operations. Overturning or tipping poses a significant risk, especially when the machine is overloaded or the boom is extended. Maintaining stability by keeping the load low and close to the machine and leveling the machine before lifting any load can help mitigate this risk. Unstable ground conditions can also increase the likelihood of overturning, emphasizing the importance of reviewing site conditions and ensuring stabilizers are firmly in contact with stable surfaces.

Electrocution hazards from live cables and overhead power lines must be carefully assessed, and precautions should be taken to maintain a safe distance from electrical hazards. Blind spots should be addressed to prevent accidents involving workers, pedestrians, or bystanders, with the use of mirrors, reversing cameras, spotters, and appropriate safety measures.

Additionally, operators should be cautious of falling material, maintain machinery and attachments properly, follow safe work procedures, use approved attachments, and avoid sudden movements that could compromise stability. Regular maintenance checks, adherence to manufacturer instructions, proper training, and licensing are essential for safe telehandler operation and accident prevention. By identifying hazards, assessing risks, and implementing appropriate control measures, operators can ensure a safe working environment and minimize the potential for accidents or injuries.

Conducting a risk assessment involves identifying potential hazards associated with the task and evaluating the likelihood of harm occurring, as well as the potential consequences. Once hazards are identified, control measures must be determined to mitigate risks effectively. This process should also consider whether a telehandler is suitable for the task or if alternative equipment should be used.

Subsequently, the method to be used for carrying out the task should be developed based on the identified hazards, assessed risks, and required control measures. This plan should be comprehensive and include consultation with relevant personnel. Contingency measures and emergency procedures must also be incorporated into the plan.

Safe Work Method Statements (SWMS) serve the purpose of outlining work activities, identifying hazards, and describing control measures to ensure high-risk construction work is carried out safely and effectively. SWMS should clearly outline the sequence of work activities, hazard identification, and control measures. The document must be easily comprehensible by those involved in the work, including supervisors, workers, and principal contractors.

Traffic management on construction sites involves establishing clear separation between pedestrians and vehicles to ensure safety. This is achieved by delineating pedestrian-only areas, providing safe designated routes for pedestrians, creating vehicle-only zones, and establishing safe vehicle routes around the site. An effective traffic management plan includes measures to keep vehicles and people apart, limit vehicle movements or speed, avoid reversing vehicles, provide safe areas for drivers, install clear signage and road markings, and ensure effective workplace communication.

To protect pedestrians, efforts should be made to prevent interaction between vehicles and people. This may include using barriers or guardrails at entrances/exits, implementing high-impact traffic control barriers, employing temporary physical barriers, establishing clearly marked footpaths or walkways, ensuring unobstructed and well-maintained pedestrian routes, and utilizing spotters when necessary.

Maintaining clear areas is crucial for safety. Workers should wear appropriate safety equipment when operating a telehandler, and the operator should remain seated in the cab during use. Access to the immediate area should be restricted using bollards or temporary fencing systems to prevent injuries from dropped tools or materials.

Developing a telehandler traffic management plan requires identifying hazards associated with telehandler use, assessing risks, and consulting with employees and health and safety representatives. Risks should be eliminated or controlled using engineering controls, administrative controls such as training and supervision, or personal protective equipment. Risk controls may include substituting telehandlers with lower-risk equipment, identifying safe travel routes, reducing telehandler-pedestrian interactions, implementing speed-limiting devices, installing warning lights and safety barriers, and providing adequate lighting and signage. Regular consultation and review of the plan are essential to ensure ongoing effectiveness and adaptation to changing circumstances.

Selecting a Telehandler and Attachments

Choosing the right telehandler is essential for ensuring efficiency and safety in operations. It involves considering various factors such as load requirements, environmental conditions, and site dimensions. Firstly, assessing the suitability of the site in terms of size and terrain is crucial. Next, determining if a telehandler is the appropriate equipment for the intended application is important. Additionally, considering the weight, dimensions, and other characteristics of both the telehandler and the loads to be lifted is necessary. Evaluating the required radii and height of lift for the intended tasks is also essential, along with determining the distance over which loads will be carried and the type of terrain. Moreover, assessing the number, frequency, and types of lifting operations to be performed is crucial for selecting the right telehandler. Considering the available space for telehandler access, operation, and stowage, including the deployment of stabilizers, is also significant. Determining if attachments such as buckets or work platforms are necessary and evaluating the impact of the operating environment on the telehandler and vice versa are further considerations. Lastly, ensuring that the operator will have adequate visibility in the operating location is essential. The selection of the telehandler and any attachments should be an integral part of the planning process.

Choosing the right attachments for telehandlers is crucial for ensuring safety and productivity. It involves several key points to consider. Firstly, determining which make and model of telehandler the attachment will be fitted to is necessary. Identifying the specific task the attachment is required for and choosing the type of attachment best suited to the application are also crucial steps. Ensuring that the attachment is approved for use on the selected telehandler and compatible with it is essential for safety. Verifying the availability of load charts and user instructions for the attachment on the specific telehandler is important. Confirming that the telehandler operator is familiar with and competent to operate the attachment is necessary for efficient use. Determining who will be responsible for fitting and removing the attachment and ensuring they are competent to do so is also crucial. Assessing any particular hazards associated with the task or location and considering whether the attachment will be sourced from the telehandler manufacturer, attachments manufacturer, or a third party are further considerations. Lastly, ensuring that the telehandler and its attachments are appropriate for the specific activity is essential for safe operations.

Figure 50: Manitou MLT 630-105 3.6 with grapple attachment. Vauxford, CC BY-SA 4.0, via Wikimedia Commons.

To confirm the suitability of telehandlers and attachments for specific tasks, a series of steps should be followed:

1. Determine Task Requirements.

2. Check Load Capacity.

3. Inspect Attachment Compatibility.

4. Conduct a Physical Inspection.

5. Perform a Functional Test.

6. Review Documentation.

7. Seek Operator Input.

8. Ensure Compliance with Safety Protocols.

9. Provide Training and Certification.

10. Maintain and Review Equipment Regularly.

Telehandler attachments are specialized tools designed to enhance the versatility and functionality of telehandlers. These attachments allow telehandlers to perform a wide range of tasks beyond their standard capabilities, making them indispensable in various industries such as construction, agriculture, landscaping, and warehousing. Here are some common types of telehandler attachments:

1. Forks: Fork attachments are perhaps the most common and basic attachments for telehandlers. They consist of two or more prongs that extend from the front of the telehandler and are used for lifting and transporting palletised loads, such as building materials, bags of goods, or stacked containers.

2. Buckets: Bucket attachments, such as shown in Figure 51, come in various sizes and configurations, including general-purpose buckets, multi-purpose buckets, and high-tip buckets. They are used for tasks such as moving loose materials like dirt, gravel, sand, or rubble, as well as for loading and unloading materials into trucks or containers.

Figure 51: Telehandler Locadour L 104 with bucket attachment. Joost J. Bakker from IJmuiden, CC BY 2.0, via Wikimedia Commons.

1. Platforms: Work platform attachments, also known as man baskets or aerial work platforms, are used for elevating personnel to perform tasks at height safely. These platforms are equipped with guardrails, access gates, and attachment points for safety harnesses, making them ideal for tasks such as maintenance, painting, or installation work.

Figure 52: Telescopic handler Merlo Roto with aerial work platform. Mattho, Public domain, via Wikimedia Commons.

1. Grapples: Grapple attachments, such as shown in Figure 50, consist of hydraulically operated jaws or claws that are used for grabbing, lifting, and manipulating irregularly shaped objects such as logs, tree branches, rocks, or debris. They are commonly used in forestry, landscaping, and waste management applications. These can include bale grippers such as shown in Figure 53.

MATERIAL HANDLING EQUIPMENT OPERATION

Figure 53: Telehandler Merlo MF 27.8 with bale gripper attachment. JoachimKohlerBremen, CC BY-SA 4.0, via Wikimedia Commons.

1. Sweepers and Brushes: Sweeper and brush attachments are used for cleaning and sweeping tasks in outdoor and indoor environments. They can be equipped with bristles or rotary brushes to sweep debris, dirt, and snow from surfaces such as roads, parking lots, warehouses, or construction sites.

2. Augers: Auger attachments are used for drilling holes in the ground for tasks such as fence post installation, tree planting, or soil sampling. They consist of a rotating drill bit attached to the end of a shaft and are powered by the telehandler's hydraulic system.

3. Crane Jibs: Crane jib attachments, also known as boom extensions or lifting jibs, are used for extending the reach and lifting capacity of telehandlers. They are commonly used for tasks such as lifting and placing heavy loads, installing roof trusses, or positioning materials at height.

4. Material Handling Arms: Material handling arms, also known as lifting booms or telescopic booms, are used for extending the reach and versatility of telehandlers. They can be equipped with various end attachments such as hooks, clamps, or spreader bars to handle different types of loads, including pipes, beams, or prefabricated components.

These are just a few examples of the wide variety of telehandler attachments available on the market. The choice of attachment depends on the specific requirements of the task at hand, such as the type of material to be handled, the desired reach and lifting capacity, and the environmental conditions of the job site. When selecting a telehandler attachment, it is essential to ensure compatibility with the telehandler model, proper installation and operation, and adherence to safety guidelines and regulations.

Figure 54: Stacking Square Bales. James T M Towill / Stacking Square Bales, CC BY 2.0, via Wikimedia Commons.

Common telehandler attachments frequently utilized in agriculture include:

1. Bucket Varieties:

    - General Purpose Buckets: Ideal for transporting loose materials like grain or silage.

    - High-tip Buckets: Specifically designed to reach over trailer sides, facilitating easy loading of grain or silage.

    - Light Material Buckets: Larger buckets suitable for handling lighter materials such as straw or hay.

2. Fork Types:

    - Pallet Forks: Employed for lifting and moving palletised goods, such as feed or fertilizer sacks.

    - Bale Forks or Bale Spikes: Tailored for lifting and transporting round or square bales securely.

3. Bale Handlers or Grippers:

    - Permit gentler handling of wrapped bales, preventing damage to the wrapping material.

4. Manure and Silage Forks:

    - Equipped with a combined fork and grab mechanism for managing materials like manure, compost, or silage.

5. Grapple Buckets or Brushes:

    - Utilized for managing silage, straw, or manure, with the grapple mechanism securing the material within the bucket.

6. Power Grab or Shear Grab:

    ◦ Convenient for both cutting silage and transporting it.

7. Lifting Jibs and Winches:

    ◦ Extend the telehandler's reach, beneficial for tasks like installing farm equipment or positioning heavy objects at elevated heights.

8. Augers:

    ◦ Employed for drilling holes in the ground, particularly useful for fence post installations.

9. Muck Spreaders:

    ◦ Attached to distribute manure or compost evenly across fields.

10. Trenchers:

    ◦ Useful for excavating trenches required for irrigation or drainage purposes.

11. Mixer Bowls:

    ◦ Attachments facilitating the mixing and dispensing of feed directly.

12. Sweepers or Brushes:

    ◦ Valuable for clearing debris, mud, or snow from farm pathways and roads.

13. Work Platforms:

    ◦ Provide elevated platforms for tasks such as tree pruning,

MATERIAL HANDLING EQUIPMENT OPERATION 173

building maintenance, or accessing tall storage areas.

14. Fertilizer Spreaders:

    ○ Aid in uniformly distributing fertilizers across fields.

15. Seeders:

    ○ Beneficial for sowing seeds over large agricultural areas.

When selecting a telehandler attachment for agricultural applications, it's critical to ensure compatibility with the telehandler model, suitability for the task at hand, and incorporation of necessary safety features. Adequate training on the operation of each attachment is also vital to maintain safety and operational efficiency.

Figure 55: Gathering bales. Evelyn Simak | Gathering the bales, CC BY 2.0, via Wikimedia Commons.

Preparing for Telehandler Operations

Preparing for telehandler operations requires adherence to specific procedures outlined in operation and maintenance manuals, manufacturer instructions, and workplace procedures. Here is a detailed explanation of each step involved:

1. Accessing Manuals and Instructions: Ensure that relevant operation and maintenance manuals, along with manufacturer instructions, are accessible. Interpret these documents to understand the proper operation, maintenance, and safety protocols associated with the telehandler.

2. Identifying Hazards and Risks: Conduct a thorough assessment to identify potential hazards and risks associated with telehandler operation. This includes considering factors such as site conditions, terrain, load characteristics, and nearby personnel. Implement safe working practices to control identified risks effectively.

3. Selecting and Using Personal Protective Equipment (PPE): Choose appropriate PPE based on the specific tasks and hazards involved in telehandler operation. Ensure that PPE is properly fitted, worn, and maintained according to workplace procedures to mitigate the risk of injury.

4. Performing Pre-Operational Checks: Conduct pre-operational checks on the telehandler as outlined in the operation and maintenance manual. Inspect for missing parts, damage, faults, or malfunctions that could affect safe operation. Address any issues identified before proceeding.

5. Rectifying and Reporting Defects: Rectify any defects found during pre-operational checks or routine maintenance. Report

any unresolved issues and tag the telehandler appropriately according to workplace procedures to prevent its use until repairs are completed.

6. Checking Telehandler Logbook: Review the telehandler logbook to confirm its accuracy, completeness, and compliance with manufacturer requirements. Ensure that all required entries are properly recorded, signed, and any necessary rectifications have been completed as per workplace procedures.

7. Assessing Weather and Work Environment Conditions: Evaluate weather conditions and the work environment to determine their impact on telehandler operations. Follow manufacturer requirements and workplace procedures to address any safety concerns arising from adverse conditions.

8. Entering the Telehandler Safely: Enter the telehandler using three points of contact to ensure stability and safety. Fasten the seat belt correctly before starting the engine.

9. Performing Start-Up Procedures: Follow workplace procedures and manufacturer instructions to perform start-up procedures for the telehandler. This includes activating safety features, checking fluid levels, and ensuring proper engine operation.

10. Conducting Operational Checks: Carry out operational checks to verify the functionality of telehandler controls, brakes, limit devices, attachments, and implements. Report any damage or defects observed during the checks and take appropriate action in accordance with manufacturer specifications and safe work procedures.

11. Checking Manoeuvrability and Serviceability: Test the telehandler controls, brakes, and attachments for manoeuvrability and

serviceability. Rectify any faults detected or report them according to manufacturer instructions and workplace procedures to ensure safe operation.

Selecting and using Personal Protective Equipment (PPE) in telehandler operation involves several essential steps to ensure the safety of operators:

Firstly, it's crucial to conduct a thorough assessment of the tasks and hazards associated with telehandler operation. This assessment entails identifying potential risks such as exposure to hazardous materials, the possibility of falling objects, or the risk of physical impact.

Once the hazards are identified, the next step is to choose the appropriate PPE needed to mitigate these risks effectively. Common PPE for telehandler operation includes hard hats to protect against head injuries, high-visibility vests for increased visibility, steel-toed boots for foot protection, gloves for hand protection, and eye protection such as safety glasses or goggles to prevent eye injuries from debris or dust.

Proper fitting of the chosen PPE is essential to ensure its effectiveness. Ill-fitting PPE can not only be ineffective but may also pose additional risks. For example, loose-fitting gloves may interfere with operating controls, while an improperly fitting hard hat may fail to provide adequate protection.

Consistent wearing of the selected PPE is crucial while operating the telehandler and when in areas where hazards are present. This includes wearing the appropriate PPE before starting any tasks and keeping it on throughout the duration of the operation to maintain protection.

Regular inspection and maintenance of PPE are necessary to ensure its effectiveness over time. This involves checking for any signs of damage or wear and tear and promptly replacing or repairing PPE as necessary. Additionally, cleaning PPE regularly to remove dirt, debris, or contaminants helps maintain its protective capabilities.

MATERIAL HANDLING EQUIPMENT OPERATION

Adherence to workplace procedures and guidelines is paramount for the proper selection, fitting, wearing, and maintenance of PPE. This includes following specific protocols for storing PPE when not in use, procedures for cleaning and disinfecting PPE, and guidelines for reporting any issues or concerns related to PPE.

Telehandler Controls

Telehandlers typically feature a variety of controls that enable operators to manoeuvre the machine safely and efficiently, as shown in Figure 56. These controls vary depending on the make and model of the telehandler but commonly include the following:

1. **Steering Wheel:**

    ◦ The steering wheel controls the direction of the telehandler. Turning the steering wheel left or right causes the front wheels to turn accordingly, allowing the operator to navigate the machine.

2. **Throttle Control:**

    ◦ The throttle control regulates the engine speed and determines the amount of power delivered to the wheels or hydraulic system. Operators can adjust the throttle to increase or decrease engine RPM (revolutions per minute) as needed.

3. **Transmission Controls:**

    ◦ Telehandlers may feature transmission controls such as a gear lever or joystick for selecting forward, reverse, and neutral gears. Operators can shift between gears to control the telehandler's speed and direction of travel.

4. **Boom Controls:**

- Boom controls operate the telescopic boom, allowing operators to extend, retract, raise, and lower the boom as required. These controls typically consist of joysticks or levers located within easy reach of the operator.

5. **Fork Controls:**

- Fork controls manage the position and orientation of the forks or attachments mounted on the telehandler. Operators can tilt the forks forward or backward, adjust their height, and angle them left or right to accommodate different loads.

6. **Hydraulic Controls:**

- Hydraulic controls operate various hydraulic functions of the telehandler, such as lifting, tilting, and rotating attachments. These controls are often integrated into the joystick or control panel and allow precise manipulation of hydraulic cylinders.

7. **Auxiliary Controls:**

- Some telehandlers may be equipped with auxiliary controls for operating additional functions or attachments, such as hydraulic couplers, winches, or hydraulic tool circuits. These controls enable operators to perform specialized tasks with greater efficiency.

8. **Parking Brake:**

- The parking brake is a safety feature that locks the telehandler's wheels in place when engaged. Operators activate the parking brake to prevent the machine from rolling unintentionally while parked or stationary.

9. **Safety Features:**

   - Telehandlers may also feature various safety features and controls, such as emergency stop buttons, horn, lights, and backup alarms. These controls are essential for ensuring operator safety and compliance with workplace regulations.

Operators typically manipulate telehandler controls using their hands and feet, depending on the design and layout of the machine's operator cab. Proper training and familiarization with the telehandler's controls are essential for safe and effective operation, as well as adherence to manufacturer instructions and safety guidelines.

Figure 56: Merlo telehandler interior. Blonder1984, CC BY-SA 3.0, via Wikimedia Commons.

Typical controls are shown in Figure 57.

MATERIAL HANDLING EQUIPMENT OPERATION

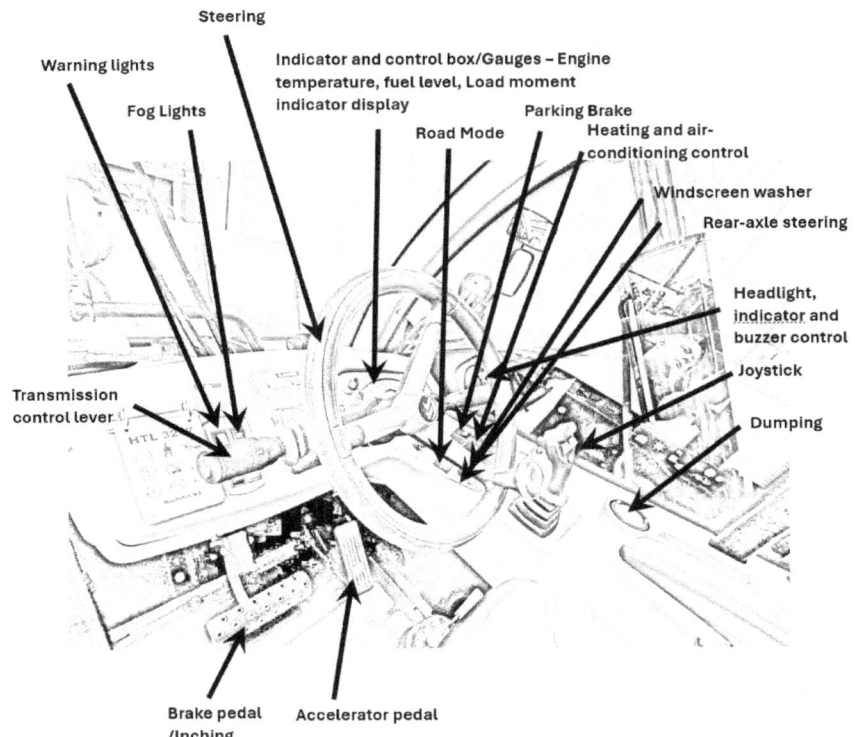

Figure 57: Example of a typical telehandler interior cabin and controls.

Starting a Telehandler

Prior to engaging the machine, it is crucial to examine all control levers, buttons, and switches. They must be clean, properly aligned, and operate smoothly without any obstructions. Should any controls seem to be sticking or malfunctioning, they may need lubrication or replacement. When uncertain about addressing such concerns, it is advisable to refer to the manufacturer's guidelines for guidance.

Below is a detailed sample start-up sequence for a telehandler:

1. **Pre-Start Checks:**

    ◦ Before entering the telehandler, conduct a visual inspection of the surrounding area to ensure there are no obstacles or hazards in the immediate vicinity.

- Ensure that the telehandler is parked on a level surface and that the parking brake is engaged.

- Check for any leaks or visible damage to the telehandler's exterior components, such as hydraulic hoses, tyres, and structural elements.

2. **Entering the Telehandler:**

- Approach the telehandler from the designated entry point, ensuring to maintain three points of contact (e.g., two hands and one foot) to safely climb into the operator's cab.

- Once inside the cab, fasten the seat belt securely to ensure personal safety during operation.

3. **Ignition and Engine Start:**

- Insert the ignition key into the designated slot and turn it clockwise to start the engine.

- Observe the instrument panel for any warning lights or indicators, ensuring that all systems are functioning properly before proceeding.

4. **System Checks:**

- Test the telehandler's various systems and controls to ensure proper functionality.

- Check the steering by turning the steering wheel left and right, ensuring smooth and responsive movement.

- Test the brakes by depressing the brake pedal and verifying

MATERIAL HANDLING EQUIPMENT OPERATION

that the telehandler comes to a complete stop without any unusual noises or vibrations.

- Activate the hydraulic controls to raise and lower the boom, extend and retract the telescopic arm, and tilt the forks or attachments (if applicable), ensuring smooth and precise operation.

5. Visibility and Mirrors:

- Adjust the seat and mirrors to ensure optimal visibility of the surrounding work area.
- Check all mirrors for clarity and proper alignment, ensuring a clear view of the telehandler's surroundings during operation.

6. Safety Features:

- Verify that all safety features, such as emergency stop buttons, horn, lights, and backup alarms, are functional and readily accessible.
- Familiarize yourself with the location and operation of all safety features, ensuring that you can quickly access them in case of an emergency.

7. Communication:

- If working in a team environment, establish communication with other personnel on the worksite using designated hand signals, radios, or other communication devices.
- Ensure that all team members are aware of your intended movements and actions while operating the telehandler.

8. Final Checks:

- Perform a final visual inspection of the telehandler and its immediate surroundings to ensure that everything is in order and that there are no safety hazards present.

- Confirm that all doors, windows, and access panels are securely closed to prevent any objects from entering the operator's cab during operation.

9. Ready for Operation:

- Once all pre-start checks have been completed, and you are confident that the telehandler is in optimal condition for operation, release the parking brake and prepare to begin your tasks according to the designated work plan and safety procedures.

By following this detailed start-up sequence, operators can ensure that the telehandler is properly prepared for safe and efficient operation, minimizing the risk of accidents or incidents during use.

Performing pre-operational checks on a telehandler is a crucial step in ensuring safe operation. These checks involve following the guidelines outlined in the operation and maintenance manual provided by the manufacturer. The purpose of these checks is to inspect the telehandler thoroughly for any issues that could compromise its safe operation.

During the pre-operational checks, operators need to carefully inspect the telehandler for any missing parts, damage, faults, or malfunctions. This includes examining components such as the engine, hydraulic systems, tyres, controls, safety features, and structural integrity. Any signs of wear and tear, leaks, cracks, or other abnormalities should be noted and addressed promptly.

Addressing any issues identified during the pre-operational checks is essential before proceeding with the operation of the telehandler. This may involve repairing or replacing damaged parts, addressing mechanical issues, or rectifying any faults or malfunctions. By addressing these issues proactively, operators can help ensure that the telehandler is in optimal condition for safe operation.

Overall, performing pre-operational checks according to the operation and maintenance manual helps identify and address potential safety hazards before they can pose a risk during operation. This proactive approach contributes to maintaining a safe working environment and preventing accidents or injuries related to telehandler operation.

Limiting devices installed on telehandlers are pivotal for maintaining safety during operations, as they are intended to prevent the machine from operating beyond its designated safe parameters. Regular testing of these limiting devices is essential to verify their proper functionality and to uphold the safety of both the operator and nearby personnel. Here is a detailed procedure for testing telehandler limiting devices:

1. Refer to the Operator's Manual: Before initiating any tests, it is imperative to consult the manufacturer's operator manual specific to the telehandler model being used. The manual will offer comprehensive instructions on how to conduct tests for each limiting device.

2. Prepare the Telehandler:

    - Ensure that the telehandler is positioned on level ground.

    - Verify that the telehandler is free from any loads or attachments that could potentially affect its balance.

    - Clear the surrounding area of other personnel.

3. Test Load Limiting Devices:

- Start the telehandler and raise a known weight, preferably approaching its maximum rated capacity.

- As the safe working load is approached, the limiting device should activate, halting further lifting or alerting the operator through an alarm.

- Note: It is crucial never to exceed the rated capacity during the testing of the limit device.

4. Test Height Limiting Devices:

- Extend the boom or lifting mechanism without any load.

- As the boom reaches its maximum safe extension, the height limiting device should activate, preventing further extension or sounding an alarm.

5. Test Reach Limiting Devices:

- Extend the boom forward without any load.

- As the maximum forward reach is approached, the limiting device should activate, either stopping further extension or triggering an alarm.

6. Test Tilt Limiting Devices:

- Attempt to tilt the telehandler's carriage or forks to their maximum angles.

- The tilt limiting device should prohibit the carriage or forks from tilting beyond the designated safe limits.

7. Inspect Visual and Audible Alarms:

- Many telehandlers are equipped with visual indicators

(lights) or audible alarms (buzzers) that activate when a limit is approached or exceeded.

- Ensure that these alarms activate as expected during the testing process.

8. Document the Tests:

- Record all test outcomes, including the date, time, telehandler model, and any irregularities observed during the test.
- Regularly scheduled tests should be documented to ensure compliance with safety regulations and manufacturer recommendations.

9. Address Any Irregularities:

- If a limiting device fails to activate or if alarms do not function as intended, cease telehandler operations immediately.
- Label the equipment as "Out of Service."
- Report the malfunction to supervisory personnel and arrange for necessary repairs.

10. Regular Maintenance:

- Recognize that limiting devices, like all components of heavy machinery, can deteriorate over time or become misaligned. Regular maintenance checks and calibrations, following the manufacturer's guidelines, are essential to ensure their longevity and effectiveness.

It is important to note that while these instructions provide general guidance, variations may exist depending on factors such as the telehandler model, brand, or configuration. Safety should always remain the top priority, and in case of uncertainty, consulting trained professionals or referring to the manufacturer's guidelines is advisable.

Operating a Telehandler

Operating a telehandler involves a series of steps to ensure safe and efficient operation, as well as the proper use of attachments. To begin, operators need to select a compatible attachment by evaluating task requirements such as load weight, dimensions, and material type. Following this, safe attachment fitting is crucial, requiring adherence to manufacturer instructions and workplace procedures to ensure proper attachment to the telehandler's lifting mechanism and secure locking mechanisms.

Quick couplers, found on some telehandlers, facilitate the rapid and effortless changing of attachments. These couplers come in two main types:

Mechanical Quick Coupler: In this type, the hitch is engaged with the attachment using the boom functions in conjunction with fork carriage tilt. Once the quick coupler and attachment are engaged, a locking pin or pins are inserted and secured with a retaining pin.

Hydraulic Quick Coupler: Similar to the mechanical quick coupler, the hydraulic version is engaged in the same manner, but the locking pin or pins are engaged hydraulically using controls within the telehandler cab.

Both types of quick couplers pose a risk of attachment detachment if the manual locking pin is omitted or if the hydraulic locking pin fails to fully engage. Instances of serious injury caused by falling attachments and misuse have been reported. Therefore, it is imperative for operators to physically verify that all quick couplers are securely locked before commencing work with a newly attached attachment.

MATERIAL HANDLING EQUIPMENT OPERATION

Regarding attachment usage, it is paramount that attachments fitted to telehandlers are utilized only for their intended purposes. An illustrative case of misuse involved using a bucket fitted to a telehandler to drive in a fence post, resulting in the post's failure and the bucket detaching and fatally injuring the person guiding the post.

When it comes to lifting suspended loads, many telehandlers can be equipped with lifting hooks or crane jibs. However, before engaging in such lifting operations, a thorough review should be conducted to ascertain if a telehandler is the most suitable lifting equipment for the task at hand.

The lifting of suspended loads must always be executed with a telehandler that is equipped with a suitable lifting hook or attachment. If an alternative method is deemed necessary, it must be justified through a comprehensive risk assessment, considering the hierarchy of control.

Any lifting hook or crane jib should be clearly marked with a Rated Capacity (Safe Working Load), which must not be exceeded. The Rated Capacity should be determined based on the lower value between the hook or jib and the telehandler. Additionally, when calculating the total weight of the load to be lifted, the weight of the lifting hook or crane jib and any lifting accessories must be factored in.

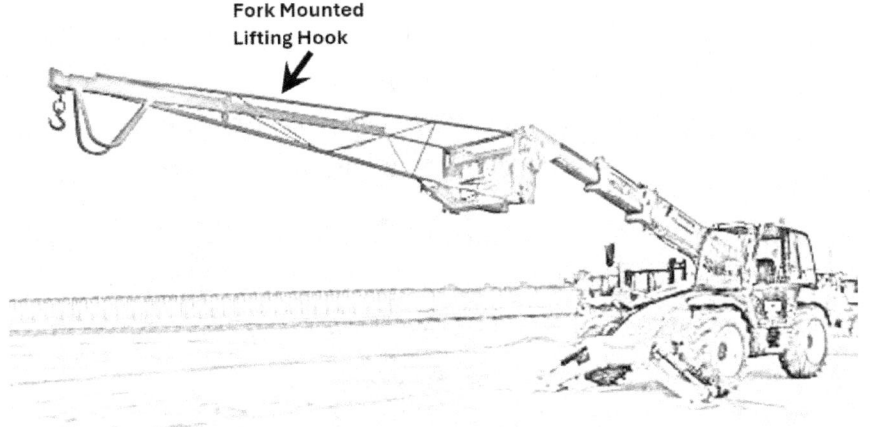

Figure 58: Example of a lifting hook attachment.

Telehandler manufacturers providing lifting hooks and crane jibs for their machines typically offer attachment/machine combination specific load charts to mitigate the risk of overload or overturn. When traveling with a suspended load, extreme caution should be exercised as any movement of the load can alter the load radius and potentially impact the stability of the telehandler.

Suspended loads should never be affixed to chains or slings over the forks or carriage. Only a securely designed, rigorously tested, and thoroughly inspected attachment should be employed for transporting a suspended load. Insecurely attached lifting accessories often lead to accidents, sometimes resulting in fatalities, particularly during lifting and traveling with suspended loads.

Utilizing a telehandler for lifting suspended loads should only occur with the presence of the appropriate load chart specifically designated for the attachment in use. Traveling with suspended loads must strictly adhere to the manufacturer's instructions, with any necessary consultation with the manufacturer conducted beforehand.

Checking a telehandler attachment for proper fitting and safe operation involves several steps to ensure efficiency and mitigate risks. This includes::

- Reviewing Manufacturer Instructions: Start by consulting the manufacturer's instruction manual for both the telehandler and the specific attachment. These manuals provide detailed guidelines on how to correctly attach and operate the equipment.

- Inspecting the Attachment: Thoroughly examine the attachment for any visible signs of damage, wear, or defects. Check the integrity of hydraulic hoses, pins, and connectors to ensure they are intact and free from damage.

- Cleaning the Connection Points: Clear any dirt, debris, or grease from the connection points on both the telehandler and the attachment to ensure a secure fit during operation.

- Ensuring Proper Alignment and Connection: Verify that the telehandler's connection points align correctly with those on the attachment. Confirm that pins, bolts, or connectors are securely in place, and ensure hydraulic connectors are firmly attached.

- Checking Safety Mechanisms: Ensure that all safety devices, such as locking pins or safety chains, are correctly installed and functional. Remove any tools or materials that could pose a hazard during operation.

- Testing the Attachment: Raise and lower the attachment to ensure it moves freely without obstruction. If the attachment is hydraulic, test its functions to ensure they are operating correctly and check for hydraulic fluid leaks.

- Checking Load Limits: Be aware of the load-bearing capacities and limitations of the attachment, as different attachments may affect the telehandler's load limits. Always refer to the attachment-specific load chart for guidance.

- Verifying Attachment Security: After testing, re-check the attachment's security to the telehandler to ensure it has not become loose or disengaged.

- Maintaining Operational Awareness: Stay vigilant for any changes in the telehandler's behaviour due to the attachment. Some attachments may impact the machine's centre of gravity, stability, or overall handling.

- Performing Routine Checks: Even after initial fitting, regularly inspect the attachment during operation breaks to ensure it remains securely connected and functions without issues. Conduct periodic maintenance checks on both the telehandler and its attachments for signs of wear or potential problems.

- Documenting the Process: Record details of the attachment fitting, including the date, time, operator name, and any observations or anomalies noted during the process.

- Ensuring Training and Supervision: Ensure that operators receive appropriate training for the specific attachment they are using. Consider providing additional training or supervision for operators using new or unfamiliar attachments to enhance safety.

Once the attachment is fitted, a thorough inspection is necessary to verify correct fitting and safe operation, checking for any signs of damage or wear. Operators must then use the attachment within its limits, adhering to design limits, load charts, and workplace procedures to prevent exceeding capacity or operating parameters. Adapting operating techniques to changing work conditions may involve adjustments in speed, boom angle, or the use of stabilizers for stability and safety.

During lifts, it's essential to conduct them within the actual capacity of the telehandler, ensuring compliance with safety protocols and load chart requirements. Continuous risk monitoring is critical, with operators remaining vigilant for potential hazards and taking proactive measures to mitigate risks.

Maintaining clear communication with other site personnel using hand signals, audible warnings, or radio communication equipment is vital during telehandler operations. Test lifts should be performed to ensure load security, telehandler stability, and correct machine operation before handling actual loads.

Moving loads safely requires following relevant telehandler movements as per manufacturer instructions and workplace procedures, exercising caution to ensure load stability throughout the operation. Safe landing of loads involves lowering them gently and ensuring secure positioning before releasing them from the attachment.

Operating on slopes necessitates following safe operating practices to travel up and down slopes, maintaining control of the machine and adjusting speed and direction as needed. Before reversing the telehandler, relevant checks for obstacles and clear visibility must be conducted, following workplace procedures for safe reversing manoeuvres.

Finally, operators must respond promptly to alarms and indicators, completing work within the equipment's actual capacity and following manufacturer instructions and workplace procedures. By following these detailed steps, operators can ensure the safe and effective operation of telehandlers and their attachments in various work environments.

Once the load is organized, positioning the telehandler to commence work is the next step. Ideally, park the telehandler on a level surface before starting work. On rough terrain, use stabilizers to level the telehandler before beginning operations. It's crucial to note that raising the boom and attachments should not exceed 1.2 meters unless the telehandler is stable. Any movement near or at the maximum operating height should be executed slowly and with deliberate care. By positioning and operating the telehandler in this manner, the risk of tipping is significantly minimized.

Limited visibility, especially when the boom is raised or when carrying large loads, coupled with poor segregation, has been identified as a major factor contributing to accidents involving pedestrians and telehandlers. Most telehandlers feature a side-mounted cab, with the boom centrally or right-mounted on the chassis. However, this cab configuration obstructs the operator's view around the machine, particularly when seated, due to cab pillars and other structural elements.

Certain stages of the loading cycle may obstruct the operator's line of sight, hindering a clear view.

Figure 59: View from the cabin of a Magni 360 slew telehandler. Adrian Bulibasa, CC BY-SA 4.0, via Wikimedia Commons.

In older telehandler designs, a high mounting for the rear of the boom made visibility to the right front quarter nearly impossible, prompting operators to drive with the boom raised for improved visibility. Modern telehandlers now feature low-profile booms that drop below the eye line when in the transport position, reducing the need to raise the boom for visibility. Supervisors should question the practice of driving with the boom raised as it heightens the risk of dynamic instability.

Operators should ensure, through appropriate means, that the area immediately surrounding the machine is clear of personnel before starting a task. This may involve exiting the cab and inspecting the machine's surroundings. Clean cab windows aid operator visibility and should be included in pre-use checks.

When selecting visibility aids, users should consider factors such as vehicle speed, site conditions, lighting, and human factors. Aids should be chosen and installed to maximize the operator's ability to perceive danger without causing confusion. The positioning of monitors and mirrors should be optimized for the operator's normal operating position, minimizing the need to look in multiple directions. For repetitive operations, additional automatic sensing systems may be beneficial to enhance safety and ergonomic considerations.

Wide angle convex mirrors are utilized to enhance visibility along the sides and rear areas of vehicles, aiding in manoeuvring and ensuring safety. In the case of telehandlers, these mirrors are strategically placed to provide views to the sides and rearward, allowing operators to assess surrounding areas before initiating movement. When selecting and installing convex mirrors, users must consider the inherent distortion in the mirror's image, which increases with the degree of convexity. This distortion can lead to inaccuracies in distance estimation, potentially compromising safety. Additionally, excessive vehicle vibrations transmitted through the mirror mountings can disrupt the image, rendering the mirror ineffective in providing clear visibility. Both factors must be carefully evaluated to ensure the effectiveness of the mirror installation.

Driving and operating a telehandler safely requires adaptability, particularly as work conditions can vary. Here is a general guide on how to effectively drive and operate a telehandler, along with techniques to modify based on changing work conditions.

Understanding Basic Operation: Prior to driving the telehandler, ensure familiarity with its controls, indicators, and alarms. Refer to the operator's manual for specific controls unique to the model.

Initial Safety Checks: Begin with a pre-operation inspection to identify any potential mechanical issues. Check brakes, tyres, lights, horn, and other safety features. Ensure all mirrors and cameras are clean and properly adjusted for maximum visibility.

Assessing Work Conditions: Observe the terrain and adjust driving speed accordingly, especially on uneven or slippery surfaces. Take note of overhead obstacles if raising the boom and be aware of other personnel or machinery nearby.

Modifying Techniques for Changing Conditions: Adapt driving techniques based on ground and weather conditions. Use 4-wheel drive on unstable terrains for better traction. Adjust speed and load handling in adverse weather conditions.

Monitoring Load Stability: Always ensure the load is secure before moving. Keep the load low to the ground to maintain stability. Be cautious when raising the boom, as it affects the telehandler's centre of gravity.

Operating in Crowded Areas: Utilize a spotter or ground guide when visibility is limited. Use the horn to alert personnel of movements and give right of way to pedestrians.

Continuous Monitoring: Regularly check instruments and gauges during operation for any signs of issues. Pay attention to unfamiliar noises, vibrations, or changes in performance.

Modifying Techniques as Needed: Adjust operations based on conditions. For example, reduce attachment height or work at slower speeds in windy conditions to maintain control.

End-of-Operation Checks: Lower attachments to the ground once the task is completed. Park the telehandler on level ground, engage the parking brake, and conduct a visual inspection for any signs of damage or wear.

General Telehandler Driving Procedures

The majority of telehandlers are equipped with steering systems that offer three modes: normal, four-wheel steer, and crab steer.

Steering in two-wheel steer mode: Starting off in two-wheel steer mode is often recommended for training purposes. In this mode, only the front wheels are engaged for steering, making it suitable for long-distance travel and highway use. It's important to emphasize that changing the steering mode should only be done while the machine is stationary to prevent transmission damage. Additionally, both front and rear wheels must be aligned straight before changing the mode, typically indicated by illuminated indicator lights.

Observation and visibility are crucial when operating telehandlers, as serious accidents often result from hazards being overlooked. Visibility to the right of the driver's cab is particularly hindered by the boom, necessitating the use of mirrors to assist with visibility, although they should not replace physically looking around.

Steering in four-wheel steer mode: Four-wheel steer mode is the most commonly used steering mode for telehandlers, offering increased manoeuvrability. It is recommended for the majority of training exercises, including manoeuvring in confined spaces while maintaining awareness of surroundings.

Steering in crab steer mode: Crab steer mode, where the machine moves diagonally, is the third steering mode available for telehandlers. While less commonly used in practice, it can be helpful for slight sideways movements to align with stacking positions. Trainees should practice left and right steering, as well as forward and backward movements, to become familiar with this mode.

Before engaging in stacking and de-stacking tasks, operators must learn to operate the hydraulic controls safely. Typically, there is one lever for raise/lower/tilt functions and another for extending the telescopic boom.

Telehandlers are equipped with safety features such as a radius plate, which provides information similar to a capacity plate on conventional machines. This plate indicates load centre and how the telescopic boom's extension affects capacity. Additionally, some machines feature a level gauge positioned above the windscreen to assist in achieving a level position. An overload warning device is standard on all telehandlers, providing both visual and audible signals if the machine becomes overloaded.

Telehandler Stacking Procedure

Approach the stack with the load positioned low and tilted backward, ensuring the wheels are as straight as possible. If the telehandler is equipped with hydraulic stabilizing jacks, lower them at this stage. Machines with a level indicator should be made level at this point.

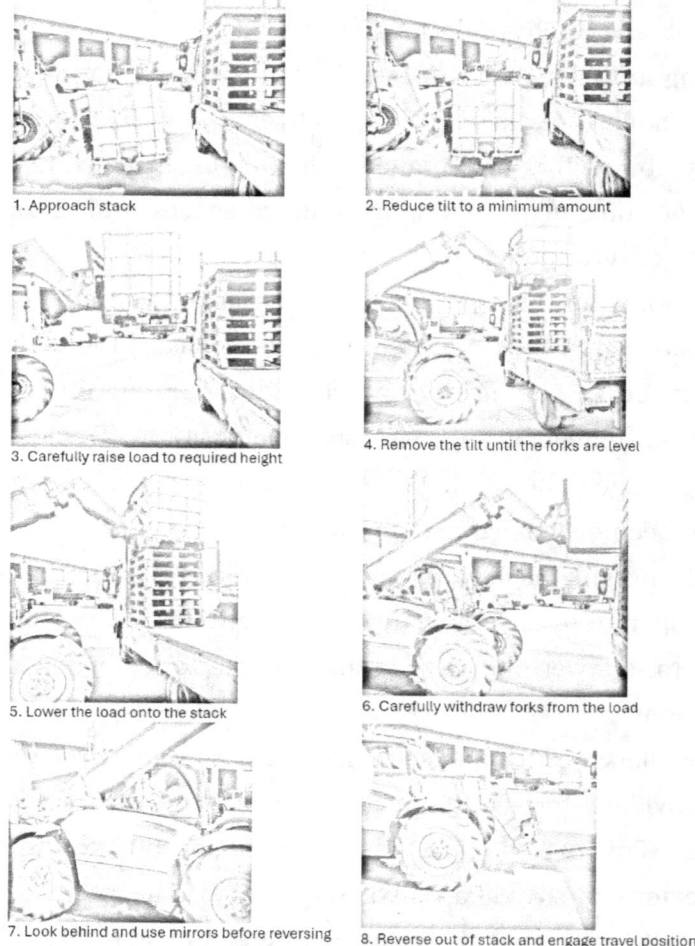

Figure 60: Stacking procedure.

Minimize Tilt: Gradually reduce the tilt to the minimum required to stabilize the load, taking care not to engage forward tilt mistakenly. Telehandlers offer a wide range of tilt options both forward and backward.

Carefully Position Load: Raise and extend the boom until the load is directly over the stack, monitoring the boom angle, extension, and overload indicator. If the overload indicator activates, immediately stop the procedure, retract the boom first, and then lower it.

Level the Load: Remove all tilt until the forks and load are level, ensuring proper alignment with the stack.

Lower the Load onto the Stack: Lower the load onto the stack by adjusting the boom angle and retracting it slightly if necessary. Exercise caution as retracting the boom may also cause downward movement, potentially posing a hazard. Some telehandlers are designed to allow the forks to "ride up" slightly in such situations.

Withdraw the Forks: Release and withdraw the forks using a combination of boom retracting and tilt angle controls, being mindful of potential hazards. If the ground is level, it's preferable to withdraw the forks by reversing the machine.

Check Behind Before Reversing: Before moving, visually inspect the area behind the machine by turning around and using mirrors to cover blind spots. Do not solely rely on mirrors for this purpose.

Reverse and Prepare for Travel: Carefully reverse out of the stacking position, lower the boom, and position the forks in the correct unladen travel position, as close to the ground as possible with rear tilt applied. Prior to reversing, thoroughly check all around, and then look in the direction of travel.

Unstacking with a telehandler involves the reverse process of stacking. One of the challenges encountered is ensuring that the forks remain level, especially when entering confined spaces such as a pack of bricks.

These machines are equipped with a tilt lock feature, which means that if the forks are level (horizontal) at the bottom, they will remain in that position at all boom heights. The most effective method to confirm the levelness of the forks is to raise them to eye level and visually inspect along the top of the forks. With some practice, achieving a horizontal position becomes straightforward. Once levelled, the tilt lever typically should not require adjustment. However, minor adjustments may be necessary as the forks penetrate the load.

Managing Loads

Performing a test lift is a fundamental safety measure when using a telehandler. It ensures the load's security, the telehandler's stability under load conditions, and the proper operation of the machine. Here's a step-by-step guide on how to conduct a test lift:

1. Pre-Inspection:

- Inspect the telehandler for any visible signs of damage or wear, focusing on components such as tyres, brakes, lights, and hydraulic systems.

- Ensure the telehandler is on stable, level ground, and deploy outriggers or stabilizers if available.

1. Check Load Data:

- Determine the weight of the load and confirm it does not exceed the telehandler's rated capacity.

- Identify the load's centre of gravity and ensure it is properly balanced and secured.

1. Start the Telehandler:

- Turn on the telehandler and allow it to run for a few minutes to ensure all systems are functioning correctly.

- Listen for any unusual sounds that may indicate issues.

1. Initial Lift:

- Raise the load a few centimetres off the ground.
- Check for any tilting or imbalance in the telehandler.
- Monitor any shifting or instability of the load.
- Ensure all hydraulic systems, such as boom extension and tilt, operate smoothly.

1. Full Extension Test:

- Extend the boom carefully to its planned operating distance for the task (avoid full extension unless necessary).
- Monitor the telehandler's stability and ensure there is no excessive swaying or movement of the load.

1. Height Test:

- Lift the load to its planned operating height.
- Observe the telehandler's stability and ensure there is no tipping.
- Watch for any unusual movement or shifting of the load.

1. Manoeuvre Test:

- With the load lifted, practice minor manoeuvres that will be performed during actual operations.
- Evaluate how the telehandler handles the load while in motion.

1. Lower the Load:

- Slowly and smoothly lower the load back to the ground.

- Check the telehandler's controls for accurate and prompt response.

1. Check Warning Systems:

- Verify that onboard warning systems, such as alarms or alert lights, are operational.

- These systems are essential as they can alert the operator if the machine approaches its operational limits.

1. Review:

- After the test lift, assess any issues or challenges encountered during the process.

- Make necessary adjustments to the operation plan or take corrective measures as required.

1. Ensure Communication:

- If working with a team, ensure all team members are familiar with communication signals and protocols.

- Clear communication is vital for safety during actual operations.

Performing a test lift is a critical step in ensuring safe telehandler operations. Safety should always be prioritized over speed, and this step should never be skipped, especially when dealing with unfamiliar loads or environments.

Telehandlers are frequently utilized for positioning suspended loads. The standard rating of a telehandler pertains to lifting unit loads on forks; hence, the standard load chart does not apply to lifting suspended loads due to variations in load centres and the impact of any side slope. Since 2010, newly manufactured machines are mandated to be equipped with longitudinal load moment control (as detailed in the operator's manual). This feature provides operators with indications concerning longitudinal stability when stationary and prevents the machine from operating beyond manufacturer-determined limits. Such machines offer enhanced safety measures when lifting suspended loads. There are two primary operating configurations (duties) for lifting suspended loads with a telehandler:

1. Lifting a suspended load with the telehandler stationary and supported on stabilizers or

2. Lifting a suspended load with the telehandler stationary, unsecured on wheels

It is strongly advised that stabilizers, if available, be consistently employed when lifting suspended loads. As both operating configurations represent specific applications of telehandler use, standard load charts for lifting unit loads on forks are not applicable. Instead, specific load charts tailored to each configuration must be referenced and followed meticulously.

It is essential for the operator of a telehandler to have precise information regarding the weight of the load to be lifted. This information can typically be obtained from various sources, including:

- The manufacturer's data plate;

- Markings directly on the load;

- Manufacturer-provided data sheets or instructions;

- Engineering drawings;

- Shipping documents;

- Direct weighing of the load.

In cases where obtaining the exact weight is not feasible, an estimation can be made by calculating the volume and referencing relevant data, as outlined in the table below. However, such estimations should be approached with caution, considering factors such as irregular shapes, composite materials, or the presence of hollow spaces containing additional materials that may shift during lifting operations.

When using a telehandler for loading or unloading tasks, ensuring the stability of the load on the vehicle or stack is crucial to prevent potential hazards. Without following the correct sequence of loading or unloading, there's a risk of instability, which could lead to injuries to nearby individuals. Loading procedures should always be carried out with unloading in mind, focusing on evenly distributing the load and working methodically from side to side. When unloading, this sequence should be reversed. Additionally, when loading uncoupled articulated trailers, priority should be given to placing the first part of the load over the rear axle before proceeding to load from the front.

Furthermore, precautions should be taken to prevent any part of the load from being dislodged by contact with the telehandler carriage, forks, or other attachments. Measures such as establishing exclusion zones or barriers can help ensure that personnel are kept clear of falling loads. Before lifting a load, it's imperative to assess its stability and security, ensuring that the forks are evenly spaced on either side of the load's centre of gravity. For long or irregularly shaped loads, the centre of gravity may be closer to the edges of the forks, increasing the risk of instability during lifting operations.

Utilization of Attachments The lifting capacity of a telehandler can be influenced by the attachment being used. While forks are commonly employed, various attachments such as truss booms, buckets, or work platforms offer different load capacities and configurations. Understanding the weight, lift height, and reach requirements, as well as the capacity of both the machine and the attachment, is essential for safe operation. Each attachment comes with its specific loading capacity, which may vary based on factors such as weight, dimensions, and load centre position. Contractors and operators must refer to the relevant load chart specific to the chosen attachment, ensuring it is readable and accessible before initiating any lifting activity.

To ensure compliance with telehandler load chart requirements and safe work procedures, the following steps should be followed:

1. Refer to the Load Chart: Consult the telehandler's load chart for maximum allowable load at different boom angles, lengths, and extensions.

2. Determine the Weight of the Load: Utilize load weighing systems or estimate the weight based on specifications if unknown.

3. Check the Load Position: Ensure the load's centre of gravity is close to the telehandler's mast or boom and evenly distributed on the forks or attachment.

4. Assess Boom Angle and Extension: Determine required boom angle and extension, cross-referencing with the load chart.

5. Consider Telehandler's Condition: Conduct a pre-lift inspection to ensure the machine is in optimal working condition.

6. Evaluate Ground Conditions: Position the telehandler on stable, level ground, avoiding soft or uneven terrain.

7. Check Attachment Positioning: Ensure attachments are securely and correctly attached, considering their weight in overall lifting capacity.

8. Adjust as Needed: Modify load weight, positioning, or boom angle if necessary to align with load chart requirements.

9. Monitor During Operation: Continuously monitor telehandler behaviour and load stability, responding promptly to any anomalies or warnings.

Travelling

It is imperative that telehandlers are driven with the boom lowered to maintain the lowest possible centre of gravity for both the machine and the load. Driving with the boom raised should never be considered standard practice due to the associated risks outlined above. Any decision to drive with the boom raised introduces additional hazards that must be carefully evaluated.

In instances where site constraints make manoeuvring impossible without raising the boom, site management should reconsider the use of a telehandler altogether or explore alternative machine options. Raising the boom solely for visibility purposes, a practice seen in the past, is outdated considering the modern design of telehandlers, which eliminates the need for such measures. Therefore, supervisors should always challenge and discourage the regular practice of driving a telehandler with the boom raised.

Travelling with a suspended load involves moving with the boom raised from its normal transport position, resulting in additional dynamic forces caused by the swinging of the load. If provided with information by the manufacturer and permitted by the site, the following guidelines should be followed:

1. Keep the boom and load as close to the ground as possible (approximately 300-500mm above the ground). Proper selection of chain or sling lengths is crucial to achieve this.

2. Extend the boom only as much as necessary to prevent the load from interfering with the front of the telehandler chassis, ensuring that the load radius remains within the limits specified

by the load chart.

3. Expect reduced visibility and plan accordingly with appropriate control measures, such as utilizing a marshaller to guide the operator.

4. Minimize load swing through careful control manipulation and maintaining slow travel speeds.

5. Exercise caution during braking and turning to avoid transmitting dynamic forces to the boom, which compromises stability.

6. Never allow slinger/signallers or other personnel to walk in front of the telehandler to stabilize a swinging load, as this poses a significant risk of tripping, falling, and being crushed by the telehandler wheels.

7. Maintain an extremely slow travel speed, never exceeding walking pace.

8. Adhere to the manufacturer's instructions for travelling on slopes and inclines, avoiding attempts to navigate inclines beyond the manufacturer's specified limits to mitigate the risk of overturning.

9. Special consideration should be given to lightweight but bulky items like roof trusses, which pose unique risks due to their size, wind susceptibility, and dynamic forces. Site-specific restrictions may necessitate raising the boom to clear fixed obstructions, adding extra risk that must be addressed in the site's risk assessment.

10. Be vigilant to avoid overhead obstructions, including power lines.

To ensure adequate traction and braking capabilities when traveling on slopes, follow these guidelines:

- When the telehandler is unloaded, the rear of the machine is the heavier end. Drive with the forks pointed downhill to maintain stability.

- Conversely, when the telehandler is loaded, the front of the machine becomes the heavier end. In this case, drive with the forks pointed uphill for better traction.

- To prevent the machine from accelerating uncontrollably on slopes, downshift to a lower gear and use the service brake as needed to maintain a slow and safe speed.

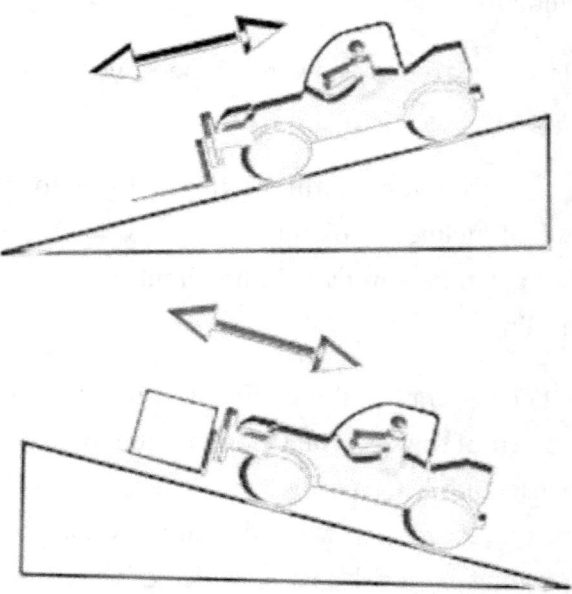

Figure 61: Correct travel directions on slopes with and without loads.

When navigating steep slopes beyond the maximum gradients outlined for planning purposes or when operating in non-standard travel modes (e.g., with the boom raised or extended), a comprehensive risk assessment is necessary. This assessment should be conducted by a competent individual who has access to the telehandler manufacturer's guidance and understands the associated risks. Operators trained in handling dynamic and raised loads, and familiar with the manufacturer's guidelines, are capable of performing this assessment.

Precautions and operating techniques for safe travel on steep slopes include:

- During job planning, carefully select routes or prepare the terrain to avoid very steep slopes, slippery surfaces, or loose terrain.

- Maintain the correct driving direction and traveling position for negotiating slopes. When carrying a load, position the load facing uphill. When unloaded, position the fork arms facing downhill.

- Avoid making turns or traversing slopes, unless the machine is specifically equipped for such manoeuvres. Descend straight down the gentlest gradient instead of driving diagonally across it.

- Never attempt to stack or de-stack a load on a slope.

- Exercise caution to avoid sharp turns while traveling on slopes.

- Be aware of the risk of overturning sideways or rearward, particularly when moving with a raised boom, even when the telehandler is unloaded.

Some manufacturers provide load charts outlining load, speed, and slope limits for traveling with a unit load on forks. These guidelines should be consulted and adhered to for safe operation.

Figure 62: *Example load chart indications of slope limits.*

Ensuring safe operations when reversing a telehandler requires careful checks to minimize potential hazards. This includes conducting a pre-operational inspection to assess the telehandler's general condition, ensuring there are no visible damages or issues. This involves examining the brakes, lights, and reverse alarm to confirm they're functioning correctly.

Clearing the rear view is crucial. Operators should ensure the rearview mirrors are clean and adjusted correctly to provide a clear view of the area behind the telehandler. Additionally, if equipped, they should ensure that any rear-view camera systems are operational and providing a clear view.

Before initiating the reverse, operators should check the surrounding area by physically inspecting the space behind the telehandler to ensure it's free from obstructions, people, equipment, or any potential hazards. They should also note any obstacles, holes, or unstable ground conditions that could pose challenges during the reversing manoeuvre.

Internally, operators need to confirm that the driver's seat and controls are adjusted correctly for the operator and that there are no obstructions hindering the operator's line of sight inside the cab.

Communication is key, especially in busy environments or when the view is obstructed. Operators should consider using a spotter or banksman to guide the reversing process and establish clear communication signals with them.

Before reversing, operators should activate any auditory or visual warning systems, like reverse alarms or flashing lights, to alert surrounding personnel.

They should also confirm that the telehandler's movement controls, such as the gear selector and steering wheel, are responsive and functioning correctly. Before initiating the reverse, they should gently test the brakes to ensure they're responsive and can halt the telehandler efficiently if needed during the reversing process.

Planning the path is essential. Operators should mentally map out their intended path, considering any turns or manoeuvres they'll need to make and any potential obstacles in their path.

When initiating the reverse, operators should proceed slowly and steadily. Quick or abrupt movements can lead to errors or accidents.

Continuous monitoring of the area behind and around the telehandler is essential as operators reverse. If equipped with a camera system, operators should alternate between using it and physically checking mirrors and surroundings.

By diligently performing these checks and maintaining a heightened sense of awareness, operators can ensure that reversing a telehandler is conducted safely and efficiently.

Completing Telehandler Operations

Completing telehandler operations includes:

1. **Attachments Removal, Cleaning, and Storage:**

    - Following manufacturer instructions and workplace procedures, detach attachments from the telehandler safely, ensuring no damage to the equipment or surroundings.

    - Clean each attachment meticulously using approved cleaning agents and tools, adhering to manufacturer guidelines to maintain optimal performance and longevity.

- Store attachments in designated areas as per workplace procedures, ensuring they are securely positioned to prevent accidents and damage, and are easily accessible for future use.

2. **Preparation for Transport:**

    - As per workplace procedures, prepare the telehandler for transport by securing loose items, retracting the boom, and removing any attachments if necessary.

    - Adhere to guidelines for loading and securing the telehandler onto transport vehicles, ensuring compliance with safety regulations and minimizing risks during transportation.

3. **Parking and Shutdown Procedures:**

    - Safely park the telehandler in a designated area away from traffic and pedestrians, ensuring the ground is stable and level.

    - Engage the parking brake, shift the transmission to neutral, and power off the engine in accordance with workplace procedures.

    - Complete any additional shutdown procedures specified by workplace protocols or outlined in the manufacturer's manual.

4. **Exiting the Telehandler:**

    - Utilize three points of contact (e.g., two hands and one foot) when exiting the telehandler, ensuring stability and minimizing the risk of falls.

- Descend from the telehandler cautiously, paying attention to surroundings and potential hazards, such as slippery surfaces or uneven terrain.

5. **Routine Shutdown Checks and Maintenance:**

   - Adhere to manufacturer maintenance instructions and workplace protocols for routine shutdown checks and maintenance.

   - Conduct inspections of fluid levels, hoses, belts, and other components, addressing any issues promptly to prevent malfunctions and ensure the telehandler's continued reliability.

6. **Post-Operational Checks and Reporting:**

   - Perform thorough post-operational checks on both the telehandler and attachments to identify any malfunctions, faults, or irregular performance.

   - Record and report any identified issues promptly and accurately, following workplace procedures for documentation and reporting to facilitate timely resolution and maintenance.

7. **Tagging Out of Service:**

   - If a defect is detected that renders the telehandler unsafe for use, follow workplace procedures for tagging the equipment out of service.

   - Attach a clearly visible tag indicating the reason for the telehandler being out of service and any necessary repair or maintenance actions required.

8. **Key Removal and Secure Storage:**

    ◦ Remove the telehandler keys from the ignition and store them securely in accordance with workplace protocols to prevent unauthorized use or access.

9. **Maintenance of Usage Records:**

    ◦ Maintain meticulous records of telehandler and attachment usage, documenting dates, times, tasks performed, and any issues encountered during operation.

    ◦ Adhere to workplace procedures for record-keeping to ensure accurate and comprehensive documentation of equipment usage and maintenance history.

Attachment Removal Safety should always come first when removing attachments from a telehandler. Before beginning the removal process, ensure that the telehandler is switched off, parked securely on stable ground, and the parking brake is engaged to prevent any accidental movement. Utilize the designated release mechanisms or levers specified by the manufacturer to detach the attachment safely. It's essential to follow the removal procedure meticulously, as some attachments may require multiple steps or sequences for proper detachment. Avoid using excessive force during the removal process, as this can potentially damage the attachment or the telehandler. If encountering resistance, carefully assess the situation to identify any obstructions or missed steps in the process.

Cleaning the Attachments Before initiating the cleaning process, conduct a thorough inspection of the attachment to check for any dirt, debris, or residues accumulated during operation. Depending on the type of attachment and the materials it's made of, select appropriate cleaning agents as recommended by the manufacturer's manual. After applying the cleaning agents, rinse off any residues thoroughly and allow the attachment to dry completely. This step is crucial for preventing rusting or corrosion, especially for metal attachments. Following the cleaning process, carefully inspect the attachment for any signs of wear, damage, or potential malfunctions. Any identified issues should be reported immediately for further evaluation and resolution.

Storing the Attachments When it comes to storing attachments, adherence to proper procedures is paramount to ensure their longevity and safety. Always store attachments in their designated areas to facilitate easy identification and minimize the risk of damage or accidents. If attachments are susceptible to damage from weather elements, ensure that storage areas provide adequate protection, especially against moisture or rust. Clearly label each attachment, particularly in workplaces where multiple similar-looking attachments are used. Some workplaces may also require maintaining a log detailing when an attachment was used, cleaned, and stored. Beyond the manufacturer's guidelines, strict adherence to workplace storage procedures or protocols is essential to maintain the integrity of the attachments.

Continuous Care Regular maintenance is key to ensuring the optimal performance and longevity of attachments. Even when not in use, periodically inspect attachments for any signs of wear or damage. Schedule routine maintenance as per the manufacturer's instructions to address any issues promptly and prevent potential failures during operation. Stay updated on any new guidelines or recommendations provided by the manufacturer regarding the care and maintenance of attachments to ensure that they continue to function safely and effectively.

Ensuring the safe transport of a telehandler involves meticulous attention to safety guidelines and adherence to workplace procedures. Here's a detailed guide on how to prepare your telehandler for transport:

    1. Consult the Manual: Always begin by consulting the manufac-

turer's manual for specific transportation guidelines.

2. Conduct a Pre-Transport Inspection: Check for any visible damage or leaks, ensure all components are in working condition, and verify the functionality of lights, brakes, and indicators.

3. Secure the Equipment: Lower the boom fully, remove any attachments if necessary, and store them separately. Ensure the forks are in their lowest position or removed and securely stored.

4. Drain Fluids if Required: Depending on the transport distance and mode, consider draining fluids to prevent leaks, following manufacturer recommendations.

5. Disengage Drive Systems: Engage the parking brake, turn off all power, remove the key, and activate any transmission disconnect features.

6. Secure Loose Parts: Remove or secure loose components to prevent damage during transit.

7. Check Tyre Pressure: Ensure all tyres are properly inflated to recommended pressure to prevent damage during loading, transit, and unloading.

8. Document Equipment Condition: Document the telehandler's condition with photographs for insurance purposes or in case of damage during transport.

9. Loading onto a Transport Vehicle: Use ramps capable of supporting the telehandler's weight, drive slowly onto the transport vehicle, and engage the parking brake.

10. Secure the Telehandler: Use heavy-duty chains, straps, or cables

to secure the telehandler to the transport vehicle, ensuring it doesn't move during transit.

11. Label as Required: Follow local regulations or workplace procedures regarding labelling for oversized loads.

12. Confirm Transport Vehicle's Readiness: Ensure the transport vehicle is in good working condition with functioning lights, brakes, and indicators.

13. Final Check: Conduct a final walk-around to ensure everything is secure and ready for transport.

Loading heavy equipment safely requires careful consideration to ensure reliability and legality. Follow these safety measures for secure loading operations:

1. Designate Responsibilities: Assign roles for loading operations, including a driver and spotter, to ensure clear communication and coordination.

2. Clean the Ramp and Trailer: Ensure ramps and trailer decks are free of dirt, oil, and debris to provide optimal traction for loading equipment.

3. Clear and Level the Loading Area: Choose an uninhabited and level space for loading operations to prevent accidents and ensure stability.

4. Begin the Machine/Ramp Line-Up: Gradually drive the equipment up the ramp onto the trailer deck, maintaining slow and steady movement.

5. Start Chaining Down Heavy Equipment: Secure the equipment to the trailer deck using tight, secure chains positioned at appropriate tie-down points, following state regulations and man-

ufacturer guidelines.

6. **Additional Reminders:** Ensure chains are fastened linearly with downward force, without slack, and matched appropriately in size and grade to prevent equipment damage and ensure compliance with safety standards.

Figure 63: Telehandler being transported via float. Frédéric BISSON from Rouen, France, CC BY 2.0, via Wikimedia Commons.

Selecting an appropriate parking location is crucial for ensuring safety when parking a telehandler. It is recommended to choose a flat and solid surface, avoiding areas near embankments, ditches, or unstable terrains. Additionally, it is preferable to select a parking location that is distanced from high-traffic zones to minimize the risk of collisions or blockages.

Once parked, the telehandler's boom should be fully lowered, and any attachments, such as forks, should be grounded. Care must be taken to ensure there is no undue tension or stress on the hydraulic parts during this process.

Before initiating the shutdown sequence, the parking brake must be engaged to prevent unintentional movement of the telehandler. The machine's transmission should be set to neutral or its specified parking mode, and any supplementary systems, such as lights or air conditioning, should be turned off.

To shut down the engine, use the ignition key or the specified shutdown switch, allowing the engine to fully cease operations before proceeding. As a security measure, it is recommended to remove the ignition key post-shutdown to prevent unauthorized usage. If the telehandler has a cabin, it is prudent to close and, if possible, lock its doors and windows.

Before departing from the telehandler, a brief inspection should be conducted to check for potential leaks, damages, or operational issues. It is essential to ensure the vicinity of the machine is free from any tools or objects that might have been used.

Certain workplaces may require the logging of shutdown timings, equipment condition, or any noticeable concerns. It is important to fill out any mandatory documentation or logs as per workplace guidelines.

In shared spaces, it may be necessary to erect barriers or cones around the telehandler as a precautionary measure. Parking the machine in a designated spot or a protected area is beneficial where possible.

Communication with relevant team members or supervisory personnel is crucial once the telehandler is parked and deactivated, especially if the machine's location might affect other operations or pathways.

It should be noted that telehandlers must never be parked on steep slopes or gradients. In emergency situations where parking on a slope or gradient is unavoidable, wheels must be chocked, and the load or forks should be left in the fully lowered or grounded position. Additionally, the parking brake performance should be considered, especially on steep or inferior surfaces, as it may not be able to hold the telehandler stationary or prevent wheel slippage.

When leaving the cab of the telehandler, regardless of the reason, it is imperative for the operator to shut off the engine and remove the key. Once operations are concluded, the telehandler should be stored in a secure location, ideally on level ground, with the handbrake engaged, the boom and fork arms or handling attachment lowered to the ground, the key removed, and the cab securely locked. The key should be stored in a safe place.

Before exiting the telehandler, it is essential to take several precautionary measures. Firstly, ensure that the telehandler is parked securely on level ground with the parking brake activated. Turn off the engine and always remember to remove the ignition key to prevent any unintended movement of the machine. Additionally, clear the operator's seat and surrounding area of any potential obstructions, debris, or tools.

When ready to exit, turn towards the cab before opening the door to facilitate a backward exit, providing better grip and stability during the manoeuvre.

Maintain a firm grip while exiting, utilizing handles inside the cab door and either on the exterior of the cab or near the steps. Begin by securely placing one foot on the highest step, ensuring it is free of mud, snow, or other slippery substances. While maintaining a firm grip, proceed to the next step with the other foot.

Throughout the descent, always maintain three points of contact with the machine, distributing weight for stability and balance as you exit. This can involve a combination of two hands and one foot, or vice versa.

Descend deliberately, one step at a time, ensuring stable footing and grip at every point. Upon reaching the last step and establishing a firm grip with your hands, step onto the ground one foot at a time.

After safely exiting the telehandler, release your grip from the handles and take a moment to double-check your balance and footing before moving away from the machine.

Prioritize safety at all times, wearing appropriate footwear with good grip and avoiding rushing, jumping off, or skipping steps, as these actions can lead to accidents even from low heights. Regular inspections of the telehandler's steps and handles are recommended to identify and address any damage or obstructions that could compromise safety.

Maintaining a telehandler effectively is fundamental to ensuring safe operations. Similar to all machinery, a telehandler experiences wear, deterioration, and potential damage over time. The maintenance process, encompassing various checks and inspections, serves to monitor, prevent, and rectify this degradation. Personnel tasked with these responsibilities must possess the requisite machine-specific training, experience, and competence in both periodic and breakdown maintenance.

Both the user and owner of the telehandler, along with any attachments used, bear the responsibility of maintaining them in a safe working condition. Typically, maintenance tasks, apart from pre-use checks, are carried out by the telehandler owner. Adherence to the manufacturer's preventative maintenance instructions is crucial for maintaining safety during usage. Checks and inspections should consider the telehandler's frequency of use and the environmental conditions it regularly encounters. Competent operators may be authorized to conduct routine pre-use and weekly checks.

Employers overseeing these checks must ensure that the telehandler is taken out of service for the required duration. Additionally, they or the authorized personnel must establish a safe work system to prevent personnel from being exposed to risks, such as inadvertent equipment operation.

Basic checks and inspections should align with company instructions and the manufacturer's recommendations. Daily pre-use checks, conducted at the start of each shift or day, focus on damage and the telehandler's correct functioning. Weekly inspections serve as additional checks to the pre-use ones and should also be recorded.

Any defect affecting the telehandler's safe operation must be reported immediately, resulting in the machine being taken out of service. Defects not immediately affecting safe operation should be reported to supervisors for timely repairs.

Routine shutdown checks and maintenance are vital for ensuring the longevity and safety of a telehandler. Following the manufacturer's maintenance instructions and workplace procedures is crucial to maintaining the machine in optimal condition. This process involves several steps:

1. **Preparing for Maintenance:** Consult the manufacturer's manual and gather necessary tools and equipment.

2. **Shutdown Checks:** Conduct visual inspections, check operating systems, verify fluid levels, and inspect tyres.

3. **Routine Maintenance:** Clean the machine, check the battery, inspect hydraulic systems, lubricate components, and replace filters.

4. **Advanced Checks:** Examine brake systems, drive train, transmission, and electrical systems.

5. **Document Maintenance Activities:** Maintain a log detailing all checks and maintenance tasks performed and report any issues.

6. **Secure the Telehandler:** Store the machine appropriately, remove the ignition key, and store it securely.

7. **Stay Updated:** Attend regular training sessions, and stay informed about manufacturer updates and guidelines.

Consistent maintenance is a proactive approach to prolonging equipment life and ensuring operator safety.

Post-operational checks are essential to ensure the telehandler and its attachments are in optimal condition for future operations. This process involves identifying and reporting any malfunctions, faults, or damage through the following steps:

1. Visual Inspection:

    - Walk around the telehandler to inspect for visible signs of damage, wear, or leaks.

    - Check the attachments for any apparent issues.

    - Ensure the stability and integrity of all moving parts, joints, and attachments.

2. Test Operational Functions:

    - Verify basic functions such as lifting, lowering, tilting, and rotating.

    - Test any specialized functions and check the functionality of the attachment in use.

3. Listen for Irregularities:

    - Start the telehandler and listen for unusual noises or sounds indicating malfunctions or damage.

    - Pay attention to vibrations, rattling, grinding, or any abnormal sounds.

4. Check Indicator Lights and Alarms:

- Confirm dashboard lights, warning alarms, and indicators are functioning properly.
- Note any warning lights that remain illuminated.

5. Review Fluid Levels and Check for Leaks:
   - Check oil, hydraulic fluid, brake fluid, and coolant levels.
   - Inspect underneath for signs of leaks.

6. Examine Tyres:
   - Check for punctures, wear, or other visible damage.
   - Ensure proper tire inflation.

7. Record Findings:
   - Document identified malfunctions, faults, irregularities, or damages thoroughly.
   - Fill out standard forms or digital reports used for this purpose.

8. Report Issues:
   - Immediately report serious issues to the supervisor or designated authority.
   - Follow workplace protocols for non-critical issues.

9. Secure the Telehandler:
   - Store in the designated area and remove the ignition key to prevent unauthorized use.

10. Review Workplace Procedures:

- Follow workplace-specific protocols for post-operation checks and reports.

These checks ensure prompt resolution of any issues, promoting a safer work environment.

Reporting Defects: Operators must report defects immediately using a predefined format, providing details like date, time, and circumstances. 'Nil Reports' should also be submitted regularly. All reports should be forwarded to the telehandler owner for informed decision-making.

Scheduled Maintenance: Site management is responsible for ensuring telehandlers are well-maintained. A scheduled preventative maintenance program, considering machine usage and environment, helps meet this requirement.

Operating Interval Maintenance: Apart from daily checks, operators should conduct maintenance at regular intervals, like every 50 or 100 hours of operation, checking items such as tyres, hydraulic filters, and engine oil.

Quarterly Maintenance: A comprehensive check every quarter should cover battery connections, electrical wiring, fork level tension, and engine air filter. Additional yearly checks may include inspecting the hydraulic tank filter. Consult the telehandler's manual for specific intervals and procedures.

Preventing accidental or unauthorized use of the machine is crucial to avoid potential accidents and hazards.

Shutdown Procedure: Commence the telehandler shutdown process by parking it on a level surface, ideally within its designated storage area. Ensure all controls are returned to the neutral position. Following these precautions, proceed to turn off the ignition. If the machine requires a specific shutdown sequence, allow it to complete this process.

Handling the Key: After confirming the telehandler's safe shutdown, proceed to extract the key from the ignition. It's advisable to briefly inspect the key for any signs of wear, damage, or deformities. Should any concerns arise, promptly report them to facilitate necessary actions, such as replacements.

Key Storage: For key storage, it is recommended to utilize a designated, secure key box or cabinet tailored for machine and equipment keys. This storage unit should be easily accessible to authorized personnel while ensuring restricted access to others on-site. Enhance security by ensuring the box or cabinet is lockable. Before placing the key inside, appropriately label it or its keyring for quick identification, especially in scenarios with multiple machines or telehandlers. Once the key is securely positioned, lock the box or cabinet.

Documentation and Access Management: Many organizations advocate for maintaining a logbook to track key storage activities. If applicable, record details such as the date, time, and responsible individual for key storage. Additional remarks can be included as necessary. It is imperative to control access to the key box or cabinet, limiting entry to trusted individuals with the appropriate authorization. Regular reviews of the access list help mitigate the risk of unauthorized entry. Furthermore, periodic checks on the storage unit ensure all keys are present, particularly in environments where multiple personnel have access.

Chapter Five

Elevating Work Platforms

An Elevating Work Platform (EWP), also known as an aerial work platform or mobile elevating work platform (MEWP), is a mechanical device used to provide temporary access to elevated areas for personnel, tools, or equipment. EWPs are commonly used in construction, maintenance, and repair tasks where working at height is required.

Elevating work platforms (EWPs) encompass various types such as scissor lifts, cherry pickers, boom lifts, and travel towers, available in both battery-powered and internal combustion engine variants. While some are tailored for use on solid, level surfaces, others are engineered for operation on rough terrain.

Individuals operating travel towers, boom lifts, or cherry pickers are required to wear securely anchored safety harnesses, whereas those using scissor lifts are exempt from this requirement.

EWPs find common applications in construction sites, warehouses, and any environment requiring mobile access to elevated areas.

EWPs typically consist of a platform or bucket attached to an extendable arm or mast, which can be raised or lowered vertically. Some EWPs also have the capability to move horizontally or rotate, providing additional flexibility in positioning workers or materials.

There are various types of EWPs, including:

1. Scissor Lifts (see Figure 64): These have a platform that moves vertically along a pair of crossed supports, resembling the shape of a scissors when extended.

Figure 64: Scissor lifts. KeepOnTruckin, CC BY 2.5, via Wikimedia Commons.

1. Boom Lifts (see Figure 65): Also known as cherry pickers, these have a telescopic or articulated arm with a platform at the end for workers to stand on. Boom lifts can reach higher and further horizontally compared to scissor lifts.

MATERIAL HANDLING EQUIPMENT OPERATION 229

Figure 65: Straight Boom Lift with telescopic boom extended. ERab123, CC BY-SA 4.0, via Wikimedia Commons.

1. Vertical Lifts (see Figure 66): These have a single mast that extends vertically, offering a more compact design suitable for indoor use or tight spaces.

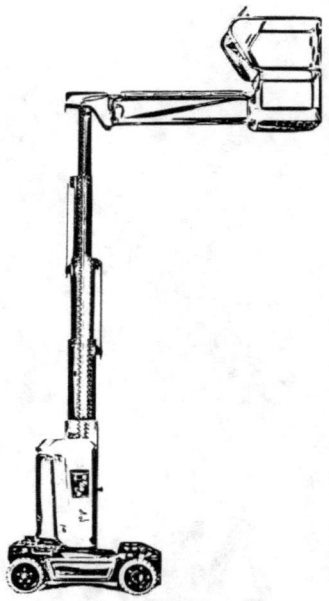

Figure 66: Vertical mast lift.

1. Personnel Lifts (see Figure 67): These are smaller, portable platforms designed for individual workers to access elevated areas safely.

MATERIAL HANDLING EQUIPMENT OPERATION

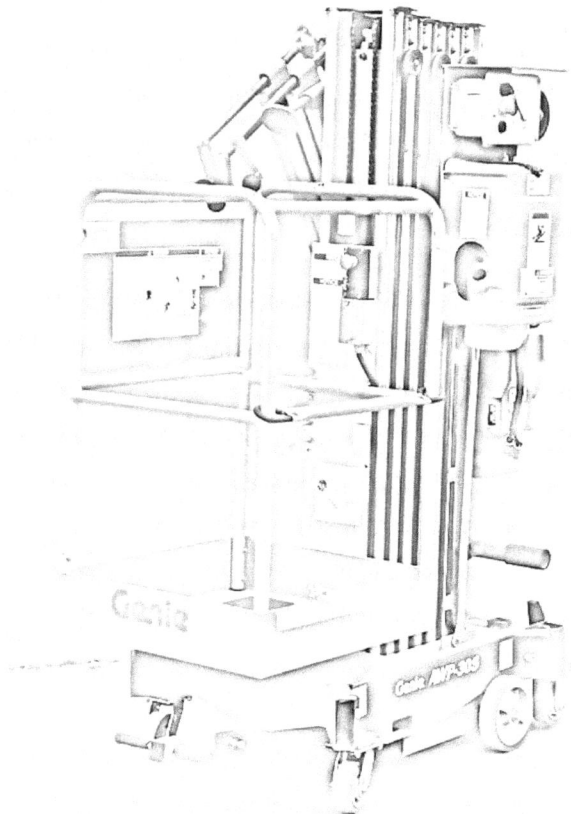

Figure 67: Personnel lift.

EWPs are equipped with safety features such as guardrails, emergency lowering systems, and overload protection to ensure the safety of workers operating at height. Proper training and adherence to safety protocols are essential when using EWPs to prevent accidents and injuries.

EWPs can also be:
- Trailer Mounted EWP: These elevating work platforms are affixed to a mobile trailer and can be towed by most vehicles equipped with a tow ball. They are equipped with manually adjustable stabilizers to ensure platform stability during operation

and offer a range of working heights up to 26 meters.

- Self-Propelled EWP With Telescoping Boom: These EWPs are self-propelled units designed for use on level slabs or firm unsealed surfaces. The platform is raised using a straight extension (telescoping) boom, with controls accessible at ground level and on the platform itself.

- Self-Propelled EWP With Telescoping Knuckle Boom (see Figure 68: These EWPs are self-propelled units suitable for deployment on level slabs or firm unsealed surfaces. The platform is elevated by a boom featuring at least two main sections connected by a knuckle joint, mounted on a turret allowing slewing. This configuration enables the boom to reach over obstacles. Both sections of the boom may incorporate telescopic extensions, and controls are available at both ground level and on the platform.

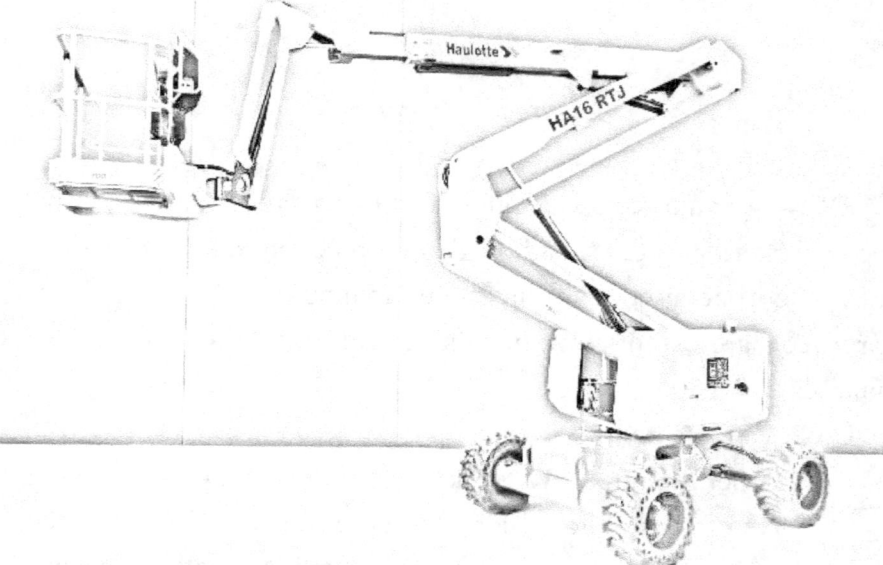

Figure 68: Self-propelled EWP with telescoping knuckle boom.

MATERIAL HANDLING EQUIPMENT OPERATION

- Vehicle-Mounted EWP (see Figure 69): These EWPs are typically trucks registered for road use, fitted with either a straight boom or a knuckle boom mounted on the truck chassis. The boom is mounted on a turret for slewing, and outriggers are installed on the chassis for stability. Controls are accessible both at ground level and on the platform.

Figure 69: Truck mounter EWP. User:Mattes, CC BY-SA, via Wikimedia Commons.

A typical telescoping boom elevating work platform (EWP) consists of several essential parts/components designed to facilitate safe and efficient operation. Here's a description of each:

1. Boom Assembly: The primary structural component of the EWP, the boom assembly extends vertically to elevate the platform to various heights. It typically comprises multiple sections that can extend or retract telescopically to reach different

heights.

2. Platform: This is the elevated work area where operators stand or perform tasks. The platform is usually equipped with guardrails, toe boards, and gates for safety. It may also have a control panel for operating the EWP.

3. Controls: The control panel allows operators to manipulate the movement of the boom, adjust the platform's height, and control other functions such as rotation (if applicable) and drive movement (for self-propelled models). Controls can be located on the platform itself and/or at ground level.

4. Base/Chassis: The base or chassis provides stability and support for the EWP. It may have wheels for mobility or outriggers/stabilizers to ensure stability while the platform is elevated.

5. Outriggers/Stabilizers: These extendable legs or arms are deployed to increase the EWP's stability, especially when working at height or on uneven terrain. They provide additional support and prevent tipping.

6. Hydraulic System: Responsible for powering the movement of the boom and platform, the hydraulic system utilizes hydraulic fluid under pressure to extend and retract the boom sections and raise/lower the platform.

7. Counterweights (Optional): In some EWPs, counterweights may be used to balance the weight of the extended boom and platform, enhancing stability and safety.

8. Safety Features: Various safety features are incorporated into the EWP design to protect operators and bystanders. These may include emergency stop buttons, overload sensors, tilt sensors,

and audible/visual alarms.

9. Power Source: EWPs can be powered by either internal combustion engines (typically for outdoor use) or electric motors (commonly used indoors). The power source provides the energy needed to operate the hydraulic system and other electrical components.

10. Telescopic Sections: In telescoping boom EWPs, the boom consists of multiple telescopic sections that can extend or retract independently or in sequence. These sections allow the boom to reach different heights while maintaining stability and manoeuvrability.

11. Rotation Mechanism (Optional): Some EWPs feature a rotating platform or turret that allows the operator to rotate the platform horizontally, providing greater flexibility and access to work areas.

Overall, these components work together to enable safe, efficient, and versatile operation of telescoping boom EWPs in various construction, maintenance, and industrial applications.

Figure 70: Parts of a typical EWP with telescoping boom. Back image - Photograph by Mike Peel (www.mikepeel.net)., CC BY-SA 4.0, via Wikimedia Commons.

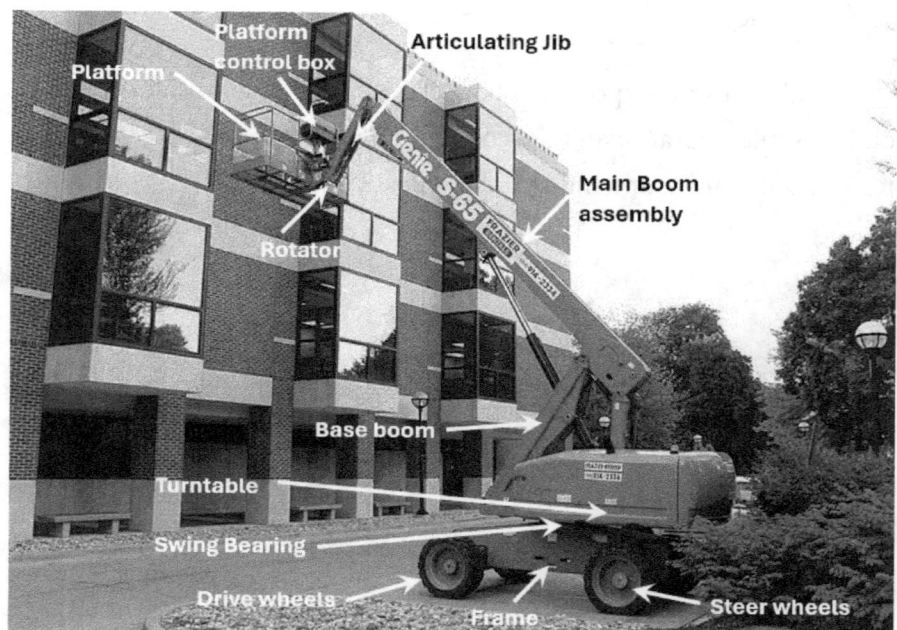

Figure 71: Parts of a typical EWP with telescoping knuckle boom. Back image - Dwight Burdette, CC BY 3.0, via Wikimedia Commons.

MATERIAL HANDLING EQUIPMENT OPERATION 237

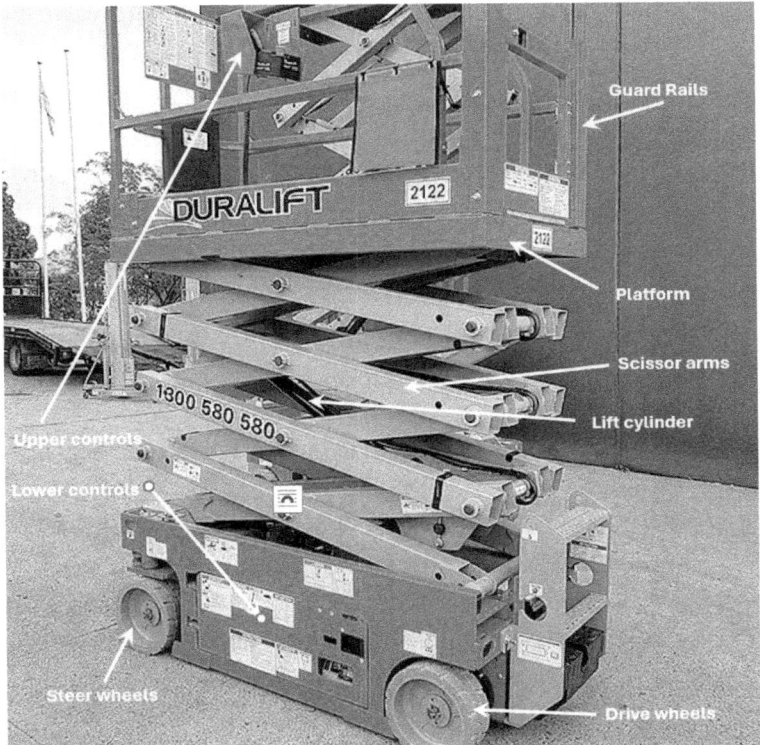

Figure 72: Parts of a typical scissor lift EWP. Back image - ERab123, CC BY-SA 4.0, via Wikimedia Commons.

Elevating Work Platforms (EWPs) operate on the principle of providing a safe and stable elevated work area for personnel to perform tasks at height. The operational principles can vary depending on the type of EWP, but they generally involve a combination of structural components, hydraulic systems, and safety features. Here's an overview of the operational principles of various types of EWPs:

1. **Scissor Lifts**:

    ◦ Scissor lifts operate using a mechanism that extends and retracts a series of crossed supports (the scissor mechanism) vertically, providing elevation to the platform.

- The scissor mechanism is powered by a hydraulic system, typically consisting of a pump, cylinders, and valves, which control the flow of hydraulic fluid to extend or retract the scissor arms.

- The platform remains level as it moves vertically, providing a stable work surface. Some models may also feature limited horizontal movement.

- Scissor lifts are commonly used for indoor maintenance, construction, and installation tasks.

2. **Cherry Pickers** (also known as Aerial Work Platforms):

    - Cherry pickers feature an articulated boom with a platform at the end, allowing for vertical and horizontal reach.

    - The boom is often mounted on a base or chassis with wheels for mobility. Some models may also have outriggers for added stability.

    - A hydraulic system powers the extension and articulation of the boom, allowing operators to position the platform precisely.

    - Cherry pickers are versatile and commonly used for tasks such as tree trimming, exterior building maintenance, and electrical repairs.

3. **Boom Lifts**:

    - Boom lifts feature a telescoping or articulated boom that extends vertically and/or horizontally, providing access to elevated work areas.

    - The boom may be mounted on a base with wheels for mobility or on a vehicle chassis. Outriggers or stabilizers are often deployed to enhance stability.

- Hydraulic systems control the extension, articulation, and elevation of the boom, allowing operators to manoeuvre the platform into various positions.

- Boom lifts are widely used in construction, maintenance, and industrial settings for tasks such as building maintenance, signage installation, and window cleaning.

4. **Trailer-Mounted EWPs:**

- Trailer-mounted EWPs are mounted on a movable trailer and can be towed by vehicles with a tow ball.

- They typically feature manually adjustable stabilizers to provide stability while in use and have a range of working heights.

- Hydraulic systems control the elevation and positioning of the platform, similar to other types of EWPs.

5. **Self-Propelled EWPs:**

- Self-propelled EWPs are equipped with their own propulsion system, allowing operators to drive them to different work locations.

- They may feature telescoping or knuckle booms, which can be extended and manoeuvered using hydraulic controls.

- Self-propelled EWPs are versatile and suitable for a wide range of indoor and outdoor applications.

In summary, EWPs operate by utilizing hydraulic systems, structural components, and safety features to provide safe and efficient access to elevated work areas. The specific operational principles may vary depending on the type and design of the EWP, but they all aim to ensure stability, manoeuvrability, and operator safety while working at height.

Planning for EWP Operations

Planning for EWP operations includes:

1. **Identifying Task Requirements:**

   - Review the work order or instructions provided to understand the scope of work.

   - Consult with relevant personnel, such as supervisors or team members, to clarify any uncertainties or requirements.

   - Conduct a site inspection to assess the conditions and environment where the EWP will be used.

2. **Assessing Work Area Ground/Surface:**

   - Inspect the ground or operating surface where the EWP will be deployed.

   - Check for any hazards or obstacles that could affect the stability or safe operation of the EWP.

   - Ensure that the surface is level, firm, and capable of supporting the weight of the EWP and its intended load.

   - Follow manufacturer requirements and workplace procedures for ground assessment.

3. Establishing EWP Capabilities:

- Determine the maximum load capacity and working height of the EWP based on manufacturer specifications.

- Assess the specific requirements of the task, including the weight of materials, tools, and personnel to be lifted.

- Ensure that the EWP is suitable for the intended work and can safely accommodate the load requirements.

4. Assessing Operating Paths:

- Identify and evaluate potential paths for operating the EWP within the work area.

- Consider factors such as overhead obstacles, confined spaces, and access points.

- Determine the most efficient and safe routes for manoeuvring the EWP to the desired locations.

5. Applying Hazard and Risk Control Measures:

- Identify potential hazards associated with EWP operations, such as overhead power lines, uneven terrain, or unstable surfaces.

- Implement control measures to mitigate risks, such as using barricades, wearing personal protective equipment (PPE), or establishing exclusion zones.

- Communicate hazard control measures to relevant personnel and ensure understanding and compliance.

6. Confirming Traffic Management Plan:

- Review the traffic management plan to ensure it aligns with the intended EWP operations.

- Confirm implementation of the plan, including any traffic control measures or signage required to safely manage vehicle and pedestrian movement in the work area.

7. **Identifying Communication Procedures:**

    - Establish communication protocols with relevant personnel involved in the EWP operation, such as ground spotters, supervisors, or other workers.

    - Determine methods of communication, such as two-way radios, hand signals, or verbal cues, based on the specific work environment and requirements.

8. **Confirming Work Coverage:**

    - Ensure that all aspects of the work/task requirements are addressed and accounted for in the plan.

    - Verify that the EWP is equipped and configured to meet the needs of the task, including necessary attachments, tools, and safety equipment.

Before commencing any work, it's crucial to ascertain the specific tasks you're required to perform. These instructions can be communicated through various channels and formats, including:

- Shift briefings.

- Handover details.

- Work orders.

- Equipment specifications.

MATERIAL HANDLING EQUIPMENT OPERATION

- Nature and scope of tasks.
- Load particulars.
- Achievement targets.
- Working conditions.
- Site lighting arrangements.
- Equipment defects.
- Hazards and potential risks.
- Coordination requirements.

Understanding these work requirements is essential as they directly impact the equipment selection and task execution methods. Having a clear understanding of the job's requirements ensures work is conducted safely and efficiently.

It's advisable to have a detailed work specification outlining the type of work and expected outcomes. Knowing the job's requirements aids in selecting the appropriate machinery and determining the necessary workforce for the task. For instance, understanding the work's height requirements and associated tasks beforehand can streamline planning efforts.

Key considerations when determining the job's scope include:
- Type of work.
- Location, including site and environmental factors.
- Work height.
- Necessary approvals.
- Timeframe for completion.

- Expected outcomes.

Performing a visual inspection of the site during pre-operational planning, if feasible, is beneficial. Alternatively, gather as much information about the site as possible before agreeing to undertake the work. This may involve asking a standard set of questions developed by your employer.

Be mindful of any special operating requirements, such as proximity to power lines or use of chemicals on the work platform. If uncertain about work requirements at any stage, consult your supervisor for clarification.

Establishing work priorities is crucial, especially when tasks involve multiple activities. The nature of the work often dictates task priorities. Your work plan should outline the sequence in which tasks will be executed, with consideration given to factors like elevation levels and safety requirements.

Adherence to workplace rules and procedures is paramount. Consult relevant personnel to understand site-specific rules and procedures, and cooperate with others by following established protocols. Consider consulting with building/site owners, government authorities, site managers, supervisors, and other trades as needed.

It's essential to be aware of regulatory requirements applicable to the work being performed from the EWP. This may involve statutory certifications or site induction training, depending on the workplace and nature of the work. Ensure compliance with occupational health and safety regulations and wear appropriate personal protective equipment (PPE) at all times, including a safety harness, helmet, steel-capped shoes, safety vest, and goggles, as required by workplace procedures and local regulations. Additional PPE may be necessary based on the specific work environment and hazards present.

MATERIAL HANDLING EQUIPMENT OPERATION

Planning includes assessing the work area and ground surface. To assess the work area ground or surface before deploying the Elevating Work Platform (EWP), follow these steps:

1. Inspect the Ground or Operating Surface: Begin by thoroughly inspecting the ground or operating surface where the EWP will be deployed. Walk around the area to visually examine the ground for any irregularities, such as bumps, holes, debris, or uneven terrain.

2. Identify Hazards or Obstacles: Look for any hazards or obstacles that could pose a risk to the stability or safe operation of the EWP. These hazards may include objects in the vicinity, overhead obstructions, soft or unstable ground, slopes, trenches, or other potential hazards.

3. Check Surface Condition: Ensure that the surface is level, firm, and capable of supporting the weight of the EWP and its intended load. Pay attention to the condition of the ground, considering factors such as stability, compaction, and suitability for bearing heavy loads.

4. Follow Manufacturer Requirements and Workplace Procedures: Adhere to manufacturer requirements and workplace procedures for ground assessment. Consult the EWP's operating manual or guidelines provided by the manufacturer to understand specific ground requirements and recommendations.

5. Document Findings: Document your findings from the ground assessment, noting any hazards, obstacles, or surface conditions that may impact the safe operation of the EWP. This documentation can be useful for reference and risk assessment purposes.

6. Take Necessary Precautions: Based on the assessment findings,

take necessary precautions to mitigate identified risks. This may involve clearing obstacles, leveling the ground, using stabilizers or outriggers, or taking other measures to ensure the stability and safety of the EWP during operation.

7. Communication and Collaboration: Communicate any relevant findings or concerns regarding the ground assessment to other personnel involved in the work operation. Collaborate with colleagues to address any identified hazards or prepare the work area for safe EWP deployment.

8. Regular Monitoring: Continuously monitor the ground conditions during EWP operation, especially in dynamic work environments or when conditions may change over time. Stay vigilant for any emerging hazards or surface changes that may affect the safety of the EWP and its occupants.

Elevating Work Platform (EWP) operations come with inherent hazards that can pose risks to both operators and bystanders. These hazards include:

1. Falls from Height: One of the most significant hazards associated with EWP operations is the risk of falls from height. Operators and workers can fall from the platform if proper fall protection measures are not in place or if they lean over the guardrails.

2. Overturning or Tip-Over: EWPs can overturn or tip over if operated on uneven ground, slopes, or if the load capacity is exceeded. This can result in serious injuries or fatalities to the operator and others in the vicinity.

3. Entrapment or Crushing: Workers can be entrapped or crushed between the platform and overhead obstacles or structures if the EWP is operated in confined spaces or near obstructions.

MATERIAL HANDLING EQUIPMENT OPERATION

4. Electrocution: Contact with overhead power lines or electrical equipment poses a significant risk of electrocution to EWP operators and workers. Accidental contact can occur if the EWP comes into close proximity with energized electrical conductors.

5. Falling Objects: Objects or materials dropped from the EWP platform pose a risk of injury to workers or bystanders below. Failure to secure tools, equipment, or materials properly can result in falling objects.

6. Mechanical Failures: Mechanical failures or malfunctions of the EWP, such as hydraulic system failure or structural defects, can lead to accidents or equipment breakdowns during operation.

To mitigate these hazards and ensure safe EWP operations, the following measures should be implemented:

1. Operator Training and Certification: Ensure that operators receive comprehensive training and certification in EWP operation, including safety procedures, hazard recognition, and emergency response protocols.

2. Pre-Operational Checks: Conduct thorough pre-operational checks and inspections of the EWP before each use to identify any mechanical defects, structural damage, or safety issues. Address any issues promptly before operating the equipment.

3. Fall Protection Systems: Implement effective fall protection systems, such as guardrails, harnesses, and lanyards, to prevent falls from the EWP platform. Ensure that workers are properly trained in fall protection measures and use appropriate personal protective equipment (PPE).

4. Stabilization and Leveling: Ensure that the EWP is set up on

stable, level ground and that outriggers or stabilizers are deployed as required to prevent tipping or overturning. Follow manufacturer guidelines for proper stabilization and leveling procedures.

5. Avoiding Electrical Hazards: Identify and assess electrical hazards in the work area, such as overhead power lines, and implement measures to maintain a safe distance from energized conductors. Use non-conductive materials and maintain safe clearance distances when working near electrical sources.

6. Communication and Signage: Clearly communicate and enforce safety rules, procedures, and signage related to EWP operations. Use warning signs, barricades, and barriers to restrict access to hazardous areas and ensure that workers are aware of potential risks.

7. Regular Maintenance and Inspections: Establish a routine maintenance schedule for the EWP and conduct regular inspections to identify and address any mechanical issues or deficiencies promptly. Ensure that only qualified personnel perform maintenance and repairs on the equipment.

Determining the lifting capacity for an Elevating Work Platform (EWP), whether it's a boom type or a scissor lift type, involves several steps. Firstly, operators should refer to the Manufacturer's Specifications, consulting the manufacturer's specifications and operation manual for the specific EWP model being used. This typically provides detailed information regarding the maximum lifting capacity, including load charts, capacities at various boom or platform configurations, and other relevant factors.

Identifying the Rated Capacity is crucial. Operators should locate the rated capacity of the EWP, typically provided in the operation manual or displayed on the EWP itself. This rated capacity indicates the maximum load that the EWP can safely lift under ideal conditions.

For boom-type EWPs, considering Boom Configuration is essential. Operators need to factor in the configuration of the boom, including the boom length, extension, and angle. The lifting capacity may vary depending on these factors, so referring to the load charts provided by the manufacturer for specific configurations is advisable.

Accounting for Platform Weight is another critical step. Operators must take into account the weight of the platform itself, along with any additional equipment, tools, or materials that will be placed on the platform during operation. Ensuring that the total load, including the platform weight and any additional loads, does not exceed the rated capacity of the EWP is essential.

Environmental Conditions must also be considered. Operators should factor in environmental factors such as wind speed, ground conditions, and slope, as these can affect the stability and lifting capacity of the EWP. Following manufacturer guidelines and load charts helps determine any necessary adjustments based on environmental conditions.

Understanding Load Distribution is vital for stability. Operators need to ensure that the load is distributed evenly on the platform to prevent tipping or instability. Avoiding overloading one side of the platform or placing heavy loads in a concentrated area is crucial for safe operation.

Regularly inspecting and maintaining the EWP is paramount. Conducting regular inspections ensures that the EWP is in proper working condition, with all components, including hydraulic systems, structural elements, and safety devices, functioning correctly. Addressing any maintenance issues promptly helps maintain safe lifting capacity.

Lastly, ensuring Training and Certification of operators is essential. Operators must be properly trained and certified in EWP operation, including understanding load capacities, load charts, and safe operating practices. Being aware of the limitations of the EWP and following all manufacturer guidelines and safety procedures is imperative.

An EWP (Elevating Work Platform) data plate typically contains essential information about the equipment, including:

1. Manufacturer Information: This includes the name, logo, and contact details of the manufacturer or supplier of the EWP.

2. Model and Serial Number: The specific model name or number of the EWP and its unique serial number for identification purposes.

3. Capacity and Load Rating: Information about the maximum load capacity of the EWP, including both platform and overall capacity, typically expressed in weight units such as kilograms (kg) or pounds (lbs).

4. Platform Dimensions: Measurements of the platform size, including length, width, and height dimensions, providing an understanding of the available workspace.

5. Power Source: Details about the power source used to operate the EWP, whether it's electric, diesel, battery-powered, or another source.

6. Operating Instructions: Basic operating instructions or guidelines may be provided on the data plate, including safety precautions, control functions, and emergency procedures.

7. Date of Manufacture: The date when the EWP was manufactured, which can be important for maintenance schedules, warranty tracking, and equipment history.

8. Compliance Information: Certifications, standards, or regulations with which the EWP complies, such as ANSI (American

MATERIAL HANDLING EQUIPMENT OPERATION

National Standards Institute) standards or CE (Conformité Européenne) marking for European compliance.

9. Safety Features: Information about safety features or systems installed on the EWP, such as emergency stop buttons, tilt sensors, overload protection, and fall arrest systems.

10. Maintenance Requirements: Recommendations or requirements for regular maintenance tasks, inspection intervals, and servicing schedules to ensure the continued safe operation of the EWP.

11. Warnings and Precautions: Hazard warnings, caution labels, or safety notices indicating potential risks, operating limitations, and precautions to be observed during EWP use.

12. Regulatory Compliance: Any additional regulatory compliance information required by local laws, regulations, or standards applicable to the region where the EWP is used.

The data plate serves as a valuable reference for operators, maintenance personnel, and inspectors, providing essential information for safe and efficient EWP operation.

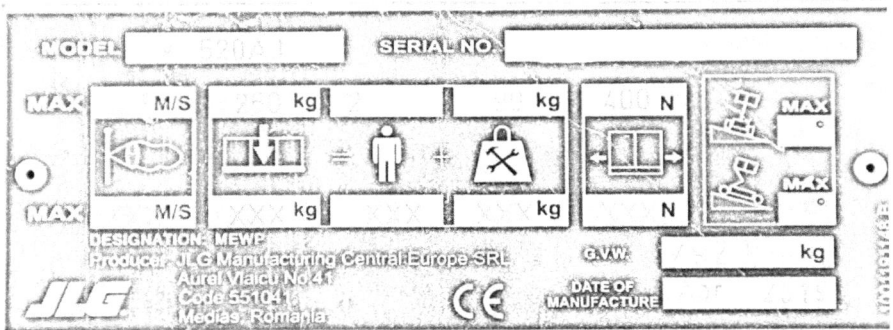

Figure 73: Sample data plate.

An EWP Operating Envelope, also known as a Range Diagram, is a graphical representation that illustrates the safe operational limits and capabilities of an Elevating Work Platform (EWP). It provides operators with a visual guide to understand the range of movement and reach of the EWP while ensuring safe operation within specified parameters.

The Operating Envelope typically depicts various factors such as maximum working height, maximum outreach, and load capacity at different boom configurations. It may also include information about platform rotation angles, allowable slopes, and environmental conditions that affect safe operation.

Operators can refer to the Operating Envelope to determine whether the EWP can safely access a specific work area or perform a particular task. By observing the boundaries outlined in the diagram, operators can ensure that they stay within the safe operating range of the EWP, minimizing the risk of accidents or equipment damage.

MATERIAL HANDLING EQUIPMENT OPERATION   253

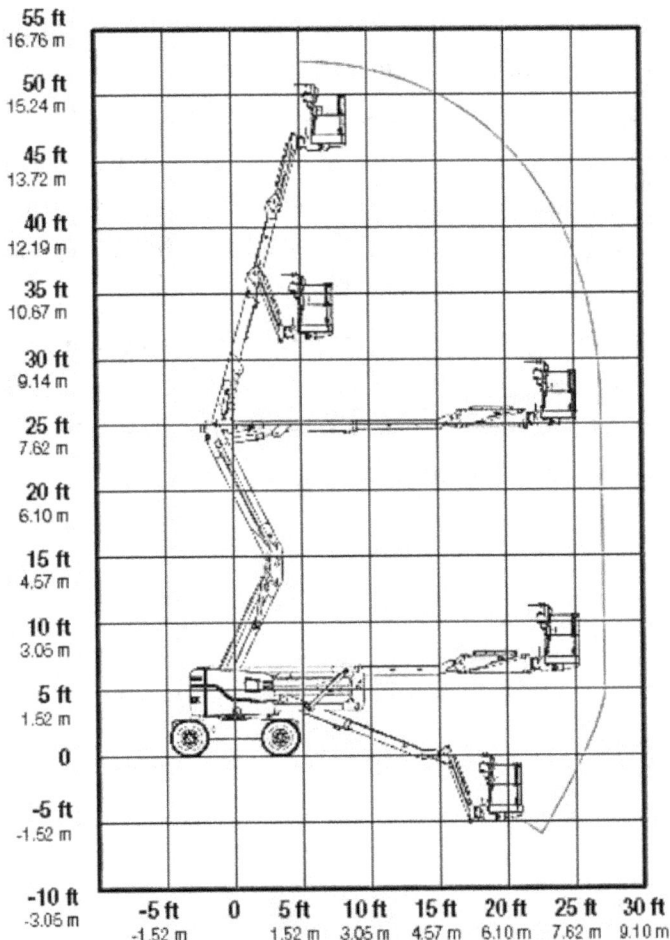

Figure 74: Sample operating envelope.

The Range Diagram is usually provided by the manufacturer and is based on the EWP's design specifications, load charts, and safety standards. It serves as an essential tool for operators to make informed decisions about EWP operation, helping to prevent overloading, tipping, or other hazardous situations.

Many boom lift EWPs exhibit a smooth 'arc-shaped' range of motion, as depicted in Figure 74. However, it's crucial to note that there are models with a 'saw-tooth' shaped operating envelope, as illustrated on the left. When operating an EWP with a 'saw-tooth' operating envelope, the operator might need to adjust (or retract) the boom to execute a successive task that necessitates moving the basket along the outer edge of the operating envelope. A range diagram also indicates whether an EWP can perform work within reach below ground level. This aspect is particularly significant for certain applications, such as working alongside or beneath a bridge, among others.

As an example of use of the operating envelope diagram, let's say that an operator needed to access a job at a reach of 10 metres when the EWP is set up 3 away from the job, they could do so as it is within the envelope, as shown in Figure 75.

MATERIAL HANDLING EQUIPMENT OPERATION

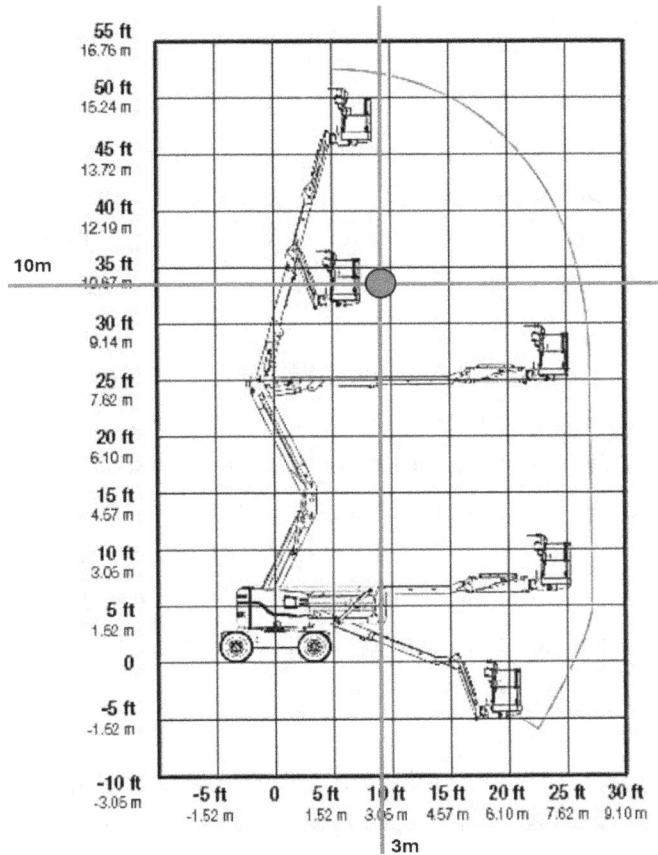

Figure 75: Job at a reach of 10 metres when the EWP is set up 3 away from the job.

When preparing to deploy an Elevating Work Platform (EWP) near an excavation or trench, it's imperative to assess the risk of trench collapse. This involves carefully considering the distance between the EWP and the excavation site. As a general safety guideline, the distance should be no less than the depth of the excavation itself. For instance, if the excavation measures 2 meters in depth, it is not advisable to set up the EWP closer than 2 meters to the trench. Alternatively, the appropriate distance may be determined by a competent individual who is knowledgeable about excavation safety protocols.

In situations where space is limited, specific precautions must be taken when positioning the EWP. These considerations include ensuring that there is adequate access for the EWP to manoeuvre in and out of the restricted space. Additionally, potential obstructions or the presence of personnel in the area should be taken into account to prevent accidents or disruptions to work operations. The use of a guide may be necessary to assist in navigating the EWP within the confined space safely.

Moreover, when setting up the EWP in a restricted area, it's essential to ensure safe slewing of the boom, considering the surrounding obstacles and clearance requirements. Sufficient space for emergency egress should also be maintained to facilitate a swift exit in the event of an emergency situation. Furthermore, if the EWP operates on diesel, it's crucial to monitor for the buildup of gas or fumes during operation to prevent potential health hazards. These precautions help mitigate risks and ensure the safe operation of the EWP in confined or restricted spaces.

Damage to tyres on mobile elevating work platforms (MEWPs) is a frequent issue, often posing challenges in determining their continued usability. MEWP tyres typically come in three types: solid, polyurethane foam-filled, or pneumatic, which are commonly found on road-going vehicles like truck-mounted and trailer lifts. It's crucial that all tyres used on MEWPs are approved by the manufacturer for their intended applications. The following guidelines outline reasonable criteria for assessing tyre condition on MEWPs.

When any of the following conditions are observed, immediate action must be taken to remove the tyre from service and arrange for its replacement: Polyurethane Foam-Filled Tyres

- Smooth, even cuts through the cord plies exceeding 10% of the tread width

- Tears or rips (with ragged edges) in the cord plies exceeding

25mm in any direction

- Punctures exceeding 25mm in diameter

- Damage to the bead area cords of the tyre

- Evidence of fluid leakage from the tyre at the valve stem, bead, or any punctures/holes

Solid Tyres
- If a cut, tear, chunk, or other discrepancy exceeds any of the following dimensions:
  - 76mm long or 10% of the tyre diameter in length, 19mm wide, or 19mm deep
  - If the metal wheel is visible at any point through the tyre tread

Air-Filled/Pneumatic Tyres
- When any cut, rip, or tear exposes sidewall or tread area cords, the tyre must be immediately removed from service. Arrangements should be made promptly for tyre replacement.

- Any defect that renders the tyre un-roadworthy, such as loss of tread or wear indicators showing, warrants tyre replacement. Note: re-treads are not recommended for vehicle-mounted MEWPs supported on pneumatic tyres.

Rims
- The rims installed on each product model are designed to meet stability requirements, including track width, tyre pressure, and load capacity. Any alterations to rim size, such as width, offset, or diameter changes, without written factory recommendations, may compromise stability and safety.

Daily inspection of tire pressures and rims is an essential component of pre-operational checks, to be carried out by a trained operator. All findings from these inspections should be meticulously recorded in the Log Book. Proper maintenance of tire pressure in air-filled tyres is paramount for ensuring maximum stability, optimal machine handling, and minimizing tire wear. Operators are advised to refer to the machine's operator's manual to ascertain the precise tire pressure requirements for that particular machine.

In the event of tire replacement, it is imperative that the new tire matches the size, ply, and brand of the original tire installed on the machine. Operators should consult the machine's Parts Manual to obtain the approved tire part number for the specific machine model. Ensuring the wheel weight matches that of the replaced wheels is critical for maintaining the machine's stability.

Unless expressly approved, substituting a foam-filled tire assembly with a pneumatic tire is not recommended. During the selection and installation of replacement tyres, it is vital to adhere to the manufacturer's recommended tire pressure. Given potential size discrepancies between tire brands, both tyres on the same axle should be identical, and all four tyres should contain the same fill media.

Preparing for EWP Operations

Effective communication with relevant personnel is fundamental to aligning the work plan with site requirements. This involves engaging in discussions with supervisors, colleagues, or other stakeholders to address tasks, hazards, and site-specific considerations, adhering to workplace procedures for consultation.

Prior to commencing work, thorough checks must be conducted to ensure that identified hazards are adequately managed. This entails verifying the implementation of safety protocols and procedures to mitigate risks, in accordance with workplace guidelines and regulations.

Inspecting, fitting correctly, and utilizing personal protective equipment (PPE) is paramount for operator safety. This step involves examining the condition of PPE, ensuring proper fitting, and adhering to manufacturer requirements and safe work procedures for its usage.

Safely accessing the EWP is essential to prevent accidents. Operators must follow manufacturer requirements and safe work procedures for entering and exiting the platform, utilizing steps, ladders, or access gates correctly and securely.

Conducting comprehensive pre-start checks is critical to ensure the EWP is in optimal working condition. This involves following manufacturer requirements and safe work procedures to inspect the machine for faults, damage, or malfunctions, ensuring its readiness for operation.

Upon starting the EWP, operators should listen for any unusual noises that may indicate mechanical issues. Adhering to safe work procedures, this step facilitates the early detection of potential problems before they escalate.

Accurate positioning of the EWP according to the work plan is vital for safety and efficiency. Operators must adhere to relevant manufacturer requirements and safe work procedures to position the platform securely and accurately within the designated work area.

Properly stabilizing the EWP is crucial to prevent accidents and ensure platform stability. This involves deploying stabilizers or outriggers as necessary, following the work plan and relevant manufacturer requirements, and adhering to safe work procedures.

Conducting operational checks from base controls ensures that all EWP functions are operating correctly. Operators should follow relevant manufacturer requirements and safe work procedures to test controls for lifting, lowering, and other essential functions.

Identifying and testing all platform controls is essential to ensure safe operation. Operators must locate, identify, and test platform controls according to manufacturer requirements and safe work procedures to verify proper functionality.

Prompt reporting of any damage or defects identified during pre-start checks or operation is crucial for maintenance and safety. Operators should follow manufacturer requirements and safe work procedures to report issues and take appropriate action to rectify them.

Thoroughly inspecting and ensuring the accuracy of the EWP logbook is essential for record-keeping and compliance. Operators must follow manufacturer requirements and safe work procedures to complete and sign the logbook accurately, maintaining comprehensive documentation.

Assessing weather and environmental conditions helps determine their impact on EWP operation and positioning. Operators should follow manufacturer requirements and safe work procedures to evaluate conditions and adjust plans accordingly for safety.

After completing site inspection, hazard identification, and pre-operational checks on the Elevating Work Platform (EWP), the next step is setting up the machine to commence work. This procedure entails several critical tasks, all of which require familiarity and competency in execution.

Before initiating setup, a final check of the work site is necessary to ensure there have been no changes since the initial inspection. The chosen setup area should be flat and capable of supporting the machine's weight. If the ground is uneven, soft, or backfilled, appropriate ground cover like steel plates or sleepers must be utilized to mitigate hazards associated with unstable ground.

MATERIAL HANDLING EQUIPMENT OPERATION

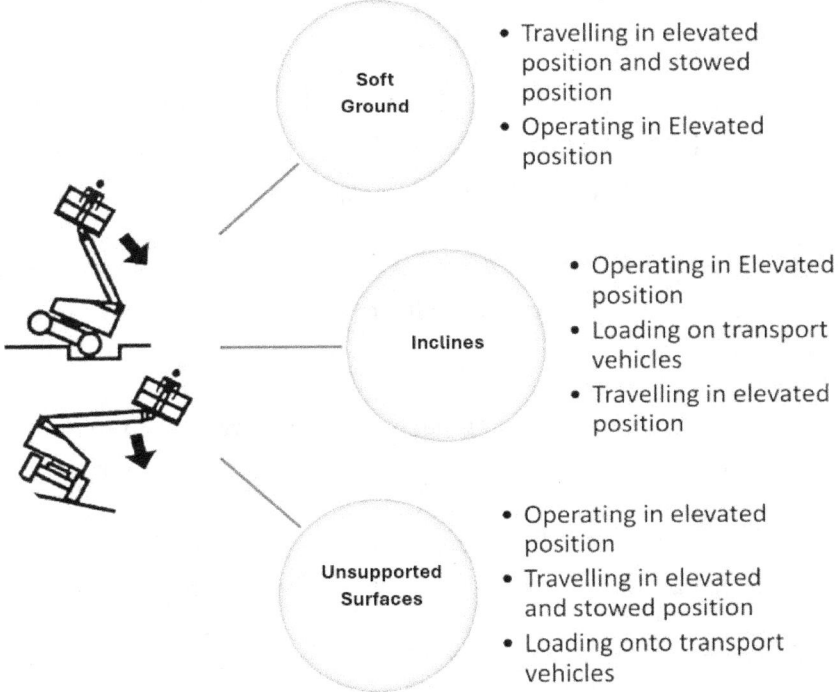

Figure 76: Conditions that can lead to roll over.

The setup procedure involves:

1. Notifying relevant personnel, such as the site foreman or safety officer, of your arrival and intentions, and discussing the work program with them to seek advice.

2. Checking environmental conditions, including wind speed, to ensure compliance with manufacturer specifications.

3. Positioning the EWP as close as possible to the designated work area while minimizing disturbance to nearby workers. An observer may assist in positioning the EWP, ensuring it is not on a slope exceeding manufacturer recommendations.

4. Applying the parking brake, placing the transmission in neutral,

and setting up all required traffic control displays and warning devices.

5. If the EWP lacks outriggers/stabilizers, chocking one pair of wheels to prevent movement. If outriggers are present, chocking the front wheels and deploying outriggers onto a firm surface.

6. Ensuring all necessary safety harnesses and lanyards are on the machine, complying with relevant standards and in good condition.

7. Checking and preparing personal protective equipment (PPE) required for the job.

8. Engaging the EWP's spring lockouts, if provided, and undoing basket and/or boom tie-down straps for free movement.

9. Ensuring all personnel are clear of the basket and boom while lowering the basket to the entry position.

Additionally, it's essential to consider risks associated with operating EWPs on inclines and soft ground. These risks include the potential for the EWP to slide, overturn, or become unstable, posing significant danger to operators and nearby individuals. Proper assessment of site conditions, adherence to manufacturer specifications, and implementation of necessary precautions are vital to mitigating these risks and ensuring safety during EWP operations.

MATERIAL HANDLING EQUIPMENT OPERATION

Figure 77: Positioning the EWP as close as possible to the designated work area. Jim.henderson, CC0, via Wikimedia Commons.

Performing pre-start checks on an Elevating Work Platform (EWP) is a critical procedure to ensure safe and efficient operation. Here's how to conduct pre-start EWP checks:

1. Consult Manufacturer Requirements and Safe Work Procedures: Begin by familiarizing yourself with the manufacturer's requirements and safe work procedures outlined in the EWP's operation manual. This will provide you with specific guidelines and instructions for conducting the pre-start checks.

2. Inspect for Faults, Damage, and Malfunctions: Thoroughly inspect the EWP for any faults, damage, or malfunctions that may compromise its safety or functionality. This includes visually examining all components, structures, and mechanisms of the machine.

3. Check Structural Integrity: Ensure that the structural integrity of the EWP is intact. Look for any signs of cracks, dents, or deformities in the chassis, boom, platform, or other structural elements. Pay special attention to welded joints and stress points.

4. Examine Hydraulic Systems: Inspect the hydraulic systems for leaks, damage to hoses, or signs of hydraulic fluid leakage. Check hydraulic cylinders, hoses, fittings, and connectors for any visible wear or damage.

5. Verify Electrical Systems: Check the electrical systems, including wiring, connectors, and control panels, for any signs of damage, corrosion, or loose connections. Test all electrical controls and switches to ensure they function correctly.

6. Test Safety Devices: Test all safety devices, including emergency stop buttons, overload protection systems, and safety interlocks, to ensure they are operational. Verify that safety features such as limit switches and proximity sensors are functioning as intended.

7. Inspect Operating Controls: Inspect all operating controls, levers, pedals, and joysticks to ensure they move freely and operate smoothly. Check for any signs of wear or damage to control surfaces and labels.

8. Examine Fluid Levels: Check fluid levels, including hydraulic fluid, engine oil, coolant, and brake fluid, and top up as necessary. Ensure that all reservoirs are filled to the recommended levels to prevent mechanical failures.

9. Test Emergency Lowering System (if applicable): If the EWP is equipped with an emergency lowering system, test it to ensure it

operates correctly. Familiarize yourself with the procedure for activating the emergency lowering system in case of an emergency.

10. Document Findings: Document any faults, damage, or abnormalities observed during the pre-start checks. Report any significant issues to the appropriate personnel and ensure they are addressed before operating the EWP.

After completing all pre-operational checks and setting up the EWP for work, the next step is to start up the machine and conduct further checks to verify the functionality of all controls and movements before commencing work. These final checks are crucial to ensuring the safe conduct of work activities and are typically guided by a supervisor or trainer who will outline each step that needs to be checked.

It is imperative to locate and thoroughly review the operations manual before proceeding with these start-up checks.

Ground Compartment Inspection: To begin the start-up checks, open the ground compartment and switch the select switch to the 'ground' position, then start the motor. Proceed to operate each of the ground control levers systematically to ensure they function correctly. The following actions need to be performed:

- Raise and lower the boom, noting any emergency lowering taps that may be present. These taps enable controlled lowering of the machine to its folded position in case of emergencies. Ensure you are familiar with their location and functionality.

- Slew the boom left and right, ensuring there are no potential hazards obstructing this movement. If the boom cannot be slewed, verify that the slew locking pin has been removed.

- Telescope the boom out to the required range for the tasks at hand and retract it back to its initial position.

- Check the auxiliary power unit on diesel and gas machines, as this is crucial in scenarios where the primary unit runs out of fuel or malfunctions. The auxiliary power unit provides the necessary power for vital functions required for descent.

- Refer to the operator's manual for guidance on lowering the machine in emergency situations if the machine lacks an auxiliary power unit or emergency lowering valves.

Emergency Lowering System Check It's essential to check the emergency lowering system before elevating the platform. Ground controls should not be utilized while personnel are working in the basket. They are strictly reserved for:

- Verifying machine operation before use.

- Conducting maintenance on the machine.

- Emergency purposes such as lowering the basket in critical situations.

To initiate the operational checks from the ground controls, a series of tasks must be performed. These include raising and lowering the basket, inspecting the auxiliary power unit on diesel and gas machines, slewing the boom left and right if applicable, and telescoping the boom to the required range. It's essential to ensure the absence of potential hazards and the removal of the slew locking pin if necessary.

Moving on to inspecting the basket controls, begin by switching the select switch to platform/basket mode. Enter the EWP basket using three points of contact, secure your harness, and don the required personal protective equipment (PPE) including a hard hat and rubber-soled steel cap shoes. Confirm the self-closing action of the platform gate, test the dead man switch, and verify the automatic leveling device along with all alarm systems.

Test each control lever in the basket systematically to guarantee smooth and accurate operation of all functions. This involves testing operations such as raising and lowering the basket, slewing left and right, telescoping the boom in and out, and performing hinging and articulating movements.

Prior to commencing work, conduct a thorough inspection of all safety devices to ensure they are operational. This includes verifying the functionality of horns/sirens, audible and visual reversing devices, operator restraint devices such as the platform gate, and any applicable lights.

Additionally, inspect any communication equipment intended for use, such as two-way radios or mobile phones, to ensure they are functioning properly.

In the event that any defects or damage are identified during the inspection process, promptly document them in the service logbook and report them to an authorized individual for further action.

Following the ground compartment checks, proceed to perform operational checks from the platform or basket. Switch the select switch to platform/basket mode, attach your harness, and wear the necessary PPE. Confirm the self-closing action of the platform gate, test the dead man switch functionality, and verify the automatic leveling device while checking all alarm systems. Confirm the 'Safe Working Load at Driving' positions and systematically test each control lever in the basket to ensure proper and smooth operation before commencing work.

MEWP Emergency Lowering Mechanisms and Emergency Processes

As the powered access industry continues to expand, various manufacturers and machine types emerge, each with its own operating and emergency lowering systems, which can differ significantly from one another. The following details outline examples of the four primary types of emergency lowering systems.

It is essential for mobile elevating work platforms (MEWPs) to have an operator's manual readily available, containing clear instructions on utilizing the machine's emergency lowering system during emergencies. It is imperative to adhere strictly to the manufacturers' operating and emergency lowering instructions provided in the manual.

All work at height should undergo thorough planning and execution in a safe manner, including the selection of the most suitable equipment for the task at hand. Additionally, there should be provisions for emergencies and rescue arrangements in accordance with the Australian Standard AS2550.10. 1.6 (f).

When operating MEWPs, ensure that the ground controls and emergency lowering system are easily accessible, especially when parked close to a structure. Familiarize yourself with the operation of emergency controls beforehand, as discovering them during an emergency may prove too late.

Emergency lowering systems are designed to be used in the event of a main power supply failure, such as a loss of fuel. If the main power supply is available, use the lower controls, but always ensure the lowering path is clear of any obstructions before attempting to lower the platform.

There are four main types of emergency lowering systems found on MEWPs:

1. Auxiliary Power Motor (APU)

2. Emergency lowering cable

3. Hand pumps

4. Bleed down valves

The images provided below depict examples of emergency lowering systems installed on MEWPs. It's important to note that different manufacturers may have their own versions of these systems.

Auxiliary Power Units Auxiliary Power Units (APUs) are typically installed on boom and scissor-type platforms. They consist of an electric motor powered by the machine's battery, connected to a small hydraulic pump. Activating the motor energizes the hydraulic pump, providing hydraulic pressure to the machine's system. Controls for the APU are usually located at both the base and platform controls and should only be used in the event of the main power source failing.

Bleed down valves are commonly installed in various types of powered access equipment. Typically, they are activated by pressing a plunger located on the cylinder. When utilizing these valves, exercise caution regarding crushing hazards as the boom lowers, and always reset the valve after use.

1. It is essential to consult the manufacturer's instructions for the emergency lowering procedure specific to the machine being used.

2. If the manual is not available with the machine, refrain from commencing daily operations. Many manufacturers offer downloadable manuals free of charge on their websites.

3. Machines vary in terms of the type and complexity of the emergency lowering system installed.

4. Prior to operating the machine, ensure that the emergency lowering system is operational by conducting a verification test.

5. Document your pre-use inspection findings in the Logbook.

6. As part of the rescue plan, always designate a competent individual at ground level who is familiar with and capable of executing the emergency lowering procedure.

When developing a rescue plan, it's crucial to consider several factors. First, identify the type of emergency lowering system installed on your machine and locate the emergency lowering controls, reviewing their usage instructions. Assign responsible individuals who are adequately trained to operate these controls and assess their accessibility while the MEWP is operational.

Instances where a rescue plan is necessary include scenarios such as operator incapacitation, failure of platform controls while elevated, overloading preventing load removal, or operator ejection and suspension in their harness. Extreme caution is warranted in cases of malfunction affecting platform, ground, and emergency lowering controls, proximity to distribution or transmission lines, risk of tip-over due to instability, or entrapment involving the operator or MEWP.

Considerations for developing a rescue plan involve ensuring a trained operator is available and appointing a competent individual familiar with the machine's controls and emergency procedures on the ground. Provide appropriate supervision and establish communication systems, determining how information will be disseminated and to whom. Have emergency contact numbers, site address, and directions for emergency services access readily available. Additionally, consider MEWP basket-to-basket rescue as a last resort, with extreme caution exercised in such situations.

An operative suspended in a harness after a fall presents a critical medical emergency. Despite being suspended, swift and effective rescue is imperative due to the risk of "Suspension Trauma" to operators in such situations. Therefore, rescue plans must be meticulously planned, practiced, and executed promptly to ensure operator safety and well-being.

Planning for work near overhead powerlines, including service lines, is crucial for ensuring safety. Elevating work platforms (EWPs) are commonly utilized for tasks near powerlines due to their capability to provide access at height. When conducting site visits before commencing work, it's essential to identify hazards and determine necessary control measures, paying close attention to any powerlines that may affect the work. Despite being a ubiquitous feature of the outdoor landscape, it's easy to overlook overhead powerlines. While engrossed in work activities, individuals may inadvertently come into close proximity to powerlines carrying high or low voltage electricity, which can be fatal upon contact.

Even when powerlines aren't visible or seem distant, the inherent danger persists. It's imperative to assume that all powerlines are 'live' and uninsulated unless confirmed otherwise as de-energized and isolated. While some EWPs feature insulated booms, this insulation may not offer sufficient protection when working near powerlines. Specific, legislated exclusion zones must be observed at all times when working near powerlines, regardless of whether the boom is insulated or not.

If work is to be carried out within these exclusion zones, a trained safety observer should be designated to warn of any encroachment beyond the specified safe distance from the powerline. Maintaining a safe distance from electrical wires is paramount to avoid turning a job into a tragedy.

Working near exposed live parts, such as overhead electric lines or underground cables, poses severe risks of injury or death. Even without direct contact, individuals are at risk due to the potential for high-voltage electricity to arc or jump gaps. Adherence to a code of practice, such as the Code of Practice - Working Near Exposed Live Parts, is essential for safety when working around electricity. This code applies to various occupations, including crane operators, painters, electrical repairers, and others working near exposed live parts or involved in activities such as vegetation clearing near overhead lines.

Exclusion zones, delineating the space around live electrical parts, necessitate the presence of a safety observer for any work that could breach these zones, ensuring heightened safety measures are upheld.

Operating an EWP

In elevating work platform (EWP) operations, ensuring safety and adherence to procedures is paramount. This includes:

1. Relevant Hazard Prevention/Control Measures Identified are Checked for Implementation: Before commencing work, it's essential to verify that the hazard prevention and control measures identified during risk assessment are implemented according to safe work procedures. This involves ensuring that safety protocols, such as barriers, signage, and personal protective equipment (PPE), are in place to mitigate identified risks effectively.

2. EWP is Safely Located at Point of Work in Work Area: The EWP must be safely positioned at the designated point of work within the work area, following safe work procedures. This entails selecting a suitable location that ensures stability and minimizes risks, such as uneven ground or overhead obstructions. Proper ground stabilization, outrigger deployment, or other stabilization measures may be necessary to enhance safety.

3. EWP Platform is Positioned for Work Tasks and Stability: Positioning the EWP platform for work tasks involves aligning it appropriately to access the work area safely. The platform must be stable, level, and securely positioned according to safe work procedures. Constant monitoring of platform stability is essential throughout the operation to detect any potential hazards or instability promptly.

4. Work Gear and Tools are Stowed and Secured: All work gear and tools must be stowed securely in designated areas within the EWP platform and properly secured to prevent accidental displacement. Safe work procedures dictate the correct storage

and securing methods to minimize the risk of objects falling from height, which could endanger personnel below.

5. EWP is Operated Using All Movements: Operating the EWP involves utilizing all movements, including lifting, lowering, telescoping, and slewing, in accordance with safe work procedures and manufacturer requirements. Operators must be trained and competent in operating the EWP and follow prescribed procedures to ensure safe and efficient operation.

6. Unplanned and Unsafe Situations are Responded to: In the event of unplanned or unsafe situations, operators must respond promptly and effectively in accordance with safe work procedures. This may involve halting operations, assessing the situation, and implementing corrective actions to mitigate risks and ensure the safety of personnel and equipment.

7. All Communication Signals are Correctly Interpreted and Followed: Proper communication is vital during EWP operations to coordinate movements and ensure safety. Operators must accurately interpret communication signals from ground personnel or other operators and follow them diligently according to safe work procedures. Clear and effective communication helps prevent accidents and enhances overall safety.

8. EWP Platform is Accessed and Egressed: Accessing and egressing the EWP platform must be done in strict accordance with safe work procedures and manufacturer requirements. This includes using designated access points, maintaining three points of contact, and adhering to safety protocols such as wearing appropriate PPE. Safe entry and exit procedures minimize the risk of slips, trips, and falls.

9. **EWP is Parked, Switched Off, and Isolated Appropriately:** After completing work tasks, the EWP must be parked, switched off, and isolated following manufacturer requirements and safe work procedures. Proper parking procedures, such as engaging the parking brake and lowering the platform to its lowest position, ensure stability and prevent unauthorized use. Isolation procedures may involve disconnecting power sources or locking control mechanisms to prevent accidental activation.

Performing an elevation:

- Ensure that your safety harness fits properly and that the lanyard length is appropriate for the type of harness and attachment points. Secure the harness lanyard to the anchor point, avoiding clipping it around the safety rail. Verify that other personnel in the basket have also donned and secured their safety harnesses.

- Check for small items, such as nuts and bolts, that may obstruct the foot switch and prevent it from operating.

- Conduct a thorough visual inspection of the surroundings, including overhead areas, to identify any overlooked obstructions or power lines. Adhere to the safety principle of "look up and live."

- Be cautious when moving the basket or boom of the EWP during operation, as it may introduce new hazards, such as closer proximity to power lines. Monitor the EWP closely to ensure that the basket and boom travel in the intended direction.

- Initiate the elevation by engaging the control lever. Avoid operating the lift at high speed, particularly in confined spaces. Note that most machines switch to creep mode after reaching a certain height. The speed of lifting, lowering, slewing, and

MATERIAL HANDLING EQUIPMENT OPERATION

telescoping is regulated by a speed controller on the dash panel.

- Elevate the EWP to the required full extension only if it is deemed safe to do so.

- Test the slewing function of the boom, if applicable, to ensure smooth operation.

- When working in confined areas, always operate the EWP in slow mode.

- Upon releasing a control lever, expect a slight delay of a few seconds before the relevant function comes to a complete stop. This delay, known as the "ramp," allows the function to decelerate gradually instead of abruptly halting. This is particularly noticeable during slewing operations, where abrupt stops could destabilize the machine.

- In case of an emergency, promptly release the dead man switch to immediately halt all functions.

Moving an Elevated Work Platform (EWP) requires careful attention due to the increased risk of destabilizing the machine. It's important to adhere to specific safety measures to ensure safe movement:

1. Avoid Moving with Outriggers Extended: Never move an EWP with its outriggers extended as it can compromise stability.

2. Apply Safety Measures:

    - Whenever feasible, retract the boom section(s) and lower the basket.

    - Ensure you are wearing your harness and securely attached to the anchor point.

    - Align the boom section with the chassis and position the basket behind the drive wheels for proper control functionality.

- Engage the turntable/basket lock.
- Verify that the travel path is clear of obstacles.
- Be vigilant for pedestrians in the travel area.
- Confirm the proper operation of warning devices.
- Check tire pressure.
- Execute steering movements smoothly.
- Stay alert for hazards such as potholes, obstructions, people, and other machinery.

3. Moving on Uneven Surfaces:

- Retract the boom fully and face it in the direction of travel.
- Ascertain the forward direction indicated by the "FWD" arrow on the machine's chassis.
- When traveling uphill, orient the platform uphill.
- Ensure the boom is fully retracted and close to the ground for long-distance travel, selecting high range speed if the surface is even.
- Exercise caution when using high speed in open areas, avoiding abrupt changes in direction.

4. Moving with an Elevated Platform:

- Ensure tools and equipment do not exceed the Safe Working Load (SWL) and keep them away from the door.

MATERIAL HANDLING EQUIPMENT OPERATION

- Be mindful of overhead obstructions and ground conditions.

- Travel at creep speed, staying vigilant for any surface irregularities.

- Avoid rough or uneven ground and lower the machine if necessary for stability.

- Check tire pressure for truck-mounted EWPs.

- Exercise caution when traversing slopes, avoiding steep inclines.

- Use the dead man switch only in emergencies, releasing it for an immediate stop.

After Movement:

- Check all gauges, lights, and switches for proper function.

- Verify the emergency stop controls and emergency lowering systems.

- Before elevating a trailer or truck-mounted EWP, ensure the cradle pin or basket strap has been removed.

Figure 78: EWP operations. Metropolitan Transportation Authority of the State of New York, CC BY 2.0, via Wikimedia Commons.

Operational Considerations include:
- Safety Protocol: It is essential to adhere to safety guidelines when operating an elevated work platform (EWP). Operators should refrain from climbing out of the elevated machine except in emergency situations. Load-bearing on handrails is permissible only if explicitly authorized by the manufacturer; however, standing on handrails is strictly prohibited to ensure operator safety.

- Equipment Misuse: Misuse of equipment can lead to severe damage and operational issues. Never utilize the EWP as an earth lead for an electric welder, as this can result in significant damage. Additionally, avoid tampering with the dead man switch by placing objects to keep it pressed, as it serves as a crucial safety device.

- Response to Malfunctions: In the event of persistent movements after bringing the controller to a neutral position, indicating a major malfunction, immediate action is required. Avoid attempting to manipulate the lever to resolve the issue. Instead, engage the emergency stop button promptly to disable the machine and seek assistance to safely lower the platform.

- Structural Considerations: When operating an EWP on an upper floor of a multi-storey building, it is imperative to verify with the site engineer that the floor can support the machine's weight. Bunting off the work area is essential to prevent additional machines from doubling the weight on a small floor area, ensuring structural integrity.

- Environmental Awareness: Operators must remain vigilant of changing environmental conditions during operations. This includes monitoring fading daylight, darkened areas, wind, storms, and lightning. If visibility becomes compromised or conditions become hazardous, work should be halted immediately to mitigate risks.

- Emergency Procedures: Familiarity with emergency procedures is crucial for swift and effective response in critical situations. If the machine's motor stops during work at height, utilize the backup battery or emergency descent device as outlined during start-up checks. In the event of an unexpected platform drop, cease operations immediately and lower the basket for inspection and repair.

- Ground Conditions and Tyre Issues: Vigilance regarding ground conditions is paramount to prevent incidents. If the EWP begins to sink into the ground despite packing, seek assistance to assess and address ground conditions promptly. Similarly, if the rubber tyres of a truck-mounted EWP start sinking into the ground, halt operations, retract and lower the boom, and seek further assistance to address the issue effectively.

In the event of inadvertent contact with powerlines, despite prior precautions, it is imperative to adhere to specific steps to ensure safety. Firstly, maintaining composure and avoiding panic is essential. Exiting the machine should be avoided as it may pose an electrification risk. Warn others to maintain a safe distance from the area. If feasible, attempt to move the machine away from the powerlines to sever contact. Subsequently, promptly descend and have the machine inspected for any damage. Notify the power authority to assess the lines for damage. In cases where breaking free from the powerlines is not possible, utilize a truck-mounted EWP with an emergency descent device (EDD) to safely descend from the basket. Ensure others in the vicinity are informed and kept at a safe distance. If there is a risk of fire or if alone, evacuating the machine onto dry ground is advisable while awaiting assistance. It is essential to inform the site manager/supervisor, who should promptly contact relevant authorities.

In the event of a colleague fainting or slumping down inside the basket, specific steps should be taken. Attempt to establish communication with the individual audibly or via phone. If the person is unresponsive, seek first aid assistance. Evaluate the work area for any hazards, such as powerlines or dangerous substances. If conditions permit, switch the machine to ground controls and lower the person down safely. In the presence of electrical hazards, refrain from touching the machine and contact the power authority for shutdown and resolution.

Upon noticing a tilt in the EWP, immediate action is necessary. Cease work and lower the platform to the ground. Exit the platform and inspect for the cause of the tilt, such as sinking packing or hydraulic ram issues. Seek guidance from a competent individual before attempting to elevate the platform again. If required, relocate the EWP to stable ground to mitigate risks.

In the event of the EWP motor cutting out, prompt response is crucial. Direct an operator on the ground to engage ground controls to lower the platform. Utilize methods such as bleeding the hydraulic valves or activating the emergency descent device, if available. For truck-mounted machines, activate the hydraulic accumulator.

Many EWPs are equipped with Emergency Descent Device (EDD) for emergency evacuations. Follow general procedures by releasing the EDD safety clip and securing it to your safety harness. Attach the EDD to the safety harness's D ring and descend cautiously using the rope, adjusting speed as needed. Ensure no one is beneath the boom or basket before activation. Familiarize yourself with specific EDD procedures for the machine and adhere to supplier requirements.

Walking Scissor Lifts come with potential risks:

1. Scissor lift platforms designed to fit through narrow openings with fixed handrails in place may lead operators to stand or crouch on the platform, risking entrapment between the handrails and door frames. Such scenarios can result in structural damage to the lift or building.

2. Driving a scissor lift up/down ramps or onto delivery vehicles/trailers while an operator stands on the lowered platform poses risks of the lift driving off the edge, ramp collapse, or bottoming out at different angles, causing the chassis to pivot and lose traction. This may lead to operator injuries due to tipping or loss of control.

3. Driving into or out of confined spaces like shipping containers or delivery vehicles can cause temporary blindness as operators transition from visible light to darkness.

Observations: Operating a scissor lift in these scenarios is common but requires a site survey beforehand and cannot be done from the platform. Risk analysis is necessary to assess hazards associated with controlling the lift from within the platform or walking beside it using an extended control cable. Walking alongside while operating the scissor lift from the platform controls should only be done if it doesn't jeopardize the operator's or bystanders' safety. Operators must familiarize themselves with manufacturer's instructions regarding "Walking the Scissor" and identify all hazards before attempting such manoeuvres.

Control Measures: Scissor lifts should only be operated from outside the platform using the upper control box under specific conditions, such as during maintenance, testing, or when guardrails are folded. If a risk assessment deems operating from the platform impractical, operators should utilize external controls. To minimize injury risks while walking with a scissor lift, operators should:

- Refer to the manufacturer's operating manual and comply with all requirements.

- Maintain a clear view of the support surface and travel route.

- Ensure the control cable is at least 1600mm long and stand at least 1000mm from the wheels.

- Hold the control box in hand rather than securing it to the machine.

- Select the slowest speed position on the Torque/Speed Select Toggle Switch.

- Limit travel speed according to conditions and maintain a safe distance from obstacles.

- Stand clear of the lift's path and avoid driving towards oneself.

MATERIAL HANDLING EQUIPMENT OPERATION

- Prevent entanglement of the control box with the lift or surrounding objects.

- Be aware of the platform's movement when controls are released and ensure others in the work area are informed.

- Maintain a safe distance from hazards and seek assistance when uncertain.

Operating Mobile Elevating Work Platforms (MEWPs) on or near water introduces additional hazards that must be identified and managed by a competent person. When selecting equipment for such tasks, hazards related to water should be considered, and a site-specific safe work method statement must be prepared, especially if there's a risk of falls exceeding 2 meters. The potential for injury from falling off the platform versus drowning if falling into water must be assessed for each site.

If the risk of drowning is higher, appropriate life jackets or personal flotation devices should be worn, and fall risks should be controlled using methods other than harnesses. While both harnesses and flotation devices may be utilized by the operator, they should not be worn simultaneously. If harnesses are necessary for other purposes, such as movement or rescue, they should not be connected to the MEWP while working near water. Instead, the occupant should connect to the attachment point once the MEWP moves away from such areas.

Efforts should prioritize preventing falls, followed by controlling fall risks. When working on a barge or pontoon, hazards such as weather conditions, barge structure failure, and MEWP tipping must be considered. Possible risk control measures include using spotters, ensuring barge stability, disabling MEWP drive functions when possible, and providing rescue equipment.

A comprehensive safe work method statement should outline communication methods, harness or flotation device usage, MEWP setup procedures, and rescue plans for personnel in water or in the basket. Information on MEWP stability on water-borne craft should be obtained from competent sources.

When working from an embankment, hazards like MEWP tipping, changing water conditions, and operator falls into water must be addressed. Risk control measures may involve trained operators, proper setup on firm surfaces, and regular ground condition checks. The safe work method statement should detail ground monitoring, slow travel practices, communication methods, and rescue plans.

Site controllers should provide relevant information on ground conditions, bearing capacity, terrain, load-bearing capability, and any local features that could impact machine stability. It's crucial to exercise caution as weather and ground conditions can vary, potentially leading to accidents if not properly assessed and managed.

Mobile Elevating Work Platforms (MEWPs) are also susceptible to lateral forces, primarily stemming from wind and manual exertion (e.g., pushing or pulling). This guidance document delineates the factors to consider in mitigating these influences within limits specified by the manufacturer.

Wind Forces: Every MEWP must prominently display its maximum wind rating, which can be found on the data/compliance plate, operator's manual, and safety decals affixed to the machine. Operating the MEWP beyond the manufacturer's prescribed limits is strictly prohibited.

It's crucial to recognize that some MEWPs are solely intended for indoor use, where wind is not a factor. Additionally, manufacturers may impose restrictions on the number of occupants when the unit is operated outdoors. Even within enclosed buildings with large openings, MEWPs can still be affected by wind forces.

Wind force increases proportionally with the square of the speed. Thus, doubling the wind speed results in a fourfold increase in force acting on the MEWP. Materials like building cladding, panels, and sheeting can act as sails, enhancing the risk of tipping over, especially during gusty conditions. Hence, attaching items such as signboards or banners to the platform, even temporarily, should be avoided.

It's essential to note that wind can be funnelled by tall structures, amplifying its intensity, even in indoor settings like large warehouses or high-rise buildings. Local wind speeds may also be influenced by factors like aircraft slipstreams at airports or high-sided vehicles on highways.

Wind poses a significant hazard during MEWP operations. Typically, wind velocity increases with elevation and can be magnified around obstacles such as buildings due to the funnelling effect. As the MEWP ascends above surrounding structures, it becomes exposed to higher strata of wind, potentially experiencing speeds up to 50% greater than those at ground level. Even if initially sheltered at lower levels, as the MEWP elevates, it becomes fully exposed to the force of the wind.

During periods of strong winds, it is advisable to refrain from operating MEWPs in areas where wind can be funnelled and intensified between gaps in buildings or structures. This concentrated wind flow can generate turbulent forces capable of destabilising an exposed MEWP. Additionally, caution is warranted when operating near aircraft slipstreams at airports and in the vicinity of high-sided vehicles on roads and motorways.

Sail Effect (Side Force Caused by Wind): Great care should be exercised when placing or attaching objects to the basket of a MEWP. Large flat surfaces have the potential to act like sails, exerting adverse effects on the machine's stability. Any accessories used must be approved by the MEWP manufacturer.

Manual Side Force:

- The maximum permissible sideways force (push or pull) applicable to or from the platform is known as side force.

- Side force is encountered during tasks such as drilling or cable pulling.

- Manufacturers specify the maximum allowable side force for the machine on the compliance plate, with force measured in Newtons (10N equals 1kg).

- Typically, a single person is allowed a side force of 200N, while two or more people may apply up to 400N.

Installation of Mesh Protection on Baskets and Handrails: The installation of mesh panels on the guardrails of MEWP baskets is sometimes viewed as an effective measure to prevent tools or materials from falling off the platform. However, it has been observed that some construction sites mandate mesh guarding as a condition for site access. Fitting mesh panels, screens, or other protective measures may increase wind loads and potentially impact the stability and strength of the MEWP. Manufacturers may offer mesh guards as a standard option for platform fitment, and these are generally recommended. In instances where suitable protection is not provided, end users should consult the supplier or manufacturer before fitting mesh guarding. Unauthorized installation of mesh guards is discouraged, as it may affect the strength, Safe Working Load, and stability of the MEWP.

Completing EWP Operations and Shutting Down the Equipment

Post-operational EWP Checks:

1. **Compliance with Manufacturer Requirements:** Following the completion of EWP operations, it is imperative to conduct post-operational checks in strict accordance with the manufacturer's guidelines. These checks typically encompass a com-

prehensive inspection of various components and systems to ensure optimal functioning and safety.

2. **Adherence to Safe Work Procedures:** Additionally, post-operational checks should align with established safe work procedures tailored to the specific EWP model and operational environment. These procedures serve to mitigate risks associated with potential equipment malfunctions or hazards arising from the work site.

3. **Thorough Inspection:** The post-operational inspection involves a meticulous examination of key EWP components, including but not limited to hydraulic systems, electrical connections, structural integrity, and safety mechanisms. Any signs of damage, wear, or abnormalities must be promptly addressed and reported.

4. **Documentation:** It is essential to document the results of post-operational checks systematically. This documentation serves as a record of compliance with manufacturer requirements and safe work procedures, facilitating accountability and traceability in maintenance and operational activities.

After completing the operation, conduct a thorough safety inspection of the machine to identify any breakages, damages, or leaks. Specifically, focus on the following areas:

- Check all hydraulic arms to ensure they are undamaged and not bent from the machine's use.

- Inspect the boom for any signs of dents or cracks in its welds and joints.

- Examine the slew ring for bending or other forms of damage.

- Assess the basket to ensure it is in optimal working condition and has not sustained any damage.

- Inspect the outriggers/stabilizers to verify they are functioning properly.

- Verify the integrity and functionality of all safety devices.

Promptly report any faults or damages to your supervisor/employer, ensuring they are documented in the log for necessary corrective measures. If required, attach warning tags to the machine to alert others of potential hazards.

Retraction, Lowering, Stowing, and Securing of EWP Boom:

1. **Manufacturer's Specifications:** Retracting, lowering, stowing, and securing the EWP boom should strictly adhere to the manufacturer's specifications outlined in the operator's manual or instructional materials. These specifications typically encompass step-by-step procedures for safe operation and storage of the boom.

2. **Safe Work Procedures:** In addition to manufacturer guidelines, safe work procedures specific to EWP operation should be followed meticulously. These procedures may include safety protocols for boom manipulation, ensuring proper equipment handling and positioning to prevent accidents or damage.

3. **Operator Competence:** Only trained and authorized personnel should be entrusted with the task of retracting, lowering, stowing, and securing the EWP boom. Adequate training ensures proficiency in executing these tasks safely and efficiently, minimizing the risk of incidents or equipment damage.

4. **Verification of Secure Stowage:** Upon completion of the process, it is essential to verify that the EWP boom is securely

stowed and properly locked in place. Any loose connections or unsecured components should be rectified immediately to prevent potential hazards during transport or storage.

Storing the Equipment: After lowering the platform, proceed to drive the machine to its designated parking spot, ensuring it is positioned safely. Lower the platform completely and power off all systems. Next, remove your harness, storing it securely in a dry location, and dismount from the machine. Retrieve your tools and equipment from the basket, and securely lock the control panel doors. Shutdown the motor and, if necessary, isolate the fuel supply. Depending on instructions from your supervisor, either connect the machine to a charging station or refuel it as required. It's advisable to defer oil and coolant checks until the following day to avoid potential oil burns or scalding from hot water.

When dealing with a truck or trailer-mounted EWP, the process for shutting down and stowing the machine follows a slightly different sequence. It is essential to adhere to the following procedures:

- Before proceeding, ensure there are no hazards below. Align the boom with the chassis and lower the bottom boom arm into the cradle. Then, bring down the top boom onto the bottom boom.

- Remove your safety harness and store it in the provided cylinder located in the corner of the basket. Replace the lid onto the cylinder.

- Exit the basket and collect and store your tools securely.

- Raise the outriggers and secure them with pins if required.

- Gather any packing materials and place them in the designated area.

- Install the boom locking pin or strap.

- Turn off the motor or disengage the power take-off (PTO) for a truck-mounted machine.

- Retrieve the keys from the EWP, lock the ground control cabinet, and ensure the keys are stored securely.

Disconnection of Safety Equipment and PPE:

1. **Sequential Disconnection:** Safety equipment and personal protective equipment (PPE) should be disconnected from the EWP platform systematically and in the reverse order of attachment. This ensures a methodical approach to equipment removal, minimizing the risk of oversight or error.

2. **Proper Handling:** During disconnection, care should be taken to handle safety equipment and PPE with caution to avoid damage or contamination. Special attention should be given to delicate components or items prone to wear, such as harnesses or safety lines.

3. **Inspection and Maintenance:** Before storage, safety equipment and PPE should undergo visual inspection for any signs of damage, wear, or degradation. Any compromised items should be promptly replaced or repaired to maintain their effectiveness and compliance with safety standards.

Application of Relevant Motion Locks and Brakes:

1. **Understanding Manufacturer Requirements:** The application of motion locks and brakes should be carried out in accordance with the specific recommendations provided by the EWP manufacturer. This entails a clear understanding of the types of locks and brakes installed on the equipment and their intended functions.

2. **Verification of Engagement:** Prior to shutdown, operators

should verify that all relevant motion locks and brakes are applied as required to immobilize the EWP effectively. This includes verifying the engagement of parking brakes, motion locks for hydraulic systems, and any other safety mechanisms designed to prevent unintended movement.

3. **Visual Confirmation:** Operators should visually confirm the engagement of motion locks and brakes before exiting the EWP or handing over control to other personnel. This visual confirmation serves as a critical safety checkpoint to ensure that the equipment is securely immobilized and ready for shutdown.

Stowing and Securing of Outriggers/Stabilizers:

1. **Proper Procedures:** Outriggers and stabilizers, if equipped, should be stowed and secured in strict accordance with manufacturer requirements and safe work procedures. This involves retracting the outriggers or stabilizers to their designated storage positions and ensuring they are securely locked in place.

2. **Systematic Approach:** Stowing and securing outriggers/stabilizers should be conducted systematically, following a step-by-step process outlined in the operator's manual or instructional materials. This ensures consistency and accuracy in the execution of these tasks, minimizing the risk of errors or oversights.

3. **Operator Vigilance:** Operators should exercise vigilance during the stowing and securing process, paying close attention to proper alignment and locking of outriggers/stabilizers. Any deviations from expected behaviour or indications of malfunction should be addressed promptly to maintain equipment integrity and safety.

The process of securing and stowing outriggers demands careful attention. It is essential to follow these procedures under the guidance of your supervisor:

- Retract the outrigger footplates.

- Bring in the outrigger beams.

- If necessary, secure the outriggers with the appropriate pins.

- Ensure the steel plates are cleaned.

- Store the packing either on the carrier or in a designated storage area for future accessibility.

Shutdown Procedure in Accordance with Manufacturer Requirements:

1. **Sequence of Shutdown:** The shutdown procedure for the EWP should be executed in strict accordance with the sequence prescribed by the manufacturer. This typically involves a series of steps to power down the equipment and deactivate its operational systems in a controlled manner.

2. **Compliance with Guidelines:** Operators should adhere to all guidelines and recommendations provided by the manufacturer regarding shutdown procedures, including the sequence of actions, timing, and safety precautions to be observed.

3. **Verification of Shutdown:** Upon completion of the shutdown procedure, operators should verify that all systems are properly deactivated, and the EWP is in a safe and secure state for storage or transport. Visual and auditory cues may be used to confirm the completion of shutdown steps and ensure compliance with manufacturer requirements.

4. **Documentation and Reporting:** It is essential to document

the shutdown procedure, including any observations or abnormalities encountered during the process. This documentation serves as a record of compliance with manufacturer requirements and may be useful for maintenance and troubleshooting purposes.

Figure 79: Genie GS-5390 scissor lift stowed and secured. Santeri Viinamäki, CC BY-SA 4.0, via Wikimedia Commons.

The proper execution of post-operational checks, boom retraction, safety equipment disconnection, application of motion locks and brakes, stowing of outriggers/stabilizers, and shutdown procedure is critical to ensuring the safe and efficient operation of EWP equipment. Adherence to manufacturer requirements and safe work procedures, coupled with operator competence and vigilance, is essential to mitigate risks and maintain workplace safety standards.

Chapter Six

Reach Stackers

A reach stacker is a specialized vehicle used in material handling and logistics operations, particularly in container terminals, ports, and freight yards. It is designed to lift and transport ISO standard containers, commonly known as shipping containers, with efficiency and flexibility.

Key features of a reach stacker include:

1. Telescopic boom: Reach stackers are equipped with a telescopic boom that can extend forward and retract, allowing them to reach containers stacked in multiple rows and tiers.

2. Spreader attachment: At the end of the boom, there is a spreader attachment that can grasp and lift containers from the top corner castings, securing them for transportation.

3. Heavy lifting capacity: Reach stackers are capable of lifting and moving heavy containers, typically ranging from 20 to 40 feet in length and weighing several tons.

4. Manoeuvrability: They are designed for manoeuvrings in confined spaces such as container yards, thanks to features like all-wheel steering and compact dimensions.

5. Versatility: Reach stackers can handle various types of contain-

ers, including standard dry containers, flat racks, open tops, and refrigerated (reefer) containers.

In essence, a reach stacker, as shown in Figure 80, plays a vital role in the efficient movement and organization of containers within terminals and storage yards, contributing to the smooth flow of goods in global trade and logistics operations.

Figure 80: Reach Stacker shifting a container. joost j. bakker from ijmuiden, the netherlands, CC BY 2.0, via Wikimedia Commons.

In the field of material handling and logistics, reach stackers have become essential equipment for the efficient movement and stacking of heavy loads, particularly shipping containers. Designed to operate in diverse environments such as ports, warehouses, and intermodal yards, reach stackers play a crucial role in container handling operations.

Electric reach stackers are powered by electric motors and utilize rechargeable batteries as their primary energy source. These machines have gained popularity due to their eco-friendly operation, emitting zero emissions and producing lower noise levels compared to diesel-powered models. Electric reach stackers excel in indoor or enclosed environments where emission and noise regulations are stringent. They offer exceptional manoeuvrability and are favoured in settings prioritizing sustainability and environmental compliance.

Applications of Electric Reach Stackers:

- Container handling in warehouses and distribution centres with strict emission regulations.

- Efficient movement and stacking of containers in industrial facilities near residential areas.

- Safe material handling in environmentally sensitive areas like ports and terminals.

Diesel reach stackers are powered by diesel engines known for their high torque, lifting capacity, and ruggedness, making them ideal for heavy-duty outdoor applications. These machines are commonly used in large port terminals and open yards where power infrastructure may be limited. Diesel reach stackers boast superior lifting capabilities and are preferred for handling heavy loads and navigating rough terrains.

Applications of Diesel Reach Stackers:

- Efficient container handling in busy port terminals with high container traffic.

- Stacking containers in intermodal yards with unpaved or uneven surfaces.

- Handling heavy loads and oversized containers in demanding industrial environments.

Figure 81: Konecranes SMV 4531 TB 5 diesel reach stacker. TeWeBs, CC BY-SA 4.0, via Wikimedia Commons.

Hybrid reach stackers combine electric and diesel components, featuring a rechargeable battery pack working alongside a diesel generator. These machines offer reduced fuel consumption and emissions compared to traditional diesel models while providing the power and versatility needed for heavy-duty operations.

Applications of Hybrid Reach Stackers:

- Environments requiring a balance between power and environmental sustainability.

- Container handling in ports and terminals with varying emission regulations.

- Efficient stacking and transportation of containers in intermodal yards with mixed indoor and outdoor operations.

In addition to electric, diesel, and hybrid models, specialized reach stackers cater to specific material handling requirements, offering unique features and functionalities tailored to various industries. Examples include:

- Laden Reach Stackers: Designed for handling loaded containers with advanced load monitoring systems and reinforced structures.

- Empty Container Reach Stackers: Optimized for stacking and moving empty containers with higher stacking capabilities and faster cycle times.

- Intermodal Reach Stackers: Equipped for seamless transportation of containers across different modes, such as trucks, trains, and ships, facilitating efficient intermodal operations.

An intermodal reach stacker is a specialized type of reach stacker designed specifically for handling containers in intermodal transportation settings. Intermodal transportation involves the movement of freight containers across multiple modes of transportation, such as trucks, trains, and ships.

Intermodal reach stackers are equipped with features and attachments that enable them to efficiently handle containers as they transition between different transportation modes. These reach stackers are designed to withstand the demands of intermodal operations and often have enhanced mobility features to navigate various terrains and loading/unloading areas.

Key features of intermodal reach stackers may include:

1. Enhanced Mobility: Intermodal reach stackers are designed to operate in diverse environments, including ports, rail yards, and distribution centres. They may have features such as all-wheel drive or adjustable wheelbases to navigate different surfaces and terrains.

2. Versatile Lifting Attachments: These reach stackers typically come with specialized lifting attachments that allow for efficient handling of containers with different sizes and configurations. This versatility is essential for the seamless transfer of containers between different modes of transportation.

3. Durability and Reliability: Given the demanding nature of intermodal operations, intermodal reach stackers are built to withstand heavy-duty use and harsh working conditions. They are constructed with robust materials and components to ensure durability and reliability over extended periods of operation.

4. Safety Features: Intermodal reach stackers may incorporate advanced safety features such as load monitoring systems, anti-collision technology, and operator-assist functionalities to enhance safety during container handling operations.

An intermodal container, often simply referred to as a container, is a large standardized shipping container designed for the transport of goods from one mode of transportation to another, typically from ship to rail or truck, without unloading and reloading the cargo. These containers come in various sizes, but the most common is the twenty-foot equivalent unit (TEU), see Figure 82, and the forty-foot equivalent unit (FEU). Intermodal containers are made of steel and are built to withstand the rigors of transportation, including being stacked on top of each other. They have standardized dimensions and are fitted with corner castings for secure handling using cranes or forklifts. The widespread adoption of intermodal containers has revolutionized global trade by simplifying logistics, reducing costs, and increasing efficiency.

Figure 82: 20 Foot Storage Shipping Container. IPLManagement, CC BY-SA 4.0, via Wikimedia Commons.

Here are the typical dimensions and maximum weights for these standard containers:

1. Standard 20-foot container (TEU):

    ○ External dimensions: 20 feet long, 8 feet wide, and 8 feet 6 inches tall (6.1 meters long, 2.44 meters wide, and 2.59 meters tall).

    ○ Internal dimensions: Slightly smaller due to wall thickness.

    ○ Maximum gross weight (including container weight and cargo): Approximately 52,910 pounds (24,000 kilograms).

2. Standard 40-foot container (FEU):

    ○ External dimensions: 40 feet long, 8 feet wide, and 8 feet

6 inches tall (12.19 meters long, 2.44 meters wide, and 2.59 meters tall).

- Internal dimensions: Slightly smaller due to wall thickness.

- Maximum gross weight (including container weight and cargo): Approximately 67,200 pounds (30,480 kilograms).

It's worth noting that there are also high-cube versions of both the 20-foot and 40-foot containers, which are taller than the standard containers:

- High-cube 20-foot container:

  - External dimensions: Same as standard 20-foot container, but taller.

  - Internal dimensions: Taller than the standard version.

  - Maximum gross weight: Similar to standard 20-foot container.

- High-cube 40-foot container (see Figure 83:

  - External dimensions: Same as standard 40-foot container, but taller.

  - Internal dimensions: Taller than the standard version.

  - Maximum gross weight: Similar to standard 40-foot container.

The actual maximum weights may vary slightly depending on regulations and specifications in different regions or by different shipping companies.

MATERIAL HANDLING EQUIPMENT OPERATION 303

Figure 83: 40 Foot High Cube Shipping Container. IPLManagement, CC BY-SA 4.0, via Wikimedia Commons.

Reach stackers are defined by their lifting capacity, wheelbase, reach, and turning radius. Lifting capacity refers to the maximum force or load that can be supported by the lift, cart, truck, or dolly. Wheelbase signifies the distance between the front and rear axles of a vehicle. Reach represents the variance between the fully-retracted and fully-extended positions of the lift or boom. Turning radius indicates the radius of the smallest circle that the vehicle can manoeuvre within.

Firstly, lifting capacity stands as a fundamental specification, denoting the maximum weight or force that the reach stacker can safely lift and handle. This capacity is crucial for determining the types and sizes of loads that the equipment can efficiently manage, ensuring optimal performance and safety in material handling operations.

Secondly, wheelbase is a critical dimension that defines the stability and manoeuvrability of the reach stacker. It represents the distance between the front and rear axles of the vehicle, influencing its balance and weight distribution. A longer wheelbase typically enhances stability, especially when handling heavy loads, while a shorter wheelbase may offer greater manoeuvrability in tight spaces.

Next, reach is a vital parameter that illustrates the extendibility and flexibility of the reach stacker's lifting mechanism. It refers to the difference between the fully-retracted and fully-extended positions of the lift or boom. A longer reach enables the equipment to access and handle loads situated further away or at higher elevations, expanding its operational versatility and efficiency.

Finally, turning radius is an essential specification that highlights the reach stacker's ability to navigate and manoeuvre within confined spaces or congested environments. It represents the radius of the smallest circle that the vehicle can turn within, affecting its agility and ability to negotiate tight corners or obstacles. A smaller turning radius facilitates enhanced manoeuvrability, enabling the reach stacker to operate efficiently in diverse work environments while minimizing the risk of collisions or accidents.

These design parameters collectively define the capabilities and performance characteristics of reach stackers, empowering businesses to select the most suitable equipment for their specific material handling requirements. By understanding and evaluating these specifications, organizations can optimize their operations, enhance productivity, and ensure safe and efficient handling of goods and materials throughout the supply chain.

Reach stackers operate on several operational principles to efficiently handle and move cargo in various material handling applications. These principles include:

1. Hydraulic Systems: Reach stackers utilize hydraulic systems to control the movement of their various components, such as the boom, lift mechanism, and steering. Hydraulic cylinders apply

force to extend or retract the boom and lift attachments, allowing for precise positioning and lifting of cargo. These systems also power the steering mechanism, enabling the reach stacker to navigate tight spaces and maneuver with ease.

2. Counterbalance: Reach stackers are designed with a counterbalance system to offset the weight of the lifted cargo and maintain stability during operation. This system typically includes counterweights strategically placed on the reach stacker's chassis to prevent tipping or instability when lifting heavy loads. By balancing the weight distribution, the reach stacker can safely handle large and unevenly distributed loads without compromising safety or performance.

3. Telescopic Boom: Reach stackers feature a telescopic boom that extends and retracts to reach and lift cargo from varying distances and heights. The telescopic design allows the reach stacker to adapt to different loading and unloading scenarios, enabling it to handle containers or other types of cargo efficiently. The boom's extension and retraction are controlled hydraulically, providing smooth and precise movement for loading and unloading operations.

4. Load-Sensing Technology: Many modern reach stackers are equipped with load-sensing technology that automatically adjusts hydraulic pressure based on the weight of the cargo being lifted. This technology optimizes energy efficiency and reduces wear and tear on the reach stacker's components by delivering the necessary force to lift the load without excess strain or power consumption.

5. Electronic Control Systems: Reach stackers feature advanced electronic control systems that enable operators to monitor

and control various aspects of the machine's operation, including lifting, steering, and safety functions. These systems often include touchscreen displays or joystick controls that provide intuitive operation and real-time feedback, enhancing productivity and safety on the job site.

By leveraging these operational principles, reach stackers can efficiently handle a wide range of cargo types and sizes while ensuring safety, stability, and precision in material handling operations.

Figure 84: Components of a reach stacker. Back image - HReuter, CC BY-SA 4.0, via Wikimedia Commons.

Much akin to the operation of a see-saw or any counterbalanced equipment, a reach stacker possesses a pivotal balance point or fulcrum. For the longitudinal (forward and rearward) axis of the machine, this fulcrum aligns with the centreline of the front tyres (Taylor Machine Works, 2024).

The principles of counterbalance can be elucidated as follows: The weight situated behind the centreline of the front tyres, as depicted in Figure 85, is akin to the weight of one child positioned at distance "D" from the fulcrum, as illustrated in Figure 86. Conversely, the weight of the boom attachment and the load itself, as depicted in Figure 85, can be equated to the combined weight of children, as showcased in Figure 86, located at distance "d" from the fulcrum.

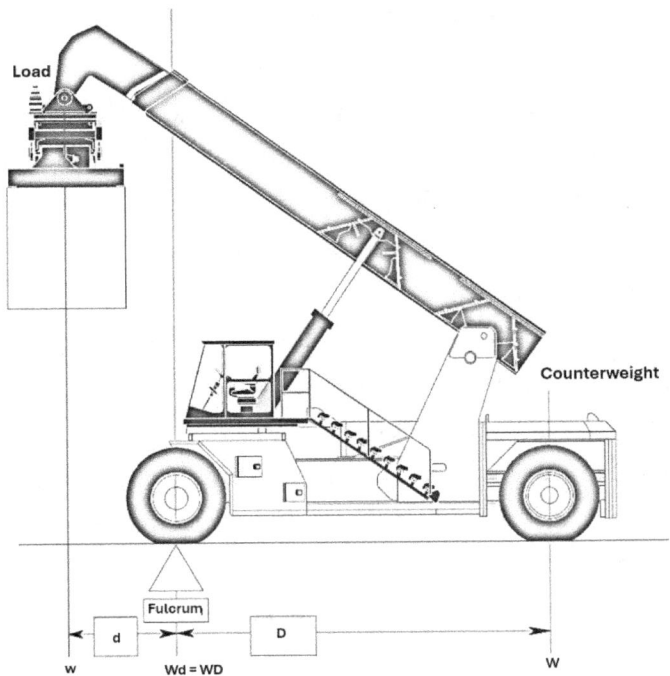

Figure 85: Reach stacker counterbalance.

Much like the dynamics of a see-saw, wherein children adjust their positions relative to the fulcrum until equilibrium is reached, a similar balance is sought within the reach stacker. This equilibrium is expressed by the equation "$w \times d = W \times D$," signifying that varied combinations of weight multiplied by distance can yield a balanced state.

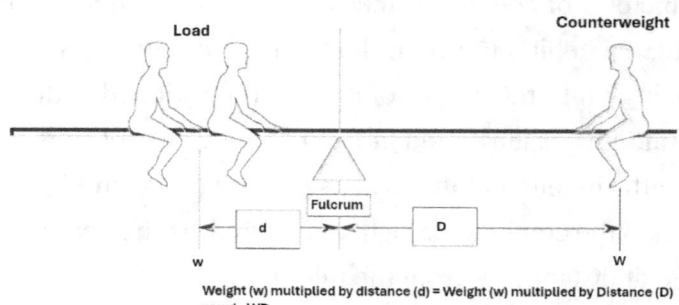

Figure 86: See-saw counterbalance.

In the context of stability principles in a reach stacker, the analogy of a see-saw remains pertinent, wherein the weight of the load and its distance from the fulcrum dictate the counterbalance requirements.

It is imperative to recognize that the reach stacker diverges in its mechanism: the weight rearward of the drive axle centreline (fulcrum), when multiplied by the distance to the centre of gravity (CG) of that weight, must consistently exceed, by a significant margin, the weight forward of the drive axle, multiplied by the distance to its CG. Approaching a balanced condition risks precarious vehicle upsets due to dynamic forces associated with stopping, traveling, or tilting (Taylor Machine Works, 2024).

Notably, the weight of the reach stacker positioned behind the fulcrum, and the CG of this weight, remain constant; hence, counterbalance remains a fixed value. Conversely, the weight of the boom and attachment remains fixed, while the distance to the CG forward of the fulcrum varies contingent on the boom's angle and extension.

As the load's moment changes with its forward location relative to the fulcrum, contingent upon the boom angle and extension, the operator must regulate these variables diligently. Ensuring that the total weight forward of the fulcrum, multiplied by the combined CG location plus other dynamic operational forces, never surpasses the reach stacker's counterbalance is essential for safe operation.

Adhering to these safety protocols and exercising sound judgment is paramount for the safe operation of the reach stacker. The equilibrium for proper operation is secure if all machine components are adequately maintained, and the operator operates the machine safely. For instance, a machine's rated capacity is calibrated for a specific combination of the machine, boom, and attachment. Any alterations to the attachment or boom could affect the capacity, necessitating a comprehensive understanding of the actual changes and resulting capacity adjustments (Taylor Machine Works, 2024).

To ensure your safety, it is essential to familiarize yourself with several key aspects regarding the reach stacker. This includes understanding the machine's dimensions, its operating capacity, and proficiency in its operation. Equally crucial is being knowledgeable about the safety features it offers, as well as adhering to safe operating procedures specific to your work site. Additionally, conducting daily checks to ensure the reach stacker is functioning correctly is imperative. Utilizing every available safety feature and consistently following safe operating procedures are essential practices. Moreover, maintaining alertness and employing common sense during operation further enhance safety measures.

The specified capacity of a counterbalanced reach stacker is valid solely under conditions where the truck is positioned on even ground, and the load is appropriately elevated and positioned relative to the front wheels. It is crucial to comprehend that this capacity diminishes, and the truck's stability is compromised under the following circumstances: when the boom is elevated, when the boom is extended, or when the truck is positioned on an incline. The stability of the reach stacker relies on the three-point suspension system of the truck, as illustrated in Figure 87.

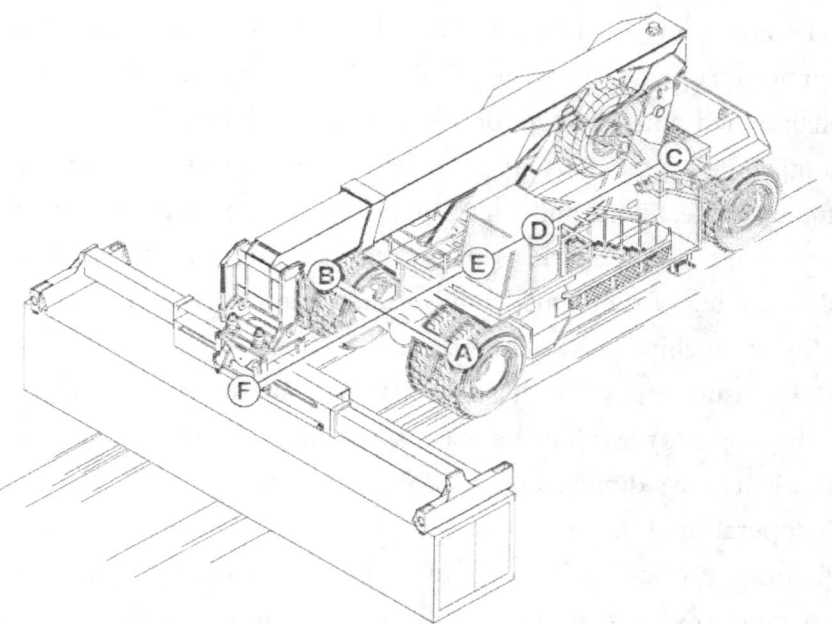

Figure 87: Reach stacker 3-point suspension system.

The truck is upheld by the tyres on the drive axle (designated as points A and B) and the pivot point of the steer axle's centreline (designated as point C). Point D indicates the centre of gravity of an unloaded truck, while point F denotes the centre of gravity of the load. Point E represents the combined centre of gravity of both the truck and the load. It is imperative that the combined centre of gravity (point E) remains within the triangular area formed by points A, B, and C for stability to be maintained. Stability is contingent upon the proximity of point E to the edges of this triangle. Should point E exceed the boundaries of the triangle for any reason, the truck risks tipping over (Taylor Machine Works, 2024).

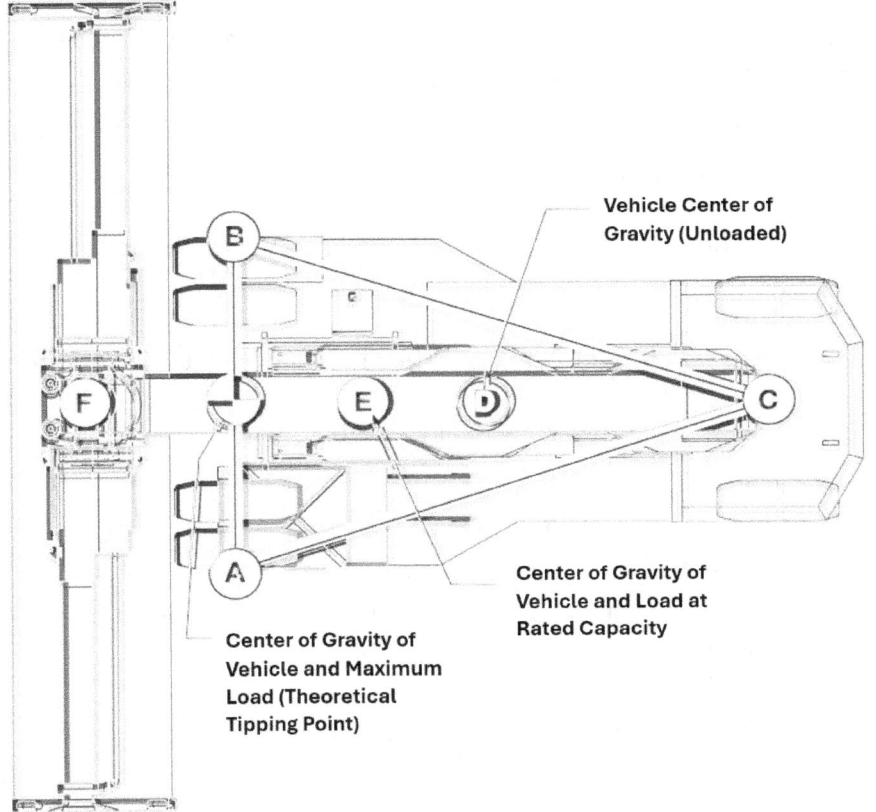

Figure 88: Forward stability.

When the vehicle is loaded, the combined centre of gravity shifts towards line A-B. Theoretically, if a load is positioned in a manner that would cause forward tipping, the centre of gravity would align at or beyond line A-B. Therefore, in practical application, it's essential to ensure that the combined centre of gravity never reaches line A-B. Rated loads are designed to maintain the combined centre of gravity well within the stability triangle. Merely increasing counterweight doesn't address forward stability concerns, as it would shift the truck's centre of gravity towards point C, resulting in decreased lateral stability. The proximity of Point E to the line connecting points A and B directly impacts forward stability. Should the combined centre of gravity cross line AB for any reason, the truck risks tipping forward (Taylor Machine Works, 2024).

These circumstances may arise when:

- The load surpasses the rated capacity designated for the current boom position.

- The boom is either lowered or extended while the load remains elevated.

- Bringing the truck to a halt while the load is elevated.

- Accelerating the truck backward too swiftly with the load elevated. It's crucial to exercise extreme caution during travel or when stacking and unstacking loads. Abrupt halts, forward tilts, or any actions leading to load shifting forward will prompt point E to advance towards line AB, thereby diminishing forward stability.

Side Stability: The distance between point E and the lines connecting points A and C, as well as points B and C, influences side stability. If point E nears or surpasses either line, the truck may tip sideways. This scenario might occur when loads are handled off-centre, stacking is performed sideways on an incline, or sharp turns are executed with the attachment elevated, either with or without a load. Therefore, extreme caution is warranted during travel, stacking, or unstacking operations, as any lateral movement or tipping due to an elevated attachment and load will cause point E to approach lines AC or BC, thereby compromising side stability.

Reach stacker operators should grasp that the rated load capacity of the machine is contingent upon both the tilt angle of the boom and the extent to which the boom is extended.

The rated load capacity of a reach stacker, which denotes the maximum weight it can safely lift and handle, is not fixed but rather dependent on various factors. Two critical factors influencing this capacity are the tilt angle of the boom and the extension of the boom. When the boom is tilted or extended, it affects the stability and weight-bearing capability of the reach stacker. Therefore, operators must consider these variables when determining whether a load falls within the safe operating parameters of the machine. Failure to account for the tilt angle and extension of the boom could lead to overloading the reach stacker, posing safety risks to both personnel and equipment. Thus, understanding the impact of these factors is crucial for ensuring safe and efficient operation of the reach stacker.

Figure 89 shows a sample reach stacker loading chart. The chart shows that as the boom is extended the maximum load decreases, with the machine operating with a boom length at 6400mm a maximum of 15 tonnes can be placed with a maximum height of 3 containers. At 1965 mm, four containers with a maximum weight of 45 tonnes can be placed with a fifth with a maximum weight of 40 tonnes.

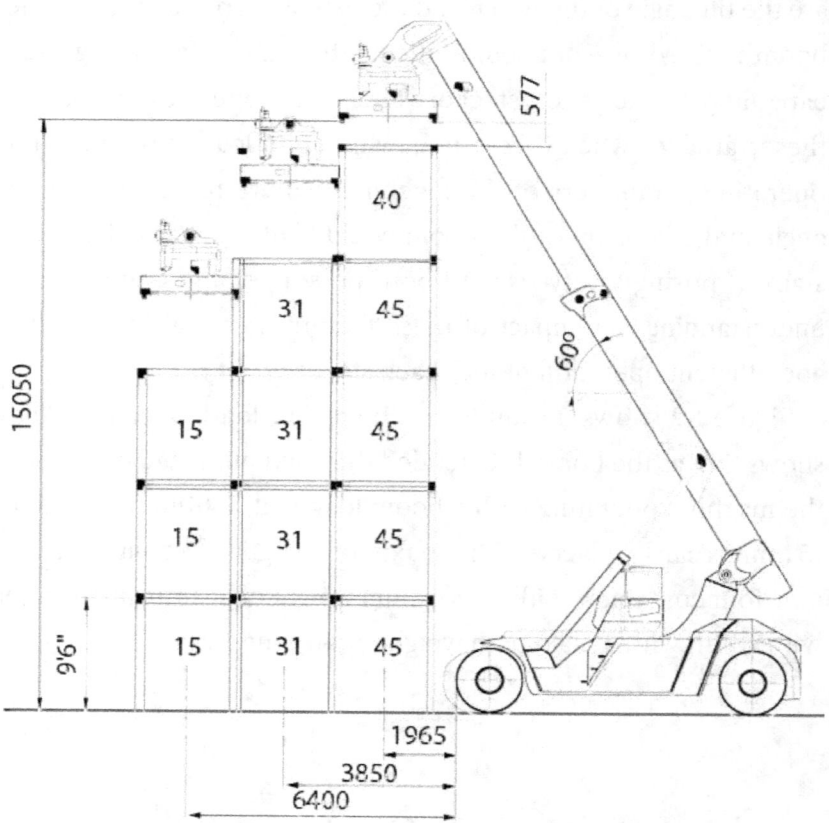

Figure 89: Sample reach stacker loading chart.

The reach stacker's load plate should also be consulted to ensure that the containers to be lifted are within the machine's capacity.

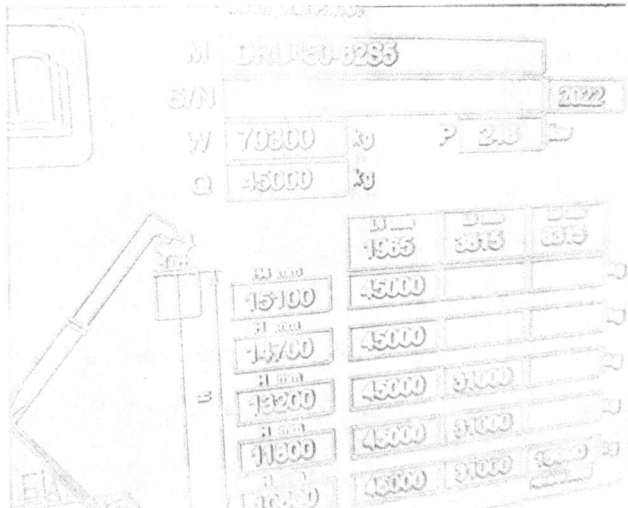

Figure 90: Sample reach stacker load plate.

Planning for Reach Stacker Operations

Operating a reach stacker involves several steps to ensure safety, efficiency, and adherence to workplace procedures. Here's a detailed explanation of each step:

1. Identify Task Requirements: Start by reviewing work orders or instructions to understand the specific tasks assigned. Confirm task requirements with relevant personnel to ensure clarity and alignment. Conduct a site inspection to assess the work area and identify any potential hazards or challenges.

2. Assess Work Area Surface: Evaluate the quality of the ground surface in the work area to determine its suitability for operating the reach stacker. Check for uneven terrain, soft spots, or obstacles that could impede safe operation. Adhere to workplace procedures for assessing ground conditions and take appropriate precautions if the surface is unsuitable.

3. Establish MRC and WLL: Refer to the reach stacker manufacturer specifications to establish the Maximum Rated Capacity (MRC) and the Working Load Limit (WLL) for the container/s and specific work/task requirements. Ensure compliance with workplace procedures and safety regulations when determining lifting capacities.

4. Assess Operating Paths: Evaluate the work area to determine suitable paths for operating the reach stacker and moving and placing containers. Consider factors such as space constraints, overhead obstacles, and the location of other equipment or personnel. Identify safe routes and operating procedures in accordance with workplace guidelines. Figure 91 shows a typical operational environment.

5. Identify Hazards and Risks: Conduct a thorough hazard identification process to identify potential risks associated with reach stacker operation. Implement appropriate risk elimination or control measures to mitigate hazards and ensure a safe working environment. Communicate identified hazards and control measures to relevant personnel.

6. Confirm Traffic Management Plan: Ensure the implementation of the traffic management plan is confirmed and understood. Coordinate with site supervisors or traffic control personnel to verify that traffic flow within the work area is managed effectively to prevent accidents or conflicts with other vehicles or pedestrians.

7. Establish Communication Procedures: Identify and establish appropriate communication procedures with associated personnel, such as spotters or ground crew. Test communication devices or signals to ensure clear and effective communication

MATERIAL HANDLING EQUIPMENT OPERATION 317

during reach stacker operations. Follow workplace procedures for communication protocols to maintain safety and coordination.

8. Confirm Task Requirements: Double-check all tasks to confirm that requirements for the relevant work area have been addressed in accordance with workplace procedures. Ensure that all necessary precautions, equipment checks, and safety measures are in place before proceeding with reach stacker operations.

Figure 91: Typical reach stacker operating environment. Trondheim Havn from Trondheim, Norway, CC BY-SA 2.0, via Wikimedia Commons.

Operating a reach stacker involves various hazards that can pose risks to personnel, equipment, and the work environment. Mitigation strategies are essential to minimize these hazards and ensure safe operation.

Here's an overview of common hazards associated with reach stacker operation and corresponding mitigation strategies:

1. **Tip-over Risk**: Reach stackers can tip over if not operated properly, especially when handling heavy loads or operating on uneven terrain.

    - Mitigation Strategy:

        - Ensure operators are adequately trained and certified in reach stacker operation.

        - Adhere to load capacity limits specified by the manufacturer.

        - Conduct pre-operational checks to ensure the reach stacker is in good condition.

        - Avoid operating on slopes beyond the manufacturer's recommended limits.

        - Use stabilizing outriggers if available and appropriate for the task.

2. **Collision Hazards**: Reach stackers operate in close proximity to other equipment, structures, and personnel, increasing the risk of collisions.

    - Mitigation Strategy:

        - Implement strict traffic management plans to separate pedestrian and vehicle traffic.

        - Use spotters or ground guides to assist with manoeuvring in congested areas.

        - Install warning devices such as horns, lights, and backup

MATERIAL HANDLING EQUIPMENT OPERATION

alarms to alert nearby personnel.

- Maintain clear lines of sight by keeping windows and mirrors clean and unobstructed.

3. **Overhead Hazards**: Reach stackers often operate in areas with overhead obstacles, such as power lines, structures, and overhead cranes.

   - Mitigation Strategy:

     - Identify overhead hazards and mark restricted zones to prevent reach stacker contact.

     - Train operators to be vigilant of overhead obstacles and maintain a safe distance.

     - Use height indicators and proximity sensors to warn operators of overhead obstructions.

     - Implement designated routes and procedures for navigating under overhead hazards.

4. **Falling Objects**: Loads being lifted by reach stackers can shift or fall, posing a risk to nearby personnel and equipment.

   - Mitigation Strategy:

     - Secure loads properly using appropriate lifting attachments and securement methods.

     - Use load backrests and attachment locking devices to prevent load displacement.

     - Establish exclusion zones around the reach stacker during lifting operations.

- Conduct pre-lift inspections to ensure loads are stable and properly positioned.

5. **Crush Hazards**: Reach stackers have moving parts and hydraulic systems that can crush or trap operators and bystanders.

    - Mitigation Strategy:

        - Implement lockout/tagout procedures when performing maintenance or repair tasks.

        - Provide adequate guarding on moving parts and pinch points.

        - Train operators on safe entry and exit procedures for the reach stacker cab.

        - Conduct regular inspections of hydraulic hoses and components for signs of wear or damage.

6. **Environmental Hazards**: Adverse weather conditions such as rain, snow, or high winds can impact reach stacker operation.

    - Mitigation Strategy:

        - Monitor weather forecasts and suspend operations during severe weather conditions.

        - Ensure operators are trained to adjust driving and operating techniques in adverse weather.

        - Maintain clear communication channels to relay weather-related updates and safety instructions.

By identifying these hazards and implementing appropriate mitigation strategies, organizations can promote a safe working environment for reach stacker operations while minimizing the risk of accidents and injuries. Regular training, effective communication, and diligent adherence to safety protocols are essential for mitigating hazards and preventing incidents.

Confirming the implementation of the traffic management plan involves several steps to ensure that traffic flow within the work area is effectively managed to prevent accidents or conflicts with other vehicles or pedestrians. Here's how to do it:

1. Review the Traffic Management Plan: Start by reviewing the traffic management plan to understand its requirements, procedures, and designated traffic routes within the work area. Ensure that you are familiar with any designated zones, signage, or barriers intended to control traffic flow.

2. Coordinate with Site Supervisors or Traffic Control Personnel: Reach out to site supervisors or designated traffic control personnel responsible for overseeing traffic management within the work area. Discuss the details of the traffic management plan and seek clarification on any specific instructions or requirements.

3. Verify Implementation: Conduct a visual inspection of the work area to verify that the traffic management plan has been implemented as outlined. Look for signs, barriers, designated traffic lanes, pedestrian walkways, and any other measures intended to regulate traffic flow.

4. Communicate with Traffic Control Personnel: Engage in communication with traffic control personnel to confirm that they are actively monitoring traffic flow and enforcing the designated traffic routes and regulations. Clarify any questions or concerns regarding traffic management procedures.

5. Address Any Issues: If any discrepancies or issues are identified during the inspection, promptly address them with site supervisors or traffic control personnel. This may involve adjusting signage, repositioning barriers, or providing additional guidance to ensure effective traffic management.

6. Ensure Understanding: Confirm that all personnel operating within the work area, including reach stacker operators, are familiar with the traffic management plan and understand their roles and responsibilities in adhering to it. Provide any necessary training or guidance to ensure compliance with traffic regulations and safety procedures.

7. Monitor Traffic Flow: Continuously monitor traffic flow within the work area to ensure that the traffic management plan is effectively preventing accidents or conflicts. Address any emerging issues or challenges promptly and make adjustments to the plan as needed to maintain safety.

By following these steps, you can ensure that the traffic management plan is successfully implemented and understood, contributing to a safe working environment for all personnel within the work area. Effective coordination, communication, and proactive monitoring are key to preventing accidents and promoting traffic safety.

Preparing for Reach Stacker Operations

Preparing to operate a reach stacker involves several crucial steps to ensure safety, compliance, and efficiency. This includes:

1. **Establish Consultation with Workplace Personnel:**
    - Consultation with workplace personnel is vital to ensure

clarity and consistency in the work plan, aligning it with site requirements. This involves open communication with supervisors, colleagues, and other relevant personnel to discuss the work plan and address any questions or concerns.

2. Check Implementation of Risk Control Measures:

- Risk control measures for identified hazards must be checked for implementation to fulfill legislative responsibilities and adhere to safe work procedures. This includes verifying that safety protocols and precautions are in place to mitigate potential risks associated with reach stacker operation.

3. Access Reach Stacker Safely:

- Accessing the reach stacker in a safe manner is essential to prevent accidents or injuries. Operators must follow manufacturer specifications and safe work procedures when approaching and entering the reach stacker cab. This includes using designated access points and ensuring proper footing to avoid slips or falls.

4. Carry Out Pre-start Checks:

- Pre-start checks are necessary to assess the condition of the reach stacker and identify any damage or defects that may affect its operation. Operators must conduct thorough inspections of key components, such as tyres, brakes, hydraulics, and safety systems, and report any issues according to manufacturer requirements and safe work procedures.

5. Check for Abnormal Noises/Operation:

- After starting the reach stacker, operators must check for any abnormal noises or operation that could indicate mechanical problems or malfunctions. This includes listening for unusual sounds and observing the machine's performance to ensure smooth and proper functioning in accordance with manufacturer requirements and safe work procedures.

6. **Carry Out Operational Checks**:

    - Operational checks are essential to confirm that the reach stacker is fully operational and ready for use. Operators must perform functional tests of controls, lifting mechanisms, steering, and other critical systems to identify any damage or defects. Any issues should be promptly reported and addressed following manufacturer specifications and safe work procedures.

7. **Determine Stability Requirements**:

    - Assessing reach stacker stability requirements for the task is crucial to prevent tip-overs or instability during operations. Operators must refer to relevant manufacturer specifications and safe work procedures to determine the appropriate configuration and operating parameters for the task at hand.

8. **Check Reach Stacker Logbook**:

    - Checking the reach stacker logbook ensures that the machine is compliant, properly maintained, and suitable for use. Operators must verify that the logbook is up-to-date, accurately completed, and signed off for any required rectifications in accordance with manufacturer requirements and safe work procedures.

9. **Assess Weather and Work Environment Conditions**:

MATERIAL HANDLING EQUIPMENT OPERATION

- Assessing weather and work environment conditions helps operators anticipate any potential impacts on reach stacker operations. This involves evaluating factors such as wind, rain, temperature, and visibility to determine if adjustments or precautions are necessary to maintain safety and efficiency.

10. **Drive to Work Area and Prepare for Container Operations:**

- Once all checks and assessments are completed, the reach stacker can be driven to the work area and prepared for container operations. Operators must follow relevant safe work procedures, including observing traffic rules, securing loads, and positioning the reach stacker appropriately for the task.

Before operating the machine, it is imperative to conduct a daily check of the work area to ensure safety and efficiency. This involves verifying several key aspects to mitigate potential risks and hazards.

Figure 92: Reach stacker work environment, loading onto rail. Gary Houston, CC0, via Wikimedia Commons.

Firstly, pedestrian safety must be prioritized by restricting access to reach stacker operation areas. Pedestrian walk paths should be clearly marked and guarded to prevent unauthorized entry into hazardous zones. Additionally, reach stacker travel lanes should be unmistakably delineated to maintain clear pathways for machine movement.

Moreover, pedestrian barriers must be securely in place to further safeguard individuals from potential hazards. It is essential that pedestrians within the vicinity wear high visibility vests and hats to enhance visibility and promote safety awareness.

For transient personnel such as truck drivers, written rules should be provided outlining protocols for dismounting trucks and remaining clear of reach stacker operations. Safe access must be facilitated to restrooms and break areas to ensure the well-being of all personnel.

Control measures should be implemented at pedestrian-machine intersections to minimize the risk of accidents or collisions. Aisleway mirrors should be installed at blind intersections and kept clean for enhanced visibility.

Figure 93: Reach stacker work environment, loading onto semi-trailer for road transport. Joost J. Bakker from IJmuiden, CC BY 2.0, via Wikimedia Commons.

Furthermore, all individuals in the work area should be well-informed about workplace dangers and adhere to established work rules. Adequate lighting is essential for visibility and should be in place throughout the work area.

Safe speed limits must be established, clearly posted, and strictly enforced to prevent accidents and maintain a safe operating environment. Additionally, reach stacker operator/pedestrian communication systems should be operational to facilitate effective communication and coordination.

Finally, operating surfaces should be inspected to ensure they are free of potholes and debris, minimizing the risk of accidents or machine damage. By meticulously checking these aspects of the work area daily, operators can help ensure a safe and productive work environment for all personnel involved.

Accessing the reach stacker safely is a critical step in preventing accidents or injuries. Operators must approach and enter the reach stacker cab in accordance with manufacturer specifications and safe work procedures to minimize risks.

To access the reach stacker safely, operators should adhere to the following guidelines:

1. Follow Manufacturer Specifications: Operators must familiarize themselves with the specific access procedures outlined by the reach stacker manufacturer. This includes understanding the designated access points and recommended entry methods.

2. Utilize Designated Access Points: Operators should use designated access points provided by the manufacturer to enter the reach stacker cab. These access points are designed to ensure safe entry and exit and may include steps, handrails, or footholds.

3. Ensure Proper Footing: Before climbing into the cab, operators should ensure they have proper footing to prevent slips or falls. This may involve checking the stability of the ground surface and using caution when stepping onto the reach stacker.

4. Maintain Three Points of Contact: Operators should maintain three points of contact (e.g., two hands and one foot, or two feet and one hand) when climbing into or out of the reach stacker cab. This helps ensure stability and reduces the risk of falls.

5. Use Handholds and Railings: Handholds and railings provided on the reach stacker should be utilized to support safe entry and exit. Operators should grip these handholds firmly to maintain

balance and stability.

Improperly mounting or dismounting the reach stacker poses a risk of slipping, falling, and sustaining serious injuries. To prevent accidents, operators should adhere to all manufacturer's access instructions. This includes facing the ladder when getting on or off the reach stacker, maintaining three-point contact with the reach stacker at all times, utilizing handrails and other grab points, and refraining from climbing on areas of the reach stacker not intended for operator travel.

Figure 94: Mount using handrails, maintain 3 points of contact and utilise PPE. Gazouya-japan, CC BY-SA 4.0, via Wikimedia Commons.

Another unsafe practice is the failure to keep the reach stacker clean, free of oil, grease, and fuel, which also poses a risk of slipping, falling, and sustaining serious injuries. To mitigate this risk, operators should follow all manufacturer's maintenance instructions. This involves keeping the reach stacker clean, using anti-slip footwear before performing maintenance, using appropriate cleaning accessories, regularly inspecting and replacing anti-slip mastic, and ensuring safety decals are in place.

Operating the reach stacker while personnel are on any part of the machine is also hazardous, as it could result in personnel falling and sustaining serious injuries. To prevent accidents, operators should verify that no one is on the reach stacker before entering the operator's cab and should be attentive to personnel entering the work area, stopping immediately if they approach or climb onto the reach stacker.

Improperly fuelling the reach stacker poses the risk of an explosion, causing serious bodily injury or death. Operators should never fill the fuel tank while the engine is running or when near an open flame, avoid overfilling the tank or spilling fuel, ground the fuel funnel or nozzle against the filler neck to prevent sparks, and ensure the fuel tank cap is replaced.

Failure to properly check for hydraulic leaks or diesel fuel leaks poses risks of severe injuries, including skin penetration or eye injury. Operators should wear heavy gloves and safety goggles when checking for leaks or damaged hoses, use a piece of cardboard or wood to detect leaks, and replace any worn or damaged hydraulic hoses immediately.

Inadequate checking of the engine cooling system poses the risk of severe burns or blindness due to spewing engine coolant. To avoid such dangers, operators should wear heavy gloves and safety goggles when inspecting engine coolant and allow the engine to cool before removing the radiator cap.

Improperly checking battery fluid levels or jump-starting engines poses risks of burns or injuries to the eyes or skin and battery explosions. Operators should wear rubber gloves and eye goggles or a face shield when handling batteries, avoid exposing batteries to arcs, sparks, flames, or lighted tobacco, and always follow the manufacturer's directions for jump-starting engines.

Putting air in a multi-piece tire and rim assembly without proper tools and training could result in the tire and rim explosively separating, causing serious injury or death. To prevent accidents, operators should avoid standing in the trajectory path while inflating a multi-piece tire and rim assembly, use appropriate tools and equipment, and allow only trained tire specialists to service tyres.

Entering the area around the steer tyres poses the risk of the tire turning or rotating, causing death or serious injury. Operators should always turn off the ignition, remove the key, and tag out the controls before entering this area and should not allow personnel to enter the area around the steer tyres while the engine is running.

Working in an area not properly vented for toxic exhaust fumes could result in death or serious injury due to exposure to toxic exhaust fumes. Operators should ensure proper ventilation, include carbon monoxide level testing in regular maintenance procedures, and use carbon monoxide detection devices as a supplementary measure.

Carrying out pre-start checks is an essential step to ensure the reach stacker is in optimal condition for safe operation. These checks are conducted to assess the overall condition of the reach stacker and identify any potential issues or defects that could compromise its performance.

Operators are required to perform thorough inspections of key components, including but not limited to, tyres, brakes, hydraulics, and safety systems. This involves visually examining each component to detect any signs of wear, damage, or malfunction. For instance, operators must check the condition of the tyres, ensuring they are properly inflated and free from cuts or punctures. They also need to inspect the brake system to ensure it is functioning correctly and capable of stopping the reach stacker safely.

Hydraulic systems play a crucial role in the operation of the reach stacker, so operators must inspect hydraulic hoses, fittings, and cylinders for any leaks, damage, or signs of wear. Additionally, they need to test the functionality of safety systems, such as lights, alarms, and emergency stop mechanisms, to ensure they are operational and effective in case of an emergency.

Any issues or defects identified during the pre-start checks must be promptly reported in accordance with manufacturer requirements and safe work procedures. This may involve documenting the findings in a pre-start checklist or maintenance log and notifying the appropriate personnel for further assessment and resolution.

By conducting thorough pre-start checks, operators can mitigate the risk of equipment failure or malfunction during operation, promoting safety and preventing potential accidents or injuries in the workplace.

Perform a daily inspection before placing the reach stacker into service, ensuring optimal safety and functionality (Taylor Machine Works, 2024):

- Ensure the parking brake is engaged and wheels are chocked if on an incline.

- Verify that the attachment is fully lowered.

- Check for all operational and safety literature located in the Vehicle Information Package (VIP) behind the seat.

- Ensure the cab is free of clutter.

- Verify that all mirrors are in place, clean, and properly adjusted.

- Check that all glass surfaces are clean and unbroken.

- Inspect steps, walkways, and handholds to ensure they are free of oil, grease, hydraulic fluid, ice, snow, debris, etc.

- Confirm that anti-slip pads are in place and free of any damage.

- Inspect tyres for damage and ensure they are properly inflated.

MATERIAL HANDLING EQUIPMENT OPERATION 333

- Check cylinders for leaks or damage.

- Test the functionality of lift, boom extension, expansion, steering, damping, sideshift, twistlocks, pile slope (if equipped), and cab raise (if equipped).

- Ensure electrical connectors, wires, cables, and junction boxes are not loose or damaged.

- Check hydraulic hoses and connectors for leaks or damage.

- Inspect the boom, attachment, and frame for cracks, broken welds, loose bolts, dents, and other damage.

- Verify attachment linkages, twistlocks, guide blocks, plungers, switches, expansion pads, etc.

- Ensure the engine compartment hood-lock is in place and functional, and the compartment is clean with hoses, clamps, and belts in place and undamaged.

- Confirm fire extinguishers are fully charged and functional.

- Inspect the operator cab structure, braces, and machine structure for breaks, cracks, or broken welds.

- Check doors and latches for good condition and functionality.

- Ensure the engine operates without unusual noise and all gauges and indicators are functional.

- Verify that air pressure is at the proper level.

- Check fluid levels as per the Maintenance Manual for the reach stacker, including fuel, engine oil, transmission oil, hydraulic fluid, coolant level, battery electrolyte, and ensure battery terminals are free from corrosion.

- Inspect filters, including the air cleaner and hydraulic fluid filters.

- Test all reach stacker functions for proper operation, including attachment expansion, pile slope (if equipped), attachment rotation, sideshift, boom lift, boom extension, and twistlocks.

- Ensure all brakes (service, spotting, and mechanical) are functional, along with steering, operator-controlled horn, alarms, beacons, and flashing beacons.

- Verify the functionality of the camera system and seat belt.

- Confirm that all daily checks outlined in the Operator's Guide have been completed.

- Ensure wheels are not chocked and check the Cab Positioning System.

Before commencing machine operation, conduct a daily inspection of the work area ensuring the following measures are in place and maintained:

- Pedestrians are prohibited from reach stacker operation zones.

- Pedestrian walk paths are visibly delineated and safeguarded.

- Reach stacker travel lanes are clearly designated.

- Pedestrian barriers are installed as necessary.

- Pedestrians are equipped with high visibility vests and hats.

- Written regulations have been provided to transient personnel (e.g., truck drivers) detailing procedures for dismounting trucks

MATERIAL HANDLING EQUIPMENT OPERATION

and staying clear of reach stacker operations.

- Safe access is available to restroom and break areas.
- Control measures are implemented at pedestrian/machine intersections.
- Aisleway mirrors at blind intersections are installed and kept clean.
- All individuals are educated about workplace hazards.
- Adequate lighting is installed throughout the work area.
- Work rules are established and enforced consistently.
- Reach stacker operator and pedestrian communication systems are functional.
- Operating surfaces are free of potholes and debris.
- Safe speed limits are established, visibly posted, and adhered to strictly.

Starting a reach stacker involves several steps to ensure safe operation. Here's a general outline of the process:

1. Pre-Start Checks:

    ◦ Before starting the reach stacker, conduct pre-start checks as outlined in the operator's manual or manufacturer's guidelines. This includes inspecting key components such as tyres, brakes, hydraulics, and safety systems for any damage or defects.

2. Ensure Safe Environment:

    ◦ Make sure the area around the reach stacker is clear of obstacles, pedestrians, and other vehicles to prevent accidents during startup.

3. Cabin Entry:

    - Approach the reach stacker's cabin from the designated entry point, ensuring proper footing to prevent slips or falls.
    - Open the cabin door and enter the operator's seat.

4. Cabin Preparations:

    - Once inside the cabin, adjust the seat, steering wheel, and mirrors to ensure optimal visibility and comfort during operation.
    - Fasten your seatbelt securely to comply with safety regulations.

5. Ignition:

    - Insert the key into the ignition switch and turn it clockwise to start the engine. Some reach stackers may have electronic ignition systems, so follow the specific startup procedure provided by the manufacturer.

6. Engine Startup:

    - After turning the key, wait for the engine to start. Monitor the dashboard gauges and indicators to ensure all systems are functioning properly.
    - Listen for any unusual noises or vibrations that may indicate potential issues with the engine or other components.

7. Warm-Up:

MATERIAL HANDLING EQUIPMENT OPERATION

- Allow the engine to idle for a few minutes to warm up, especially in colder temperatures. This helps ensure proper lubrication and fluid circulation throughout the engine and hydraulic system.

8. Functional Checks:

    - While the engine is idling, perform functional checks of critical systems such as steering, brakes, lifting mechanisms, and lights to ensure they are operating correctly.

    - Test the horn, headlights, turn signals, and other safety features to verify their functionality.

9. Monitor Systems:

    - Continuously monitor the dashboard gauges and indicators during startup and warm-up to ensure all systems are operating within normal parameters.

    - Be vigilant for any warning lights or abnormal readings that may indicate issues requiring further inspection or maintenance.

10. Ready for Operation:

    - Once the reach stacker has been started, warmed up, and all systems have been checked, it is ready for operation. Follow safe operating procedures and adhere to all relevant safety guidelines and regulations while using the reach stacker.

A reach stacker typically features various controls designed to operate its different functions efficiently. Here's an overview of the common controls found in a reach stacker:

1. Steering Wheel: Allows the operator to steer the reach stacker.

Turning the steering wheel left or right controls the direction of movement.

2. Accelerator Pedal: Controls the speed of the reach stacker. Pressing the accelerator pedal increases speed, while releasing it slows down or stops the vehicle.

3. Brake Pedal: Used to apply the brakes and slow down or stop the reach stacker. Some reach stackers may have separate pedals for service brakes and parking brakes.

4. Gear Shift Lever: Selects the appropriate gear for forward or reverse movement. Reach stackers typically have multiple gears to accommodate different driving conditions and loads.

5. Hydraulic Controls: Operate the hydraulic system responsible for lifting and lowering containers. These controls include levers or buttons to extend, retract, tilt, and rotate the lifting mechanism.

6. Lift/Lower Controls: Controls the vertical movement of the lifting mechanism. Operators can raise or lower containers using these controls.

7. Reach Controls: Adjusts the reach or extension of the lifting mechanism. Operators can extend or retract the lifting arms to accommodate containers of various sizes.

8. Twistlock Controls: Engages or disengages the twistlocks, which secure containers to the lifting mechanism. This control ensures containers are securely locked in place during transport.

9. Auxiliary Controls: Operate additional features or attachments, such as spreaders, side shifters, or pile slope adjustments, depending on the reach stacker's configuration.

10. Horn: Activates the horn to alert nearby personnel or vehicles of the reach stacker's presence.

11. Lights and Wipers: Controls the headlights, turn signals, and windshield wipers to ensure visibility in different lighting and weather conditions.

12. Display Panel: Provides essential information such as engine status, fuel level, hydraulic pressure, and diagnostic alerts. Operators can monitor the reach stacker's performance and address any issues promptly.

These controls may vary depending on the specific model and manufacturer of the reach stacker. It's crucial for operators to familiarize themselves with the layout and operation of the controls before operating the reach stacker to ensure safe and efficient handling of containers.

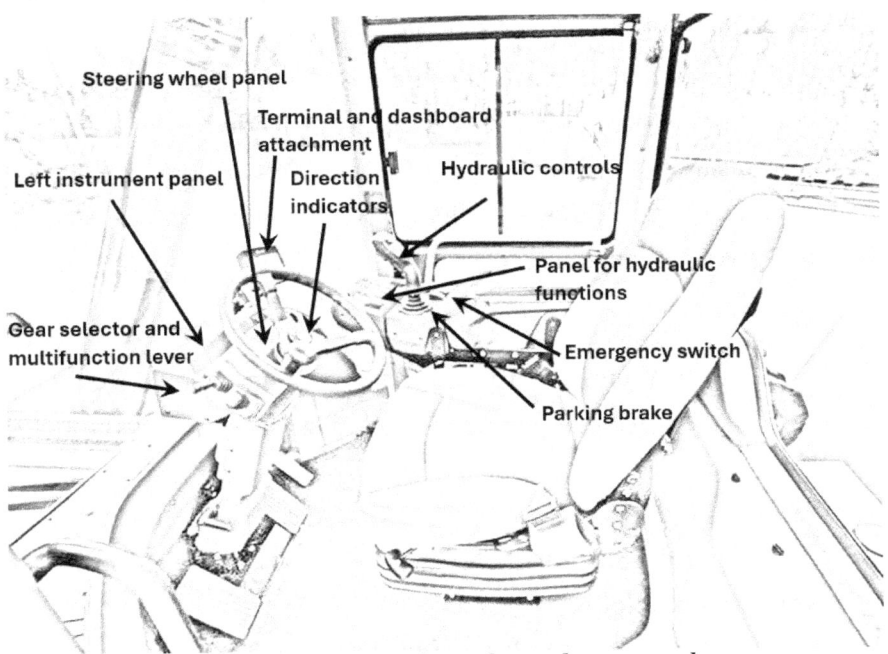

Figure 95: Typical reach stacker controls.

Performing operational checks is a crucial step to ensure the reach stacker is in optimal condition and safe for use. These checks involve testing various operational aspects such as controls, lifting mechanisms, steering, and other critical systems. By conducting these tests, operators can identify any potential damage or defects that may compromise the machine's functionality or pose safety risks. Any issues detected during the operational checks should be reported promptly and addressed following the guidelines provided by the manufacturer and safe work procedures. This ensures that the reach stacker is fully operational and ready for safe use in the workplace.

Operating a Reach Stacker

Operating a reach stacker involves a series of steps to ensure the safe and efficient handling of containers. This includes:

1. Determine Container Lifts: The container lifts are determined within the Maximum Rated Capacity (MRC) of the reach stacker, ensuring that the weight of the container does not exceed the machine's lifting capacity. This is done in accordance with safe work procedures to prevent overloading and maintain operational safety.

2. Position Container Spreader: The container spreader is safely positioned over the container, following directions from associated personnel if applicable. The spreader is aligned properly to ensure a secure grip on the container, minimizing the risk of accidents during lifting. This step is crucial for safe and effective container handling.

3. Latch Spreader onto Container: The container spreader is latched onto the container securely, ensuring that it is properly

locked in place before lifting. Additionally, the reach stacker is stabilized appropriately to maintain balance and prevent any tilting or instability during the lifting process. This step is essential for safe lifting and transport of containers.

4. Conduct Test Lift: Before proceeding with full-scale lifting operations, a test lift is carried out in accordance with safe work procedures. This involves lifting the container slightly to ensure that the spreader is securely attached and that the reach stacker can handle the weight without any issues. Any abnormalities or concerns are addressed before proceeding further.

5. Safely Mobilize Containers: Containers are safely mobilized using best mobile practices and relevant reach stacker movements. This includes carefully manoeuvring the reach stacker to transport the container to its destination, following predefined routes and avoiding obstacles or hazards in the work area. Safe work procedures are strictly adhered to during this process to minimize risks and ensure operational safety.

6. Monitor Container and Reach Stacker Movement: Throughout the lifting and transport operations, constant monitoring of container and reach stacker movement is essential. Operators closely observe the position and stability of the container, as well as the performance of the reach stacker, to detect any issues or deviations from the planned operation. This proactive approach helps prevent accidents and ensures smooth operation.

7. Interpret Communication Signals: All required communication signals are correctly interpreted, used, and followed while operating the reach stacker. Effective communication between operators and associated personnel helps coordinate movements and ensure safety during container handling operations.

8. Lower and Land Container Safely: Once the container reaches its destination, it is safely lowered and landed in accordance with safe work procedures. This involves carefully lowering the container to the ground or onto a designated surface, ensuring a smooth and controlled descent to prevent damage or accidents.

9. Disconnect Spreader and Prepare for Next Task: Finally, the container spreader is disconnected from the container and positioned safely and efficiently for the next task. This may involve retracting the spreader arms and preparing the reach stacker for further operations, following safe work procedures to maintain a safe working environment.

Operating a reach stacker entails avoiding several dangerous actions to prevent accidents or injuries. Here's how to avoid these risks:

1. Braking or Accelerating Too Hard: Apply brakes smoothly and evenly, and accelerate in a similar manner to prevent the machine from tipping over due to abrupt changes in momentum. Quick braking or acceleration can shift the balance of the machine and the load, leading to instability.

2. Turning Too Sharply: Make turns smoothly and evenly, steering the wheel slowly to avoid tipping the machine. Sharp turns can cause instability, especially when the load is securely attached, potentially leading to a tip-over.

3. Raising Load in Excessive Wind: Avoid raising the load to high elevations when wind velocity is excessive (wind speeds of 30 mph or greater). The load can act as a sail in high winds, exerting excessive force and potentially causing the machine to tip over.

4. Operating on Uneven Surfaces: Do not operate the machine on uneven surfaces or in unstable yard conditions where control

MATERIAL HANDLING EQUIPMENT OPERATION

can be lost. Report pot holes or obstacles to supervisors, and avoid running over boards, rocks, or trash on the yard to prevent machine jerking or tipping.

5. Extending or Lowering Boom Improperly: Lower the load vertically by retracting the boom as it is being lowered. Observe the load being lifted and adhere to the rating plate values to prevent tipping accidents caused by improper boom handling.

6. Traveling with Load Raised Too High: Lower the load immediately after clearing a stack and travel with the load in the lowest possible position that allows good visibility. Never travel with the load higher than the operator's line of sight to prevent tip-over accidents.

7. Not Wearing Seat Belt: Always travel with the seat belt properly fastened to prevent death or serious injury in the event of a tip-over or collision with a fixed object. Additionally, do not allow riders on the machine for safety reasons.

8. Jumping from Moving Machine: Remain seated in the operator's station with the seat belt securely fastened whenever the machine is in motion. In the event of a tip-over, do not jump from the machine; instead, brace your feet firmly, grip the steering wheel tightly, and lean away from the direction of the fall to minimize the risk of injury.

9. Handling Off-Center Load Improperly: Always lift the load properly according to established procedures and use the attachment side shift to balance the load before traveling. Never attempt to lift an out-of-balance load without extreme caution to avoid accidents resulting in serious injury or death.

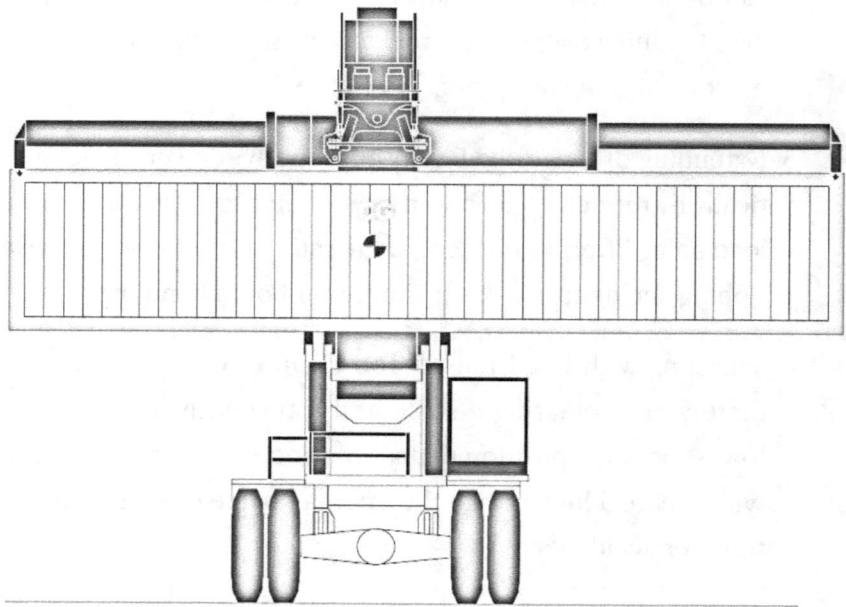

Figure 96: Correctly handling off-centre load.

Operating or parking the reach stacker in an area with excessively steep slopes or insufficient strength to support the machine's weight poses significant risks. Control of the machine can be lost, leading to potential shifting and overturning of the machine and its load. To avoid this danger, operators should refrain from operating on steep grades not designated for reach stacker operation. When navigating grades, loaded trucks should ascend with the load upgrade, while unloaded trucks should descend with the load engaging means downgrade. Additionally, the load and load engaging means should be tilted back if applicable, and raised only as far as necessary to clear the road surface. If the load obstructs forward visibility on ramps, a ground guide should assist the operator, and the horn should be sounded while traveling slowly. It is essential to ensure that travel lanes are always clearly marked, and the mixing of pedestrians and industrial trucks is avoided.

Traveling with the reach stacker when the elevating cab is not fully lowered poses serious risks, including the possibility of striking pedestrians and causing severe injury or death. To avoid this danger, operators should fully lower the cab after checking beneath it and in the stair area. The boom should be properly positioned before traveling, and the operator should refrain from traveling until they have a clear view of the path ahead.

Traveling with the reach stacker when the manually positioned cab is not securely locked in the rear position can lead to the cab moving unexpectedly, potentially causing injury to personnel or property damage. To mitigate this risk, operators must always ensure that the cab is securely locked in the rear position before operating the reach stacker.

Lifting a load that exceeds the rated capacity of the reach stacker poses severe risks, including the potential for death, serious injury, or damage to surrounding equipment or structures. To prevent accidents, operators must be aware of the reach stacker's rated capacity as indicated on the detailed rating plate. They should also verify the weight of the trailer or container being lifted. If the load appears heavier than indicated on the bill of lading or if lifting the load presents difficulties, operators should refrain from continuing the lift and seek guidance from their supervisor.

Raising the load directly over the reach stacker cab presents significant dangers, including the risk of the container coming loose and causing harm to the operator. To avoid this danger, operators should extend the boom to maintain proper clearance between the load and the cab. It is crucial never to position the load behind the front edge of the cab to prevent accidents and injuries.

A reach stacker typically uses a spreader attachment equipped with twistlocks to lock onto a container for lifting. The twistlocks are mechanical devices designed to securely fasten onto the container's corner castings, which are standardized attachment points located at each corner of the container.

Here's how the process generally works:

1. Approach: The reach stacker positions itself close to the container, aligning the spreader attachment with the corner castings.

2. Engagement: The spreader attachment, often controlled hydraulically or mechanically by the operator, moves down onto the container, aligning the twistlocks with the corner castings.

3. Locking: Once properly aligned, the twistlocks engage with the corner castings, securing the container to the spreader attachment. This locking mechanism ensures that the container remains securely attached during lifting and transportation.

4. Lifting: With the container securely locked onto the spreader attachment, the reach stacker can then lift the container vertically, using its lifting mechanism and hydraulic system.

5. Transport: Once lifted, the reach stacker can manoeuvre and transport the container to its desired location within the terminal or yard, maintaining a secure hold on the container until it is ready to be stacked or unloaded.

The use of twistlocks provides a reliable and standardized method for locking onto containers, ensuring safe and efficient handling by the reach stacker operator.

Lifting a container without ensuring that all four twistlocks are fully locked poses significant risks. There is a possibility that the container could fall from the attachment, resulting in death or serious injury to ground personnel or causing physical damage to the container, the reach stacker, or other yard equipment. To avoid this danger, operators must ensure that the proper amber indicating light on the attachment is illuminated before locking the twistlocks. If the green light goes out while the load is raised, it is essential to set the container down and correct the problem before continuing operations. Referring to the Operator's Guide for proper procedures is recommended to ensure safe handling practices.

Leaving the reach stacker with a load suspended poses significant risks as the lift system could drift down unexpectedly, potentially causing the load to interfere with yard traffic or strike equipment below, resulting in death, serious injury, or physical damage. To avoid this danger, operators must never leave the cab while the load is suspended. It's crucial to lower and release the load before exiting the cab and park the reach stacker in a safe, level area, applying the parking brake, neutralizing the controls, shutting off the power, and removing the key. If parked on an incline, blocking the wheels is necessary for added safety.

Improperly traveling on grades can lead to loss of control over the machine and the load, posing serious risks. To mitigate this danger, operators must ascend or descend grades slowly, ensuring loaded trucks are driven with the load upgrade and unloaded trucks are operated with the load engaging means downgrade. Additionally, the load and load engaging means should be tilted back if applicable and raised only as far as necessary to clear the road surface. It's essential to use a ground guide if the load blocks forward visibility on ramps, sound the horn, and travel slowly, ensuring clearly marked travel lanes to prevent accidents involving pedestrians and reach stackers.

Backing away from the load in a rack or stack without complete release of the load can result in death, serious bodily injury, and property damage. To prevent such incidents, operators must ensure the load is properly placed and completely released from holding devices before backing away from the stack. Slowly backing away while visually checking if the load is being pulled with the machine due to incomplete release is crucial. Regular inspection of holding devices for proper action before each day's service is also essential to ensure safe operations.

Starting the engine despite a "Do Not Operate" tag on the controls poses significant risks, potentially causing harm to maintenance personnel or rendering the reach stacker unsafe for operation. Operators must never start a reach stacker with such tags in place. Instead, they should confirm completion of all work, ensure personnel clearance, and have the responsible individual remove the tag before proceeding with operations. Similarly, operating the reach stacker while personnel are on any part of the machine poses serious risks of falls, collisions, or crush injuries, emphasizing the importance of thorough safety checks before operation and continuous vigilance during work.

Operating a reach stacker in areas without proper overhead clearance can lead to electrocution, equipment damage, or property damage. Operators must understand the risks associated with inadequate clearance and take necessary precautions, such as ensuring sufficient headroom, designing ergonomic machine paths to avoid overhead obstructions, and using qualified ground guides near power lines. In the event of contact with electrical lines, following proper safety procedures, such as not stepping down from the vehicle and seeking assistance from the power company, is crucial to prevent accidents and minimize risks.

Traveling forward with a load that blocks visibility can result in accidents involving pedestrians, emphasizing the importance of maintaining clear visibility while operating the reach stacker. Operators must drive forward only if they can maintain a clear view of the path of travel and resort to reversing if the load obstructs forward vision. Adhering to defined travel positions, using indicators for proper load positioning, and carrying loads at appropriate heights are essential safety measures to prevent accidents caused by impaired visibility.

MATERIAL HANDLING EQUIPMENT OPERATION

Moving a machine without clearing all blind spots can lead to accidents resulting in death or serious injury. Operators must never move the machine without thoroughly checking all possible blind spots to ensure no one is too close to the machine or load. Relying solely on mirrors while backing up or traveling in reverse can also lead to accidents, emphasizing the need for operators to look in the direction of travel rather than relying solely on mirrors for visual guidance. Mirrors should only be used for reference of potential hazards, with operators maintaining a clear view of the path of travel at all times to prevent accidents and ensure safe operations.

Relying solely on cameras while backing up or traveling in reverse poses significant risks, potentially resulting in death or serious injury to individuals nearby. To mitigate this danger, operators should refrain from traveling in reverse unless necessary for stacking and retrieving containers. Moreover, they must never depend solely on cameras for visual guidance during manoeuvring in reverse, as the camera image may be distorted by weather conditions and lighting. Following OSHA regulations, operators should prioritize looking in the direction of travel and use cameras only for providing advice on potential hazards approaching the machine from the rear at a distance. Overreliance on cameras for visual guidance can exacerbate blind spots, making it imperative for operators to always look in the direction of travel and maintain a clear view of the path ahead, both when stationary and in motion.

Failing to ensure the path of the machine's tailswing is clear can lead to accidents causing death, serious injury, or property damage. Operators must refrain from operating the machine or moving the load if other individuals are near the machine or load and understand the concept of machine tailswing. As steer axles on reach stackers are situated at the rear, turning the machine can cause significant swing at the back, resulting in unexpected movements that may inadvertently strike bystanders. Operators should be mindful that tailswing may be greater than anticipated and refuse to operate the machine if bystanders are present. Initiating turns on the inside of aisles to ensure adequate clearance for tailswing, slowing down, sounding the horn at blind corners, and ensuring the path of the machine's tailswing is clear are essential safety measures to prevent property damage and ensure the safety of individuals in the vicinity.

Concluding Reach Stacker Operations

Finishing up operating a reach stacker involves several critical steps to ensure the safety of personnel and equipment. These include:

1. Securing the Reach Stacker Boom and Container Spreader: Before lifting any containers, it's essential to ensure that the boom and container spreader are properly secured according to manufacturer specifications and safe work procedures. This involves inspecting the locking mechanisms and ensuring they are engaged securely. The container spreader should be positioned correctly over the container, and all locking devices should be activated to prevent accidental disengagement during lifting operations.

2. Applying Relevant Motion Locks and Brakes: Motion locks and brakes play a crucial role in stabilizing the reach stacker during operations. Before lifting or moving any loads, operators must apply the appropriate motion locks and brakes as required by manufacturer specifications and safe work procedures. This typically involves engaging the parking brake and any additional motion locks provided by the manufacturer to prevent unintended movement of the machine.

3. Raising and Securing Stabilizers (if Fitted): If the reach stacker

is equipped with stabilizers, they must be raised and secured according to manufacturer specifications and safe work procedures. Stabilizers help distribute the weight of the load and provide additional stability, especially when handling heavy containers or operating on uneven terrain. Operators should ensure that stabilizers are properly deployed and securely locked in place before proceeding with lifting operations.

4. Parking and Shutting Down the Reach Stacker: After completing the lifting or handling tasks, the reach stacker should be parked in a safe location to avoid hazards and shut down following safe work procedures. This typically involves selecting a level surface away from traffic or pedestrian areas. The operator should engage the parking brake, neutralize the controls, and turn off the engine according to manufacturer recommendations. Additionally, any attachments or lifting mechanisms should be returned to their stowed positions to prevent damage and ensure safety during storage.

5. Carrying Out Post-Operational Checks: Once the reach stacker is parked and shut down, operators need to perform post-operational checks to assess the condition of the equipment. These checks should be conducted in accordance with manufacturer specifications, legislative responsibilities, and safe work procedures. Operators should inspect key components such as the engine, hydraulics, brakes, lights, and safety systems to identify any damage or defects that may have occurred during operation. Any issues should be reported and addressed promptly to ensure the reach stacker remains in safe working condition.

6. Securing the Reach Stacker Against Unauthorized Use: Finally, it's essential to secure the reach stacker to prevent unauthorized access or use, as required by legislative obligations, responsi-

bilities, and safe work procedures. This may involve locking the cab, removing the ignition key, or implementing additional security measures such as immobilizers or access controls. By securing the reach stacker properly, operators can reduce the risk of accidents and ensure that only authorized personnel can operate the equipment.

Parking the reach stacker in an unsafe area, such as locations not designated for reach stacker travel or on steep grades, poses significant risks. Potential consequences include collisions with moving trucks or railcars, pavement damage from tire breakage, or unintended rolling downhill if the parking brake fails. Such incidents could result in severe injury to ground personnel or damage to the reach stacker and surrounding equipment. To mitigate these dangers, it's crucial to always park the reach stacker in a level, safe area away from rail tracks and truck lanes, ensuring the surface can support the tire loads adequately. Additionally, when parking on an incline, securely place wheel chocks against the tyres before leaving or servicing the reach stacker.

MATERIAL HANDLING EQUIPMENT OPERATION

Figure 97: Reach stacker parked up in designated area. AlfvanBeem, CC0, via Wikimedia Commons.

Chapter Seven

Truck Trailer Side Loader

A truck trailer side loader, also known as a side-lift trailer or side loader trailer, is a specialized type of trailer used for transporting shipping containers. Unlike traditional trailers that require cranes or forklifts for loading and unloading containers, side loader trailers have built-in hydraulic lifting mechanisms that allow them to lift containers from the side of the trailer onto the ground or onto other surfaces, such as the bed of a truck or a loading dock.

Here's how a typical truck trailer side loader works:

1. Approach and Positioning: The side loader trailer is manoeuvred into position alongside the container that needs to be loaded or unloaded. The operator ensures that the trailer is parked on stable ground and properly aligned with the container.

2. Engagement: The operator activates the hydraulic lifting mechanism of the side loader. This mechanism typically consists of one or more sets of hydraulic arms equipped with lifting pads or cradles that engage with the bottom corners of the container.

3. Lifting: The hydraulic system raises the container off the ground,

lifting it clear of the trailer chassis. The lifting process is controlled by the operator to ensure smooth and stable movement.

4. Transport: Once the container is lifted, the side loader trailer can transport it to its destination. The trailer may be driven to a storage area, a loading dock, or directly to another truck for onward transportation.

5. Lowering: Upon reaching the desired location, the operator carefully lowers the container using the hydraulic controls. The container is lowered onto the ground or onto the receiving surface with precision to ensure safe placement.

6. Release and Disengagement: After the container is securely placed, the hydraulic arms disengage from the container, and the lifting mechanism retracts back into its stowed position.

7. Retraction and Stowage: The side loader trailer is then ready to be retracted from the container, and the hydraulic arms are stowed away. The trailer can either be prepared for another loading operation or driven away empty.

Truck trailer side loaders offer several advantages, including increased efficiency, reduced reliance on external lifting equipment, and improved safety during loading and unloading operations. They are commonly used in shipping yards, distribution centres, and other logistics facilities for handling standard ISO shipping containers.

Figure 98: Truck trailer side loader fitted to a semi-trailer with container loaded. Bahnfrend, CC BY-SA 4.0, via Wikimedia Commons.

These trailers are equipped with lift modules or cranes that are integrated into the trailer chassis. Alternatively, these lifting components can be mounted on a sub-frame typically attached to a truck.

Constructed from high-tensile steel, the lift modules are engineered to deliver robust strength capabilities. They feature wide-reaching stabilizer jibs and legs controlled by a hydraulic unit, which can be powered either by the tractor's power take-off (PTO) system or by an Auxiliary Power Unit (APU).

Figure 99: Unloaded side loader trailer. 111 Emergency from New Zealand, CC BY 2.0, via Wikimedia Commons.

The lift modules are capable of smoothly sliding inward or outward to accommodate containers of various lengths, including 20 feet, 40 feet, or 45 feet positions.

A conventional container side lifter, as shown in Figure 100, typically features an inline model equipped with stabilizer legs and lifting jibs. Alternatively, some models come with a dual side loader along with either dagger legs or leg-over stabilizers.

Container side lifters can also be classified based on the chassis design, including (Anster, 2024):

- Lattice Chassis: This original design is distinctive and highly favoured. It boasts a low tare weight while providing excellent strength, making it a preferred standard option.

- I-Beam Chassis: Introduced as an alternative chassis benchmark, this design offers customers another option to consider based on their specific requirements and comparisons with other designs.

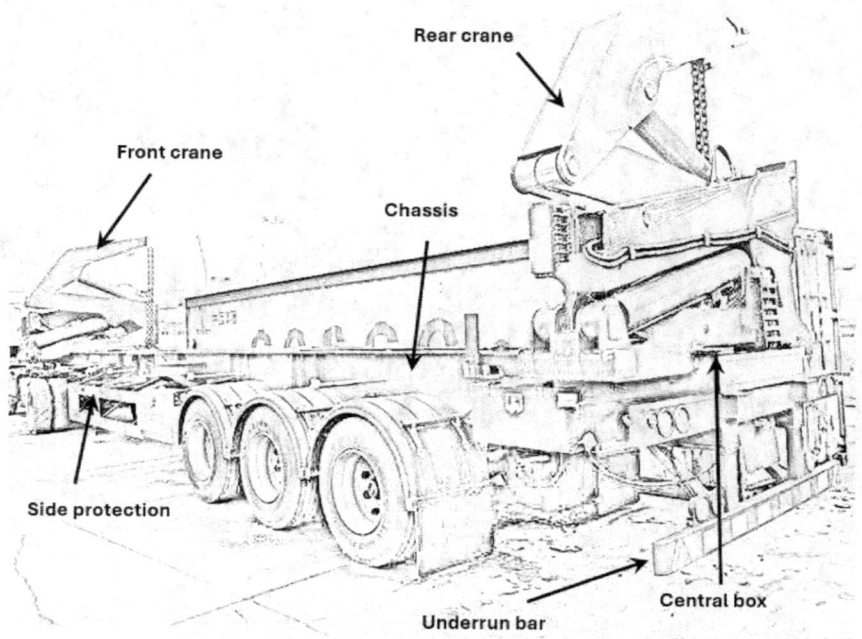

Figure 100: Components of a conventional side loader.

A side loader incorporates several key features (Anster, 2024):
- Lifting Cranes – also referred to as crane lift modules (see Figure 101), these are hydraulically powered cranes responsible for lifting cargo or containers from various surfaces, including the ground, other vehicles, loading docks, railway wagons, or directly from the top of another container. This lifting capability extends to and from the chassis, and the cranes are typically positioned atop the Side lifter Chassis. They are equipped with hydraulic motors or cylinders to facilitate movement along the chassis, accommodating containers of different lengths during loading and unloading operations.

- Driving Power Unit – typically, these cranes are powered by a diesel or gasoline engine mounted on the trailer. Alternatively, they can be powered by a Power Take-Off (PTO) from the tractor or truck.

- Stabilizing Legs – hydraulic legs used to support fully laden shipping containers during lifting operations, ensuring vehicle stability and preventing tilting. These legs are adjustable to accommodate operations on uneven terrain, providing enhanced safety margins and load limits when stacking containers. They can be extended and tilted to enhance capabilities in confined spaces such as trailer decks.

- Chains – chains attached from the cranes' upper part to the corner castings at the container base during lifting operations. Special connecting devices enable the locking of two 20ft containers together, allowing the side lifter to transport them as a single 40ft container.

- The Cab/Tractor – used to tow the trailer and, in some cases, provide power via the PTO. Additionally, it supplies compressed air for the side lifter's wheel brakes. The side lifter typically relies on connection to the tractor for operation, as the tractor provides essential compressed air for the trailer brakes and extra stability during lifting operations.

- Chassis – crucial structural component managing the weight of loaded cargo/containers and supporting the cranes.

- Remote Control – a device operated with buttons and joysticks, connected via a multi-pair electric wire or radio signal. This enables the driver-operator to manoeuvre around the container and view the unit from various angles during lifting operations.

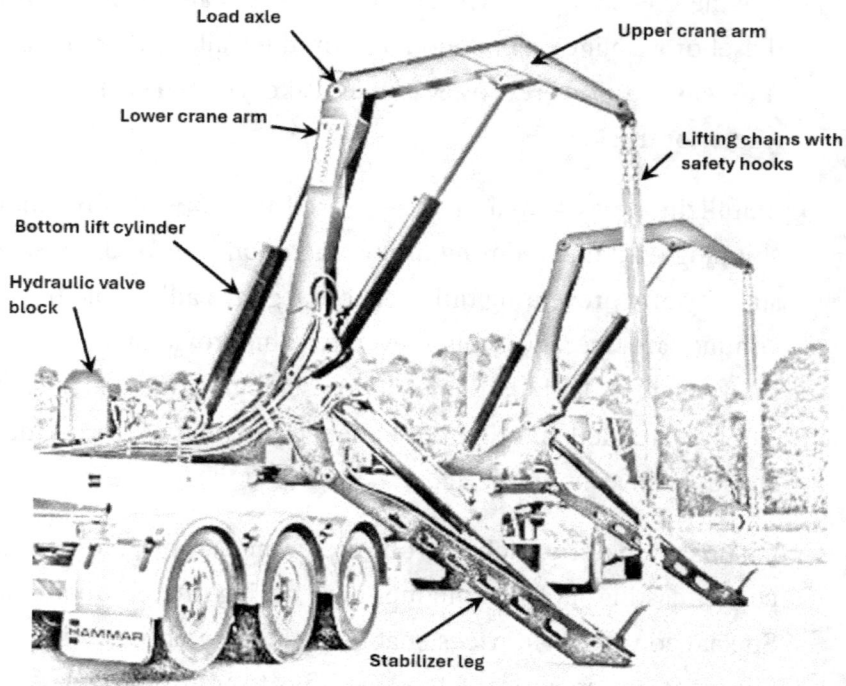

Figure 101: Crane Lifting Module.

The crane lifting module consists of two main components: the stabilizer leg assembly and the crane arm assembly. Hydraulic power provided by the power pack assembly allows the module to move longitudinally along the chassis. It can be securely locked in fixed positions along the chassis to accommodate different container sizes. Both the modules and lifting arms are constructed from high tensile steel, comprised of continuously welded box sections. Pins located within lubricated glacier bearings facilitate the movement of all module parts and can be replaced as needed.

The crane arms are equipped with pilot-operated, over-centre, manual valve controls. These controls are pre-set by the manufacturer to handle shock loads and prevent exceeding the safe working load. The over-centre valves have several functions: a. Prevent movement of the

MATERIAL HANDLING EQUIPMENT OPERATION

crane arms unless there is a pressure signal from the main hydraulic valve. b. Maintain consistent movement and load control during lowering, regardless of cylinder pressure. c. Securely hold the load in position in case of hydraulic system pressure loss or hydraulic hose failure.

The stabilizer leg assembly is essential for providing the necessary stability for lifting loads with the crane arms. Once deployed, these stabilizer legs not only support the load during lifting operations but also prevent the trailer chassis from tilting or twisting. Depending on the available operating space and surface conditions, the stabilizer legs can be deployed at various distances from the chassis. The farther they are deployed from the chassis, the greater the lifting capacity. Each stabilizer leg assembly can be operated individually or simultaneously, with separate joystick controls for each module.

Figure 102: Stabilizer leg assembly extended placing the load. Daniel Linsbauer, CC BY-SA 3.0, via Wikimedia Commons.

By utilizing different combinations of leg extensions and tilt angles, the operator has multiple options for positioning the stabilizer feet. These feet can be placed on the ground at maximum reach to maximize lifting capacity, or at minimum reach for minimal lifting capacity. They can also be positioned underneath the deck of a companion vehicle or on the deck of a companion vehicle or rail car.

To ensure safety, a stabilizer leg interlock system is installed to prevent lifting loads without deploying the legs. When the load handling system is activated, an audible warning sounds and a warning light on the crane lifting module illuminates until both stabilizer legs are deployed. Additionally, each stabilizer leg housing is equipped with a plunger switch that activates when there is positive downward pressure on the foot, automatically disabling certain crane lifting functions until the foot is properly engaged.

Proximity switches mounted on the stabilizer leg housings trigger warning lights on both the remote control and main control panel if the leg is tilted beyond the optimal stability point. This alerts the operator to reduced stability, indicating that lifting should not proceed. If a stabilizer foot loses contact with the ground during lifting operations, audible and visual warnings are activated, and relevant hydraulic functions are disabled until the issue is resolved.

Once the stabilizer legs are appropriately deployed, the arm assembly of the crane is employed to lift and manipulate the load. Each arm within the assembly can be controlled independently or collectively, with individual joysticks on the controller dedicated to controlling each arm.

Each crane arm assembly is equipped with a lifting chain system, comprising two chain legs featuring 16 mm diameter links. Each chain leg is outfitted with a chain shortener and a container lifting lug. These chain legs are connected to the clevis using pins, with the clevis attached to a pivot pin located on the top arm of the crane arm assembly. The container lifting lugs are designed for both right-hand and left-hand operation, determined by the placement of the roll pin on the lifting lug. This roll pin prevents accidental dislodging of the lifting lug from the container corner lifting block. When positioned at the end of the container, the lifting lugs should be affixed to the lower left and right corner lifting blocks with the roll pin facing outward. Incorrect fitting of the lifting lugs may lead to the container becoming loose during lifting operations. Additionally, the chain shorteners are installed to allow for adjustment of the chain legs' length when lifting and stacking containers atop one another.

The pneumatic system is responsible for supplying pressurized air to operate both the trailer braking system and the engine throttle control. It ensures that the trailer brakes remain engaged while the MHE-CSL is in operation. Additionally, a hold back protection valve is installed to safeguard the trailer brake system and isolate the auxiliary pneumatic system if the trailer air pressure drops below a predetermined level.

Mounted beneath the chassis, the trailer pneumatic system consists of three storage reservoirs that are replenished by the air compressor on the prime mover. The engine speed control, integrated into the power pack, is activated and regulated by a solenoid actuated air cylinder. In its default state with no air pressure applied, the engine operates at an idle speed. However, when any of the hydraulic functions of the loader system are activated, the air cylinder elevates the engine speed accordingly.

A pneumatic engine run/stop control solenoid, linked to the key switch and emergency stop button, supplies system air pressure to activate the engine speed control cylinder. This cylinder necessitates air pressure for the engine to function and is spring-loaded to the stop position. Disengaging the key switch or pressing the emergency stop button releases the air from the speed control cylinder, causing the throttle to move to a position where fuel is cut off, effectively stopping the engine.

The hydraulic system functions by delivering pressurized hydraulic oil to operate the hydraulic cylinders installed on the crane lifting modules. This system is comprised of several key components:

- Hydraulic Oil Reservoir: Attached to the power pack sub-frame, the reservoir includes features such as a return oil filter, breather assembly, and taps for reservoir isolation from the hydraulic system.

- Hydraulic Pump: Hydraulic pressure is generated by a tandem, geared hydraulic pump directly linked to the engine.

- Unloader Valve: A high-speed and load-sensed unloader valve assembly is integrated into the system.

- Filtration: Inline high-pressure and return oil filters are installed to maintain hydraulic oil cleanliness.

- Proportional Control Valves: Each crane lifting module is equipped with a Danfoss proportional control valve, which responds to electrical signals from the control modules.

- Traverse Cylinders: Two hydraulic cylinders connect the crane lifting modules to the trailer chassis, allowing longitudinal movement along the chassis to accommodate different container sizes.

- Stabilizer Leg Cylinders: Each lifting module features two hydraulic cylinders to operate the stabilizer legs, providing tilting and extension/retraction actions. Double check valves ensure load system safety in case of hose failure.

- Lifting Cylinders: Two hydraulic cylinders on each crane lift module operate the crane arms. Over-centre valves, preset at the factory, prevent exceeding the safe working load and cushion shock loads.

- Over-centre Valves: These pilot-operated valves prevent arm movement without a pressure signal, maintain load control during lowering, and secure cylinder position in case of hydraulic system pressure loss or hose failure.

- Solenoid Operated Dump Valve: Activated by joystick controllers and emergency stop buttons, this valve controls load sense pressure by dumping it to the reservoir when de-energized.

- Pressure Gauge: The system pressure is monitored via a pressure gauge located on the rear face of the rear crane lifting module.

Planning for Side Loader Operations

Planning to operate a container side loader efficiently and safely, the following should be followed:

1. Identify Task Requirements:

    - Review work orders or equivalent documents to identify task requirements.
    - Confirm the lift plan with associated personnel, ensuring clarity and understanding of responsibilities.
    - Conduct a site inspection to assess the work area and identify any potential hazards or obstacles.

2. Confirm Work Area Suitability:

    - Verify the quality of the operating surface in the work area to ensure it is suitable for the vehicle loading crane's operation.

    - Conduct ground suitability checks in accordance with workplace procedures to prevent accidents or damage to the equipment.

3. Establish Load Capacity and Limits:

    - Determine the Rated Capacity (RC) of the vehicle loading crane and the Working Load Limit (WLL) of the lifting gear based on manufacturer requirements.

    - Match the load/s and task requirements with the established RC and WLL to ensure safe lifting operations.

4. Assess Operating Paths:

    - Evaluate and determine appropriate paths for operating the vehicle loading crane and moving and placing loads within the work area.

    - Consider factors such as clearance, obstacles, and terrain conditions when determining operating paths.

5. Identify and Control Hazards:

    - Conduct relevant hazard identification to identify potential risks associated with the lifting operation.

    - Apply appropriate risk elimination or control measures to mitigate identified hazards.

    - Advise relevant personnel of potential hazards and control measures to ensure a safe working environment.

6. Confirm Traffic Management Plan:

    - Verify the implementation of the traffic management plan for the work area to ensure the safety of personnel and equipment.

    - Follow established procedures for traffic management to prevent accidents and maintain smooth operations.

7. Establish Communication Procedures:

    - Identify appropriate communication procedures and protocols for coordinating lifting operations with associated personnel.

    - Test communication systems to ensure clear and effective communication during lifting tasks.

8. Confirm Task Requirements:

    - Double-check all task requirements to ensure they align with the needs of the relevant work area and comply with workplace procedures.

    - Verify that all necessary preparations have been made before proceeding with lifting operations.

9. Obtain Equipment Information:

    - Gather information required to ensure compliance with manufacturer requirements for the inspection, use, maintenance, and storage of lifting equipment and gear.

    - Interpret and apply manufacturer guidelines to ensure the

safe and effective operation of the equipment.

Operating a container side loader involves various hazards that operators need to be aware of to ensure safety. These hazards can be categorized into different types:

Mechanical Hazards:

- Pinch Points: Operators face the risk of getting caught in pinch points between moving parts of the crane arm assembly or during the deployment and retraction of stabilizer legs.

- Entanglement: There is a potential for entanglement in lifting chains, cables, or other moving components, as well as in the stabilizer leg assembly during deployment or retraction.

- Crushing Hazards: Operators may encounter crushing hazards between containers and the crane arm assembly or during stabilizer leg deployment or retraction.

- Hydraulic Hazards: Risks include hydraulic fluid leakage leading to slips or falls, and hydraulic system failures causing unexpected movements of the crane arm or stabilizer legs.

Fall Hazards:

- Falls from Height: Operators face the risk of falls from the crane arm assembly when operating at elevated positions or from the trailer or container during loading or unloading operations.

- Falls on the Ground: Slips and falls may occur due to uneven or slippery ground surfaces, as well as during stabilizer leg deployment or retraction.

Struck-By Hazards:

- Struck by Moving Parts: There is a risk of being struck by the crane arm assembly or stabilizer legs during operation, as well

MATERIAL HANDLING EQUIPMENT OPERATION

as by containers or cargo being lifted or moved.

- Struck by Falling Objects: Objects falling from the crane arm assembly or stabilizer legs, as well as containers or cargo slipping or falling during loading or unloading, pose hazards.

Electrical Hazards:
- Electrical Shocks: Operators may come into contact with live electrical components or overhead power lines, and malfunction of electrical controls can lead to electrical hazards.

Ergonomic Hazards:
- Repetitive Strain Injuries: Strain from repeated operation of controls and awkward postures during stabilizer leg deployment or crane arm operation can lead to ergonomic injuries.

Environmental Hazards:
- Weather Conditions: Slippery surfaces due to rain, snow, or ice, as well as reduced visibility during adverse weather conditions, pose risks.

- Noise: Exposure to high levels of noise generated by the operation of the equipment can result in potential hearing damage.

Traffic Hazards:
- Collisions: Collisions with other vehicles, equipment, or structures in the work area, as well as with pedestrians or workers on foot, are potential hazards.

- Visibility: Limited visibility while operating the container side loader and blind spots that may obstruct the view of surrounding hazards contribute to traffic hazards.

Preparing for Side Loader Operations

Preparing to operate a container side loader requires careful consideration and adherence to various procedures to ensure safety and efficiency. Here's a detailed explanation of how to carry out specific tasks:

1. Consultation with Workplace Personnel: Establish and maintain communication with workplace personnel to ensure that all crane and lifting operations align with site requirements outlined in the lift plan and workplace procedures. This consultation ensures clarity and consistency in operations.

2. Checking Risk Control Measures: Verify that risk control measures for identified hazards are implemented according to the lift plan and safe work procedures. This involves regular checks to mitigate potential risks associated with crane and lifting operations.

3. Accessing Crane Controls: Safely access the vehicle loading crane controls in accordance with manufacturer requirements and safe work procedures. Proper training and understanding of control systems are essential to operate the crane safely.

4. Pre-Start Checks: Conduct pre-start checks on the vehicle loading crane to ensure its proper functioning. Report any damage or defects, and take appropriate action as per safe work procedures and manufacturer requirements to address issues promptly.

5. Setting up the Crane: Set up the vehicle loading crane correctly, including any lifting gear, according to the lift plan and relevant manufacturer requirements. This includes referring to load charts and following safe work procedures to ensure proper configuration.

6. Setting up Boom/Jib and Lifting Gear: Configure the boom/jib and lifting gear as required, following specific manufacturer requirements and safe work procedures. Proper setup ensures the crane is ready for safe lifting operations.

7. Stabilizing the Crane: Ensure the vehicle loading crane is stabilized appropriately according to the lift plan, relevant manufacturer requirements, and safe work procedures. Proper stabilization is crucial for safe and efficient lifting operations.

8. Operational Checks: Perform operational checks to verify the crane's performance. Report any damage or defects, and take appropriate action in accordance with manufacturer requirements and safe work procedures to maintain operational integrity.

9. Inspecting the Crane Logbook: Inspect the vehicle loading crane logbook to ensure it is correct for the crane type, completed, and signed. Any required rectifications should be signed off in accordance with manufacturer requirements and safe work procedures.

10. Assessing Weather and Work Environment: Evaluate weather and work environment conditions to determine their impact on vehicle loading crane operations. Adhere to manufacturer requirements and safe work procedures to mitigate risks associated with adverse conditions.

11. Identifying Load Weight: Determine the weight of the load by identifying, calculating, or estimating it accurately. This information is crucial for safe lifting operations and load management.

12. Calculating Derated WLL: Calculate the derated Working Load

Limit (WLL) of lifting equipment resulting from selected slinging techniques. This ensures that lifting operations remain within safe load limits.

13. **Identifying Suitable Lifting Points and Slinging Techniques:** Identify appropriate lifting points and slinging techniques based on load characteristics and operational requirements. Proper selection minimizes the risk of load instability and ensures safe lifting.

14. **Preparing Lifting Equipment and Gear:** Prepare lifting equipment and gear for safe use by inspecting and ensuring they are in good condition. This includes checking for defects and ensuring proper rigging and attachment.

15. **Confirming Load Destination:** Confirm the load destination for stability, ensuring it can bear the load safely. Prepare the destination for safe access and landing of the load, adhering to manufacturer requirements and safe work procedures.

Performing daily equipment inspections is crucial for enhancing safety and ensuring proper functionality. During the inspection, check the following (Hammar, 2017):

- Ensure that the king pin is securely attached to the fifth wheel.

- Verify that container hooks, chains, and twist locks are intact and operating correctly.

- Confirm that operating levers on the crane control valve block move smoothly and return to the neutral position automatically.

- Check for any leaks in the hydraulic system hoses, fittings, and components.

- Monitor the hydraulic oil level in the tank.

- Examine the tyres for any signs of damage or abnormal wear.

- Assess the functionality of the braking system.

- Verify that all lighting components are operational.

- In sub-zero temperatures, drain the air tanks unless equipped with automatic venting valves.

- Inspect the side loader for any damage that could pose a risk of personal injury or material damage.

- Ensure that the emergency stop function is working correctly.

If any deficiencies are identified during the inspection, they must be addressed before putting the side loader into operation. It's important to note that this is only a daily function and safety check. For more detailed maintenance procedures, refer to the separate service manual. Additionally, for lubrication and care of axles, suspension, and brakes, consult the accompanying service documents provided by each respective manufacturer.

COUPLING: Prior to putting the side loader into service, it is advisable to perform brake adjustment between the truck and trailer. This practice ensures a consistent braking effect, thereby prolonging the lifespan of the braking system. Before connecting the side loader, ensure that the upper part of the fifth wheel is well lubricated. Reverse the truck to confirm proper engagement and positioning of the king pin. During transportation of the side loader, always connect the brake couplings and the statutory electrics (lighting) and ABS contacts. Regularly inspect all lighting components, such as indicators and brake lights, to ensure they are functioning correctly. Address any malfunctions promptly. Always verify that the cranes are fully closed before transporting the side loader and ensure that the parking legs are fully cranked up. Before driving away, release the parking brake; the pressure in the air tanks must be approximately 5 bar for the brakes to disengage. The location and appearance of the couplings may vary depending on the market.

UNCOUPLING/PARKING: Park the vehicle in a suitable location on level ground and engage the parking brake. Disconnect all contacts, air, and hydraulic connections between the side loader and the truck. Gradually lower the parking legs until the side loader is almost lifted from the fifth wheel. If the ground is soft, utilize support pads. Release the lock on the fifth wheel and carefully drive the truck away.

PARKING LEGS: The parking legs feature a telescopic design and are equipped with two gears: a working gear with high efficiency and a fast gear with a high gear ratio. Use the fast gear when cranking the legs down to the ground or raising them from the ground. The working gear is employed to adjust the height when a load is applied.

Conducting Side Loader Operations

Whether transferring loads to other trucks, trailers, or offloading them onto the ground, the side loader container enables versatile handling options, including double-stacking containers on loading platforms. Conducting container loading and unloading operations on the ground minimizes the risk of injuries and eliminates the need for additional machinery, leading to reduced waiting times and streamlined operations. Furthermore, the side loader container eliminates the necessity for ground preparation using other types of machinery, resulting in significant cost savings for operations and considerable time savings for manufacturers, importers, and distributors. As an example, Figure 103 shows a side loader being used to transfer a container to a rail car.

MATERIAL HANDLING EQUIPMENT OPERATION

Figure 103: Transferring a container from the trailer to a rail car. BOXmover.eu, CC BY-SA 4.0, via Wikimedia Commons.

As a result, logistics companies, independent transport operators, and fleet managers regard the side loader as the most cost-effective equipment solution.

To operate a container side loader effectively:

1. Determine Lifts within Crane Capacity:

    ○ Identify lifts within the Rated Capacity (RC) of the vehicle loading crane by referencing the load chart/s, see Figure 105 for an example, and lift plan.

2. Position Boom/Jib and Hook Block:

    ○ Safely position the crane arms over the container according to directions from associated personnel, if applicable, and in alignment with the lift plan and safe work procedures.

3. Connect Lifting Equipment:

- Connect lifting equipment to the container, see Figure 104 for an example, and operate them safely as per the lift plan, safe work procedures, and manufacturer requirements.

4. Conduct Test Lift:

- Perform a test lift following safe work procedures to ensure the equipment functions properly and the load is stable.

5. Transfer Loads:

- Transfer loads using relevant crane movements and tag lines as needed, adhering to the lift plan and safe work procedures.

6. Monitor Load and Crane Movement:

- Continuously monitor the load and crane movement, operating the crane safely according to the lift plan and safe work procedures.

7. Follow Communication Signals:

- Interpret and follow all required communication signals accurately while operating the crane, in accordance with the lift plan and safe work procedures.

8. Lower Load Safely:

- Lower the load safely and land it in the designated area, following the lift plan and safe work procedures.

9. Disconnect Lifting Gear:

- Disconnect lifting gear from the load and position the crane safely and efficiently for the next task, adhering to the lift plan and safe work procedures.

10. Inspect Equipment:

    - Inspect lifting equipment and gear for defects, and isolate, tag, and report any defective items for maintenance or repair.

During lifting operations, it is advised to maintain a distance of 0.4 m between the side loader and the container to optimize the side loader's full lifting capacity (Hammar, 2017). The side loader should be positioned on stable, level ground. If the ground is not sufficiently stable, support pads of appropriate size and strength should be placed beneath the stabilizer legs. The ground should ideally be horizontal, with maximum recommended inclinations as follows: longitudinal inclination of chassis, ±1cm/m; longitudinal inclination of underlying ground, ±2cm/m; and transverse inclination, ±5cm over the width of the trailer. When handling a container on a slope, the driver must ensure that the side loader remains stable without any risk of slipping lengthwise or sideways. If the side loader is equipped with a RAISE/LOWER function, it should be utilized to achieve a horizontal chassis position as much as possible. In situations deviating from the recommended guidelines, a risk assessment should be conducted, as incorrect handling may result in significant material damage and personal injury. For further guidance on handling containers on slopes, refer to the separate chapter dedicated to this topic. Additionally, it is essential to ensure that the crane's position relative to the trailer and container size is correct.

Figure 104: Container placement with side loader. Borivoj.sourek, CC BY-SA 4.0, via Wikimedia Commons.

As a general guide, to connect the crane arm and chain to a container using a side loader:

1. Position the Side Loader:

   ◦ Park the side loader on firm, level ground, ensuring stability and safety during the loading process.

2. Prepare the Crane Arm:

   ◦ Ensure that the crane arm is properly positioned and aligned with the container to be lifted.

3. Extend the Crane Arm:

   ◦ Use the crane controls to extend the crane arm towards the container until the lifting hook is directly above it.

MATERIAL HANDLING EQUIPMENT OPERATION

4. Position the Lifting Chain:

    - Lower the lifting chain or cables from the crane arm so that they can be attached to the container's lifting points.

5. Attach the Lifting Chains:

    - Securely attach the lifting chains or cables to the designated lifting points on the container. These lifting points are typically located at the corners of the container and are designed to withstand the weight of the container when lifted.

6. Verify Connection:

    - Double-check that the lifting chains are securely attached to the container's lifting points and are not twisted or tangled.

7. Test Connection:

    - Conduct a test lift with the crane to ensure that the connection between the crane arm and the container is secure and stable. Lift the container slightly off the ground to verify that it is properly attached and balanced.

8. Adjust as Needed:

    - If necessary, make any adjustments to the position of the crane arm or the attachment of the lifting chains to ensure a secure connection.

9. Proceed with Lifting:

    - Once the connection is verified and secure, proceed with lifting the container using the side loader, following all safety protocols and operational procedures.

10. Monitor During Lifting:

   - Continuously monitor the container and crane during the lifting process to ensure stability and safety until the container is properly positioned or placed at its destination.

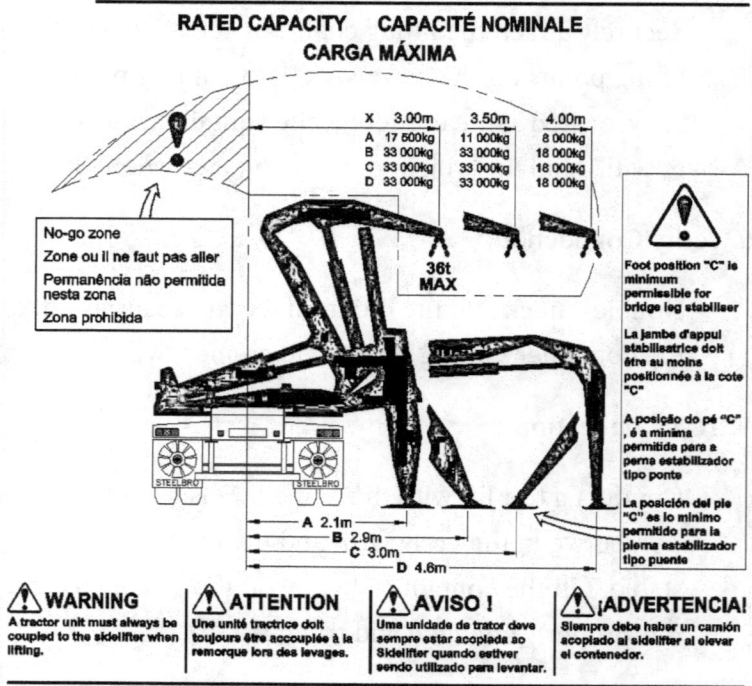

Figure 105: Sample capacity chart for a side loader.

Figure 105 shows that the weight that can be lifted diminished with respect to how far form the trailer it is being placed.

MATERIAL HANDLING EQUIPMENT OPERATION

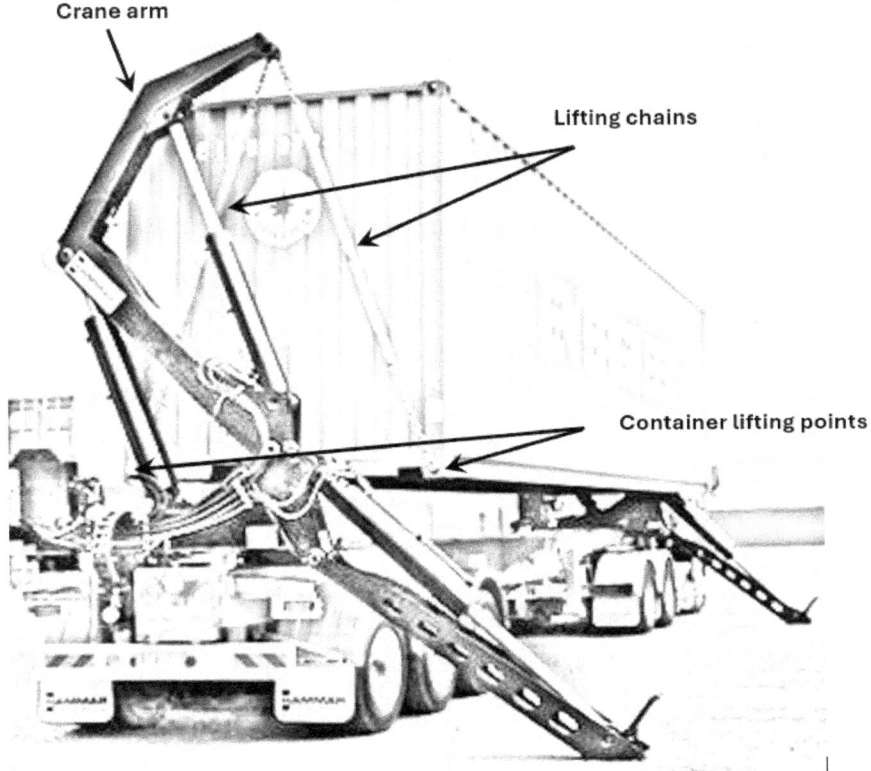

Figure 106: Connection to container.

Completing Side Loader Operations

To stow and secure lifting gear and associated equipment, apply relevant motion locks and brakes, secure stabilizers, and stow plates or packing on a container side loader, follow these steps:

1. Stow Lifting Gear:

    ◦ Ensure that all lifting gear, including chains, hooks, and cables, are properly stowed in their designated storage areas and positions on the side loader.

- Use any provided securing mechanisms, such as hooks or straps, to secure the lifting gear in place to prevent movement during transit.

2. Secure Associated Equipment:

- Any associated equipment, such as tag lines or slings, should also be stowed securely to prevent them from becoming loose during transportation.

- Ensure that all compartments or storage areas are properly closed and latched to prevent items from falling out during transit.

3. Apply Motion Locks and Brakes:

- Engage relevant motion locks and brakes on the side loader as per the manufacturer's instructions and safe work procedures.

- Verify that all motion locks and brakes are functioning correctly and securely locked in place.

4. Stow and Secure Stabilizers:

- If the stabilizers were deployed during operation, retract them back into their stowed position as per manufacturer requirements.

- Secure the stabilizers using any provided locking mechanisms or straps to prevent them from moving during transit.

5. Secure Plates or Packing:

- If plates or packing materials were used during the lifting operation, ensure they are properly stowed and secured on the side loader.

- Use straps or securing devices to prevent plates or packing materials from shifting or falling off during transportation.

6. Perform Shutdown Checks:

- Conduct shutdown checks in accordance with safe work procedures and manufacturer requirements.
- Verify that all systems are powered off, and all controls are in the neutral position.
- Check for any signs of damage or defects and report them as necessary.
- Ensure that the side loader is in a safe and secure condition for transit or storage.

By following these steps, operators can effectively stow and secure lifting gear and associated equipment, apply necessary motion locks and brakes, stow and secure stabilizers, stow plates or packing, and perform shutdown checks on a container side loader in accordance with manufacturer requirements and safe work procedures.

Figure 107: Sideloader stowed and set for road transport. Lav Ulv from Viby J, Denmark, CC BY 2.0, via Wikimedia Commons.

Chapter Eight
Pushback Tugger Truck

A pushback tugger truck, also known as a pushback tractor or pushback tug, is a specialized vehicle used in aviation and ground handling operations at airports. These vehicles are designed to push back aircraft from gates or parking positions, allowing them to manoeuvre away from the terminal building or other structures. Examples of these trucks are shown as Figure 108 and Figure 109.

Figure 108: Japan Airlines Pushback tractor. 221.20, Public domain, via Wikimedia Commons.

Pushback tugger trucks typically feature a powerful diesel engine and are equipped with a tow bar or tow hitch at the front. They attach to the nose landing gear of the aircraft and use hydraulic power to push the aircraft backward.

The main purpose of pushback tugger trucks is to assist in aircraft taxiing, especially in congested areas where aircraft may have limited space to manoeuvre. By pushing the aircraft back, these vehicles help optimize the use of available space on the apron or taxiway and facilitate the efficient flow of air traffic at the airport.

MATERIAL HANDLING EQUIPMENT OPERATION 387

Figure 109: pushback vehicle at Sheremetyevo International Airport. Alf van Beem, Public domain, via Wikimedia Commons.

Pushback tugger trucks are operated by specially trained ground handling personnel and play a crucial role in the safe and efficient movement of aircraft on the ground. The primary function of a pushback tractor is to assist in aircraft pushback operations, which occur after an aircraft lands on the runway and taxis to an aircraft stand, also known as an aircraft bay or airport gate. This is where passengers disembark, and various servicing tasks are performed to prepare the aircraft for its next operation.

Once all servicing activities are completed, the aircraft needs to be reversed from the aircraft stand in order to return to the runway for take-off. The pushback tractor facilitates this process by attaching one end of a towing hook to the aircraft and the other end to the tractor. Upon receiving clearance from the pilot, the tractor driver initiates the pushback operation, guiding the aircraft to the correct position on the taxiway.

Aside from pushback operations, pushback tractors serve other purposes within airport operations. They are utilized to transport aircraft to and from maintenance hangars, where maintenance activities are performed. These tractors are essential for moving aircraft safely within enclosed hangar spaces, where it is not safe to operate aircraft engines due to the risk of foreign object debris ingestion.

Figure 110: Towing into hangar. Buyung koto, CC BY-SA 3.0, via Wikimedia Commons.

Pushback tractors are also employed to reposition aircraft between different parking bays at the airport. This may be necessary to accommodate changes in flight schedules or to optimize gate utilization. Additionally, pushback tractors are utilized in instances where an aircraft parks incorrectly on an aircraft stand, necessitating repositioning to align with the designated centreline and stop positions.

In all cases, pushback tractor operations are conducted with utmost attention to safety and efficiency, ensuring that aircraft movements on the ground are carried out smoothly and in accordance with established procedures (Aviation Learnings, 2020).

The origin of the term 'tractor' dates back to the early days of aviation when airplanes would land on open fields rather than the concrete runways commonly used today. Upon landing, the nearest available tractor on the field would be connected to the aircraft to facilitate its movement. Although engineers later developed specialized vehicles for this purpose, the name 'tractor' persisted and continues to be used today (Aviation Learnings, 2020).

It may seem logical that an aircraft, equipped with its own engines, should be capable of reversing itself from the aircraft bay and moving independently around the airport. After all, no pushback tractor is required to manoeuvre an aircraft from the runway to the airport gate upon landing. These questions raise valid points that warrant scientific explanations.

Beginning with the pushback operation, let's explore why an aircraft cannot reverse itself from the bay. Most airliners are equipped with a reverse thrust mechanism that theoretically allows for reverse movement. Pilots use this mechanism to decelerate the aircraft after landing. However, utilizing reverse thrust for ground movement poses significant safety concerns. The design of an aircraft bay positions airport buildings and facilities in front of the aircraft. While aircraft engines generate thrust by expelling high-velocity air behind the aircraft, utilizing reverse thrust would direct this force toward airport structures, including passenger boarding bridges. Consequently, for safety reasons, aircraft cannot reverse themselves and necessitate the use of an aircraft pushback tractor to manoeuvre them away from the bay.

While it's evident why aircraft cannot reverse from the bay, the question remains as to why they cannot move from one point to another on the airport grounds independently. The answer lies in the economic considerations of jet engines versus pushback tractors for ground movement.

Aircraft jet engines are optimized for high-speed flight, not low-speed ground movement at typical taxiing speeds of 10-30 km/hr. Operating at lower speeds significantly impacts their fuel efficiency, as jet engines are inherently less efficient at low speeds compared to their optimal cruising speeds. Conversely, pushback tractors are equipped with diesel engines, gearboxes, and chassis specifically designed for high torque and low-speed operations. Their fuel consumption is far lower than that of jet engines when operating within the typical speed range for ground handling activities.

Given these factors, airlines and ground handling agencies prefer to utilize pushback tractors for on-ground manoeuvring of aircraft due to their superior efficiency and suitability for low-speed operations.

A conventional pushback tractor is a vehicle powered by a diesel engine and designed with a chassis that maintains a low profile close to the ground. This design is intentional to prevent collisions with the nose of aircraft and to maintain a low centre of gravity, which enhances stability.

During a pushback operation, the pushback tractor attaches itself to the aircraft using a towing hook, typically located on the nose landing gear, known as the NLG. It accomplishes this by pushing the aircraft in reverse.

The chassis of the pushback tractor is engineered to be as close to the ground as possible to ensure that the force exerted during the pushback operation remains in a straight line. This helps prevent the bending of the towing bar, which we will discuss shortly.

If the force applied is not in a straight line, the pushback tractor may exert more pressure on the towing hook, causing it to bend, rather than effectively pushing the aircraft.

MATERIAL HANDLING EQUIPMENT OPERATION

The pushback tractor is recognized for its large wheels, which serve to enhance the contact patch of its tyres, ensuring sufficient traction during the process of aircraft pushing or towing. Similar to how a person with sturdy footing is better equipped to push a heavy object, the effectiveness of a powerful diesel engine in pushing an aircraft hinges on the traction provided by its tyres.

Figure 111: Large wheels and tyres enlarging the contact patch. Trepel Airport Equipment, Attribution, via Wikimedia Commons.

A conventional pushback tractor is constructed to be exceptionally heavy. For instance, a pushback tractor designed for wide-body aircraft can weigh in excess of 50 metric tonnes.

This substantial weight is not solely attributable to its own components but also includes additional ballast weight incorporated into the tractor's chassis. This addition enhances traction by augmenting the coefficient of friction, thereby minimizing wheel slippage during operations.

A pushback tug, example shown as Figure 112, typically consists of several main components essential for its operation. These components work together to facilitate the movement of aircraft on the ground. Here are the main components of a pushback tug:

1. Engine: The engine provides the power necessary to drive the pushback tug. It can be either gasoline or diesel-powered, depending on the specific model and manufacturer. The engine generates the torque required to move the tug and the attached aircraft.

2. Transmission: The transmission transfers power from the engine to the wheels of the pushback tug. It allows the operator to control the speed and direction of movement by shifting between different gears.

3. Hydraulic System: The hydraulic system is responsible for powering various functions of the pushback tug, such as raising and lowering the tow bar, adjusting the height of the tug's chassis, and operating any hydraulic brakes or steering mechanisms.

4. Chassis: The chassis forms the framework of the pushback tug and provides structural support for the other components. It is typically made of durable materials such as steel or aluminium to withstand the stresses of towing heavy aircraft.

5. Tow Bar: The tow bar is a critical component that connects the pushback tug to the aircraft's nose landing gear. It is usually a sturdy steel bar with attachments at both ends to secure it to the tug and the aircraft. The tow bar transmits the force from the tug to the aircraft, allowing the tug to push or pull the aircraft.

6. Braking System: The braking system allows the operator to control the speed and stopping of the pushback tug. It may include hydraulic or pneumatic brakes that act on the tug's wheels to slow down or stop its movement.

7. Steering Mechanism: The steering mechanism enables the operator to manoeuvre the pushback tug accurately. It may utilize

MATERIAL HANDLING EQUIPMENT OPERATION

hydraulic or mechanical systems to turn the front wheels of the tug, allowing it to navigate tight spaces and make precise adjustments during pushback operations.

8. Operator Controls: Operator controls, such as a steering wheel, throttle, brake pedals, and hydraulic control levers, enable the operator to control the movement and functions of the pushback tug effectively. These controls are typically located within reach of the operator's seat for ease of use.

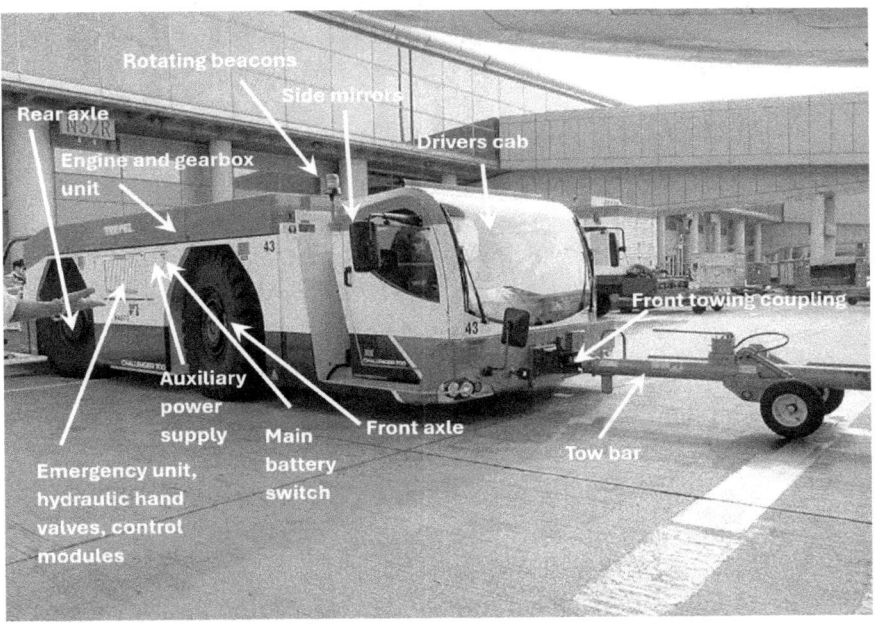

A vehicle with text overlay

Description automatically generated with medium confidence

Planning and Preparing for Pushback Tug Operations

From the standpoint of planning and preparing for pushback tugger operations, this includes:

1. **Selection and Use of Personal Protective Equipment (PPE):**

    - Review workplace procedures to determine the specific PPE requirements for pushback tugger operations.

    - Select appropriate PPE such as high-visibility vests, safety goggles, steel-toed boots, and ear protection based on the identified hazards and workplace policies.

    - Ensure proper fitting and use of the selected PPE during all pushback tugger operations as per workplace procedures.

2. **Pre-operational Checks of Tug:**

    - Refer to workplace procedures and manufacturer instructions for the detailed checklist of pre-operational checks.

    - Inspect the tugger for any visible damage, leaks, or signs of wear and tear.

    - Check the condition of tyres, brakes, steering mechanism, and lights.

    - Verify the functionality of essential components such as engine, transmission, and hydraulic system.

    - Confirm that all safety features, including emergency stop buttons and alarms, are operational.

3. **Topping up Fluid Levels:**

    - Refer to the manufacturer's guidelines to identify the specific fluids that need to be checked and topped up.

    - Use appropriate fluid types and quantities as recommended by the manufacturer.

- Check fluid levels such as engine oil, hydraulic fluid, coolant, and brake fluid, and top up as required to maintain optimal levels for safe operation.

4. **Rectification or Reporting of Equipment Faults and Malfunctions:**

    - Immediately address any equipment faults or malfunctions identified during pre-operational checks.

    - For minor issues that can be rectified on-site, follow the procedures outlined in the manufacturer's instructions or workplace guidelines.

    - For major or complex faults that require professional intervention, promptly report them to the relevant personnel as per workplace procedures.

    - Document all identified faults, actions taken for rectification, and any reported issues for compliance with regulatory requirements and future reference.

An important aspect of planning is ensuring that the pushback tug's capacity is sufficient to pushback the particular aircraft. Manufacturers produce pushback tractors in various models, configurations, and capacities to accommodate diverse aircraft types and airport conditions. These variations stem from several key factors:

1. **Maximum Aircraft Weight:**

    - The capacity of a pushback tractor is influenced by the maximum weight of the aircraft it needs to manoeuvre.

    - Aircraft weight varies based on size and loading condition, often measured by the Maximum Take-off Weight (MTOW).

- For instance, smaller aircraft like the Airbus A320 have an MTOW around 70 metric tons, while larger planes like the Airbus A380 exceed 500 metric tons. Higher MTOW requires a more powerful pushback tractor.

2. Apron Surface Slope:

    - The slope of the apron surface where the pushback operation occurs affects tractor capacity.
    - Ideally, apron surfaces are flat, but slight slopes are common, posing challenges for pushback operations.
    - Typically, pushback tractor capacity is assessed considering a maximum slope of 2%.

3. Number of Running Engines:

    - Prior to pushback, pilots often start one or both jet engines at idle speed to prepare for taxiing and take-off.
    - Pushback tractors must contend not only with the aircraft's weight and slope but also with the thrust generated by idling jet engines.

4. Surface Condition:

    - Surface conditions, such as snow or rainwater on the apron, impact traction and power requirements for pushback tractors.
    - Slippery surfaces reduce traction, necessitating additional ballast weights to enhance traction and stability.
    - Adverse conditions, particularly in locations like Chicago O'Hare International Airport during extreme winter weather,

MATERIAL HANDLING EQUIPMENT OPERATION

demand careful consideration.

Aircraft manufacturers provide towing requirements in their manuals, often presented in chart form, combining these factors to determine the necessary capacity of pushback tractors. Airlines and ground handling agencies maintain a fleet of pushback tractors tailored to serve various aircraft types and operating conditions.

Considering the factors influencing the need for pushback tractor capacity, the primary specifications of a pushback tractor encompass:

- Drawbar Pull

- Tractor Weight

- Maximum Aircraft Weight it can handle

These specifications are interdependent, each influencing the others. Here's how:

Drawbar pull denotes the horizontal pulling force exerted by the pushback tractor, typically measured in kilo Newtons (kN). A higher drawbar pull rating signifies a more potent tractor capable of handling larger aircraft. This metric relies on the tractor's diesel engine power and chassis robustness.

The weight of the pushback tractor reflects its ability to maintain traction while the engine operates. Analogous to a weightlifter needing sturdy footing to exert force effectively, the tractor's weight ensures traction, preventing wheel spinning and optimizing engine power utilization.

Manufacturers specify both the base weight of the tractor and its "ballasted weight." Ballasted weight refers to additional mass added to enhance traction, particularly useful in challenging conditions like rainy weather.

The combination of drawbar pull and tractor weight dictates the maximum aircraft weight the pushback tractor can manage, as well as the aircraft families it's compatible with.

For a practical illustration, let's examine various models of pushback tractors manufactured by Trepel, a renowned GSE brand (Aviation Learnings, 2020):

- Challenger 150: Supports aircraft up to 160 metric tonnes, with a drawbar pull of 101 kN. It weighs 9 tonnes and can be ballasted up to 15 tonnes. Compatible with Airbus A320 & Boeing 737 Family.

- Challenger 280: Suitable for aircraft up to 300 metric tonnes, offering a drawbar pull of 209 kN. It weighs 24 tonnes, with a ballasted weight of 28 tonnes. Compatible with Airbus A350 & Boeing 787 Family.

- Challenger 430: Designed for aircraft up to 380 metric tonnes, providing a drawbar pull of 304 kN. It weighs 27 tonnes and can be ballasted up to 43 tonnes. Compatible with Boeing 777 Family.

- Challenger 550: Capable of handling aircraft up to 450 metric tonnes, offering a drawbar pull of 369 kN. It weighs 50 tonnes, with a ballasted weight of 60 tonnes. Compatible with aircraft up to Boeing 747-800, the Jumbo Jet.

- Challenger 700 (see Figure 113: Supports aircraft up to 600 metric tonnes, with a drawbar pull of 498 kN. Weighing 40 tonnes, it can be ballasted up to 70 tonnes. Compatible with Airbus A380, the largest passenger airliner in the world.

Figure 113: Trepel Challenger 700. Trepel Airport Equipment, Attribution, via Wikimedia Commons.

In conventional pushback operations, a pushback tractor connects to the nose landing gear of the aircraft using a basic tool known as a tow bar.

This tow bar is a cylindrical steel rod equipped with hooks at each end. One end securely engages with the towing hook on the aircraft's nose landing gear, while the opposite end connects to the pushback tractor. The pushback tractor exerts force on the aircraft's nose landing gear through this tow bar, see Figure 114.

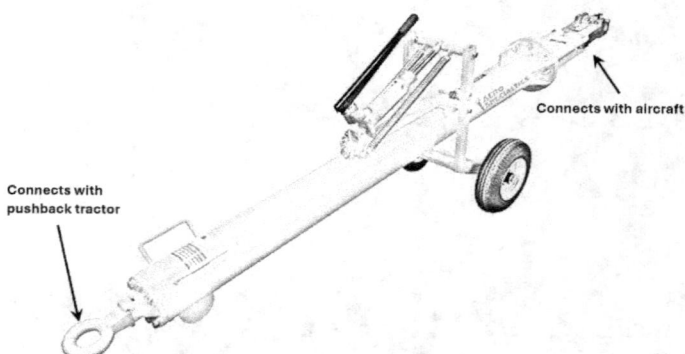

Figure 114: Pushback towbar.

Various aircraft models feature distinct nose landing gear designs, making it necessary to use specific tow bars tailored to each aircraft type. Tow bars are only compatible with aircraft families sharing similar nose landing gear configurations.

Airlines and ground handling agencies equipped with conventional pushback tractors maintain a stock of towing bars to accommodate the diverse range of aircraft in their fleet. Tow bar manufacturers prioritize safety by integrating a crucial feature into their designs: the shear pin.

The shear pin serves a singular purpose: to safeguard the aircraft's nose landing gear and the pushback tractor from excessive forces during towing operations. Positioned within the tow bar head connected to the aircraft's nose landing gear, the shear pin maintains alignment between the tow bar tube and head under normal conditions. However, if forces exceed safe limits, the shear pin shears, causing the tow bar head to collapse. This misalignment is immediately evident to the pushback crew, prompting them to halt the operation.

Vigilance is essential as shear pin failure may go unnoticed amid the noisy airport environment, underscoring the importance of regular inspections by the pushback crew.

MATERIAL HANDLING EQUIPMENT OPERATION

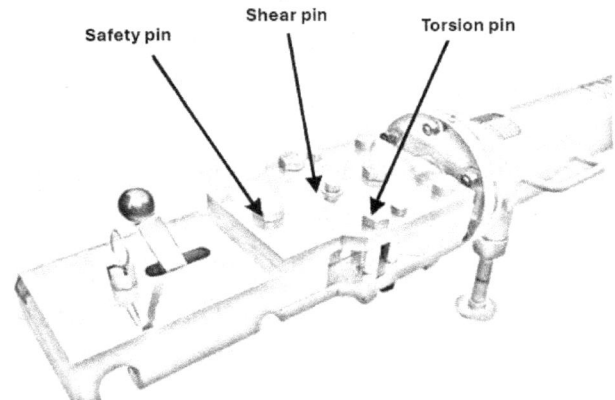

Figure 115: Location of shear pin.

As shown in Figure 115, the shear pin is specifically crafted to alleviate the threat posed by excessive force exerted on the shaft during pushing or towing operations, serving as a protective measure against potential damage to the aircraft. Meanwhile, the torsion pin serves to restrict the degree of angular displacement when pushing or pulling the aircraft, effectively curbing the risk of excessive axial force that may compromise the aircraft's integrity. Additionally, the safety pin is implemented to address the aftermath of shear pin and torsion pin failures, mitigating the potential for substantial damage to the aircraft resulting from their breakage.

The Tow Bar Less (TBL) Pushback Tractor, as shown in Figure 116 represents a significant advancement in pushback tractor technology, eliminating the need for a tow bar in aircraft manoeuvring operations. Instead of relying on a tow bar, the TBL tractor employs a hydraulic system to raise the aircraft's nose wheel assembly off the ground and support it using its own chassis. This innovative design allows the tractor to tow the aircraft to its destination without the use of a tow bar, releasing the nose wheel assembly upon arrival. By bearing a substantial portion of the aircraft's weight on its chassis, the TBL pushback tractor negates the need for additional ballasts typically required for conventional models, resulting in a lighter overall weight.

Primary advantages of Tow Bar Less (TBL) Tractor (Aviation Learnings, 2020):

1. Enhanced Fuel Efficiency: TBL tractors are notably lighter compared to conventional towing tractors, resulting in improved fuel efficiency. Unlike conventional tractors, which carry the weight of a tow bar even when not in use, TBL tractors operate without this additional burden, leading to fuel savings.

2. Cost-Effective Maintenance: The reduced weight of TBL tractors translates to cost savings on maintenance. With decreased strain on components such as the engine, gearbox, and chassis, wear and tear are minimized, resulting in lower maintenance costs compared to conventional tractors.

3. Inventory Simplification: TBL tractors eliminate the need for maintaining an inventory of tow bars, as they do not require engagement with the aircraft's towing hook. While there are various models of TBL tractors available based on their weight handling capacity, they generally accommodate multiple aircraft types without the necessity of tow bars.

Figure 116: Towbarless aircraft tractor (Goldhofer AST-3) pushing back aircraft A319-100. Bundesstefan, CC0, via Wikimedia Commons.

Performing pre-operational checks of the tug involves several crucial steps to ensure its safe and efficient operation:

1. Consult Workplace Procedures and Manufacturer Instructions: Begin by referring to the workplace procedures and manufacturer instructions to obtain a detailed checklist of pre-operational checks. This checklist will outline specific items that need to be inspected before the tugger can be used.

2. Visual Inspection: Conduct a visual inspection of the tugger to identify any visible damage, leaks, or signs of wear and tear. Pay close attention to areas such as the body, engine compartment, hydraulic system, and any other relevant components.

3. Check Key Components: Inspect the condition of essential components including tyres, brakes, steering mechanism, and lights. Ensure that tyres have adequate tread depth and are properly inflated. Test the brakes to verify their functionality and inspect the steering mechanism for any abnormalities. Ad-

ditionally, check that all lights are working correctly.

4. Verify Functionality of Mechanical Systems: Verify the functionality of critical mechanical systems such as the engine, transmission, and hydraulic system. Start the engine and listen for any unusual sounds or vibrations. Shift through the gears to ensure smooth operation of the transmission. Test the hydraulic system by operating any hydraulic functions to confirm proper functioning.

5. Confirm Safety Features: Confirm that all safety features of the tugger are operational. This includes verifying the functionality of emergency stop buttons, alarms, and other safety mechanisms. Test each safety feature to ensure they function as intended and can be activated in case of an emergency.

Conducting a visual inspection of the tugger is essential for identifying visible damage, leaks, or signs of wear and tear. To ensure thoroughness, it's crucial to adopt a systematic approach by visually scanning the entire tugger, leaving no area overlooked during the inspection process. This systematic method helps in covering all aspects of the vehicle, from the body to the engine compartment and beyond.

Begin by inspecting the exterior body of the tugger, scrutinizing it for any dents, scratches, or damages, particularly focusing on vulnerable areas like the front bumper and sides of the vehicle. Moving on, open the engine compartment to examine the engine thoroughly for leaks, corrosion, or damage to various components such as hoses, belts, and connectors. This inspection also involves checking for oil or coolant leaks and ensuring tight connections to mitigate potential issues.

Additionally, delve into examining the hydraulic system, paying close attention to detect leaks, damaged hoses, or loose connections. Verify hydraulic fluid levels and be vigilant for any signs of contamination or discoloration, indicating potential internal problems within the system. Finally, inspect other pertinent components like the transmission, steering system, electrical wiring, and braking system for wear and tear, loose connections, or abnormalities that could compromise the tugger's performance or safety. Documenting all findings during the visual inspection aids in tracking the tugger's condition over time and facilitates informed decisions regarding maintenance or repairs to uphold its safe and efficient operation.

To check key components of the tugger effectively, follow these steps:

1. Inspect Tyres: Begin by examining the tyres to ensure they are in good condition. Check for adequate tread depth and look for any signs of wear or damage. Additionally, ensure that the tyres are properly inflated according to the manufacturer's specifications. Proper tyre inflation is crucial for optimal traction and safe operation of the tugger.

2. Test Brakes: Next, test the brakes to verify their functionality. Apply the brakes while the tugger is stationary and ensure that it comes to a smooth and controlled stop. Listen for any unusual sounds or sensations, which may indicate brake issues. Additionally, check the brake fluid level and inspect brake lines for leaks or damage.

3. Inspect Steering Mechanism: Inspect the steering mechanism for any abnormalities or signs of wear. Turn the steering wheel from lock to lock and check for smooth operation without any binding or resistance. Ensure that the steering system is properly lubricated and that all components are securely fastened.

4. Check Lights: Finally, inspect all lights on the tugger to ensure they are working correctly. This includes headlights, taillights, brake lights, turn signals, and any other auxiliary lights. Test each light individually to verify functionality, and replace any bulbs that are burnt out or flickering. Proper lighting is essential for

visibility and safety, especially during nighttime or low-visibility conditions.

5. To verify the functionality of critical mechanical systems in the tugger, it's essential to follow a systematic approach that ensures each system is thoroughly tested for optimal performance and safety. Begin by focusing on key components such as the engine, transmission, and hydraulic system.

6. Firstly, start the engine and carefully listen for any unusual sounds or vibrations that may indicate potential issues. A smooth and consistent engine sound is typically indicative of proper functioning. Additionally, observe the engine's idle behaviour to ensure it remains stable without any fluctuations or irregularities.

7. Next, shift through the gears to assess the transmission's functionality. Move the transmission lever through each gear position, from park to drive and reverse, ensuring smooth engagement and disengagement without any hesitations or grinding noises. Proper transmission operation is crucial for efficient movement of the tugger.

8. Finally, test the hydraulic system by operating any hydraulic functions available on the tugger. This may include raising or lowering hydraulic arms, extending or retracting hydraulic cylinders, or activating any other hydraulic mechanisms. Observe the hydraulic system's response to these commands, ensuring that movements are smooth, controlled, and without any signs of fluid leaks or pressure issues.

9. Throughout this verification process, pay close attention to any abnormal behaviour or indications of mechanical malfunction.

MATERIAL HANDLING EQUIPMENT OPERATION

Document any observed issues and prioritize addressing them promptly to prevent further damage or safety hazards. By systematically verifying the functionality of these critical mechanical systems, you can ensure the tugger is in optimal condition for safe and efficient operation in the workplace.

Controls in a pushback tug are used for manoeuvring and operating the vehicle safely and effectively during aircraft pushback procedures. These controls typically consist of various components that allow the operator to control the movement and operation of the tug. Here's an overview of the typical controls found in a pushback tug:

1. Steering Wheel: The steering wheel allows the operator to control the direction of travel of the pushback tug. By turning the steering wheel, the operator can steer the tug in the desired direction, whether it's straight ahead, left, or right. The steering wheel is crucial for manoeuvring the tug accurately, especially in tight spaces such as aircraft parking areas.

2. Accelerator and Brake Pedals: Similar to those found in automobiles, the accelerator pedal controls the speed of the pushback tug by adjusting the engine throttle. Pressing the accelerator pedal increases the engine speed, while releasing it reduces speed. The brake pedal is used to slow down or stop the tug's movement when necessary. Proper coordination between the accelerator and brake pedals is essential for smooth and controlled operation of the tug.

3. Transmission Controls: Pushback tugs may have manual or automatic transmissions, each with its set of controls. In manual transmissions, the operator uses a gear lever or selector to shift between different gears, such as drive, reverse, and neutral. In automatic transmissions, the controls may include a gear selector or buttons for selecting the desired driving mode.

4. Hydraulic Controls: Many pushback tugs are equipped with hydraulic systems that control various functions, such as raising and lowering the towing arm or other hydraulic attachments. These controls may consist of levers, switches, or buttons located within easy reach of the operator. Proper operation of the hydraulic controls is crucial for safely attaching and detaching the aircraft during pushback procedures.

5. Emergency Stop Button: An emergency stop button or switch is a safety feature that allows the operator to quickly stop the tug's movement in case of an emergency or unsafe condition. Pressing the emergency stop button activates a system-wide shutdown, bringing the tug to a halt to prevent accidents or injuries.

Pushback tugger operation involves various hazards that pose risks to both personnel and aircraft. Mitigation strategies are essential to minimize these risks and ensure safe operations. The following are some common hazards associated with pushback tugger operation along with corresponding mitigation strategies:

1. Collision Hazards:

- Hazard: Collisions with stationary objects, other vehicles, or aircraft can occur during manoeuvring.

- Mitigation: Operators should undergo comprehensive training on safe driving practices and be familiar with the layout of the apron. Clear pathways and designated parking areas should be established to minimize the risk of collisions. The use of spotters or ground personnel to guide the tugger can also enhance safety.

2. Equipment Failure:

MATERIAL HANDLING EQUIPMENT OPERATION

- Hazard: Mechanical failures or malfunctions of the pushback tugger can lead to accidents or damage to aircraft.

- Mitigation: Regular maintenance and inspections of the tugger should be conducted to identify and address any potential issues before they escalate. Pre-operational checks should be performed diligently to verify the functionality of essential components. Immediate reporting and rectification of any equipment faults or abnormalities are essential to prevent accidents.

3. Slips, Trips, and Falls:

   - Hazard: Operators and ground personnel may encounter slippery surfaces, uneven terrain, or obstacles, increasing the risk of slips, trips, and falls.

   - Mitigation: Adequate lighting and signage should be provided to improve visibility and alert operators to potential hazards. Proper housekeeping practices, such as keeping work areas clear of debris and maintaining well-marked walkways, can help prevent slips and trips. Personal protective equipment (PPE), including non-slip footwear, should be worn to minimize the risk of falls.

4. Weather Conditions:

   - Hazard: Adverse weather conditions such as rain, snow, or strong winds can impact visibility, traction, and overall safety during tugger operation.

   - Mitigation: Operators should monitor weather forecasts and exercise caution when operating in inclement weather conditions. Reduced speeds, increased following distances, and heightened awareness of surroundings are recommended in adverse weather. In extreme conditions, operations may need to be suspended until conditions improve to ensure the safety of personnel and aircraft.

5. Communication Issues:

- Hazard: Inadequate communication between operators, ground personnel, and aircrew can lead to misunderstandings or errors during pushback operations.

- Mitigation: Clear communication protocols should be established, including standardized hand signals, radio communication procedures, and pre-operation briefings. Training programs should emphasize the importance of effective communication and situational awareness among all personnel involved in tugger operations.

By implementing these mitigation strategies and maintaining a proactive approach to safety, organizations can minimize the hazards associated with pushback tugger operation and ensure the well-being of personnel and the integrity of aircraft. Regular reviews of safety protocols and continuous training are essential to address emerging risks and maintain a culture of safety within the workplace.

Operating a Pushback Tug

To manoeuvre the tug to the aircraft and position it for ground manoeuvres or push-out operations, operators adhere to workplace procedures by carefully navigating the tug to the designated location. This involves coordinating with ground maintenance personnel and following established pathways to ensure safe and efficient movement around the aircraft parking area. Once in position, the tug is aligned with the aircraft according to workplace protocols to facilitate smooth coupling.

Coupling the tug to the aircraft is executed in strict accordance with workplace procedures to ensure a secure connection. Operators verify the compatibility between the tug and aircraft, confirming proper alignment and attachment of the tow bar or other coupling mechanisms. Attention to detail is crucial during this process to prevent potential damage to both the tug and the aircraft, with operators following manufacturer instructions to ensure a safe coupling procedure.

During operation, the tug is handled in strict compliance with workplace procedures and manufacturer instructions. Operators are trained to operate the tug controls effectively, manoeuvring the vehicle with precision and caution. Regular monitoring of the tug's systems and performance ensures optimal functionality throughout the operation. Moreover, operators remain vigilant for any signs of hazards or malfunctions, promptly addressing any issues in accordance with workplace protocols and occupational health and safety regulations.

Identifying hazards associated with tug operation is a fundamental aspect of workplace safety. Operators are trained to recognize potential risks such as uneven terrain, obstacles, or inclement weather conditions that may pose a threat to safe operation. By adhering to work health and safety (WHS) or occupational health and safety (OHS) regulations, operators implement appropriate precautions to mitigate these hazards, including wearing personal protective equipment and implementing hazard management strategies.

During aircraft ground manoeuvres or push-out operations, operators follow the directions of ground maintenance personnel and aircrew meticulously. This involves clear communication and coordination to execute manoeuvres safely and efficiently, minimizing the risk of accidents or damage to the aircraft. Upon completion of required operations, the tug is uncoupled from the aircraft following workplace procedures, and operators manoeuvre the tug to its allocated parking or storage area. Once parked, the tug is shut down in accordance with established protocols, ensuring proper maintenance and readiness for future haulage activities.

The individuals involved in the pushback operation comprise:

- Pilots

- Pushback tractor driver

- Headset operator

- Two wing walkers, positioned on either side of the aircraft

- One tail walker

While the pilot holds ultimate responsibility for the operation, they lack a clear view and spatial awareness during the pushback process. Consequently, the pilot does not directly control the aircraft's reversal from the stand. Instead, the speed, turning angle, and other aspects of the pushback movement are managed by the pushback tractor driver. However, the driver, situated within the tractor, focuses on vehicle control and manoeuvring.

In this context, the key communicator and overseer of ground activities for the pilot is the headset operator. Constantly connected to the cockpit via a headset device linked to a port on the nose landing gear, the headset operator facilitates communication between the pilot and ground personnel.

Clearance for initiating the pushback is granted by the control tower. Subsequently, coordination between the pilot and the headset operator determines the pushback's commencement. Once all parties are prepared, the headset operator signals the pushback tractor driver to initiate the operation.

MATERIAL HANDLING EQUIPMENT OPERATION 413

Figure 117: Aircraft pushback operation, with a pushback tractor and its driver at the forefront, accompanied by a headset operator walking alongside the tractor. Additionally, another ground crew member is seen walking behind the tractor. Rafale20307, CC BY-SA 4.0, via Wikimedia Commons.

Prior to commencing the aircraft pushback operation, safety measures are initiated with a thorough walkaround visual inspection of the aircraft by the pushback crew. This procedure, crucial for both ramp and flight safety, entails a meticulous examination of the aircraft's exterior to detect any irregularities or anomalies. Such observations could include improperly closed cargo doors or unreleased chocks from the rear landing gear wheels. These seemingly minor details hold significant importance in ensuring ramp safety, and the vigilant scrutiny of a trained individual can greatly reduce the risk of aircraft pushback accidents. Once the walkaround check is completed, the pushback equipment is prepared, and the crew readies themselves for the operation.

Importance of Correct Towbar Engagement in Aircraft Pushback Safety: Despite its simple appearance as a non-motorized piece of equipment, the towbar plays a critical role in ensuring safe engagement with the aircraft during pushback operations. The sequence of steps involved in setting up the pushback tractor and towbar necessitates careful consideration for safety. It is imperative that the towbar be engaged first with the aircraft before attaching it to the pushback tractor.

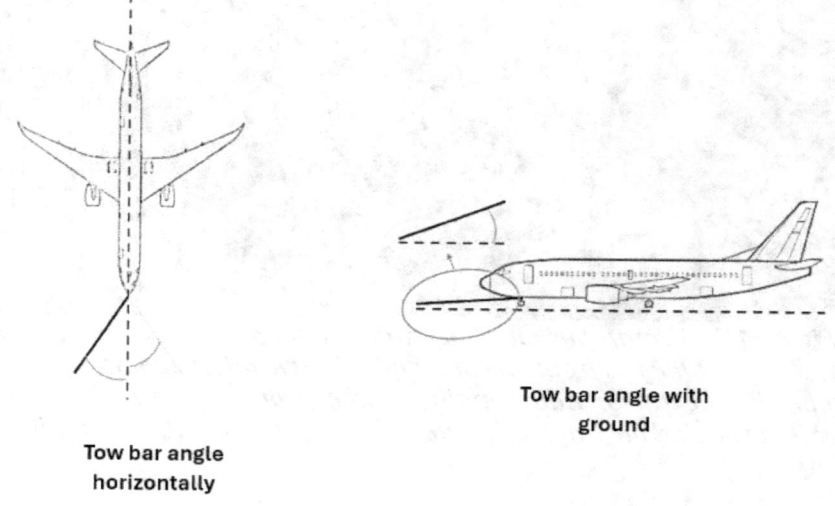

Tow bar angle with ground

Tow bar angle horizontally

Figure 118: Tow bar angles.

This sequence is essential as it allows for proper alignment of the towbar with the aircraft's line of symmetry, ensuring correct engagement. Consequently, the pushback tractor is then adjusted to establish the connection, utilizing the aircraft and towbar as reference points. Additionally, attention must be paid to the angle of engagement of the towbar, particularly its alignment with both the aircraft's line of symmetry and the ground. While the former angle governs the steering of the aircraft during pushback, the latter angle must be minimized to mitigate the risk of towbar snapping due to buckling forces.

The removal of aircraft chocks should only occur once the towbar and pushback tractor have been securely engaged with the aircraft, and the pushback tractor driver is present inside the vehicle. This precaution is vital as the chocks serve to prevent aircraft movement should the brakes be released from the cockpit. Without proper engagement of the pushback tractor, the aircraft's brakes become the sole barrier to prevent unintended movement. Mistakenly releasing the brakes could result in uncontrolled aircraft rolling, posing risks such as collision with the tractor or causing injury to personnel.

Numerous incidents worldwide underscore the importance of this protocol, where accidents involving aircraft running over individuals have occurred due to the premature removal of chocks and inadvertent release of brakes. Once the pushback tractor is correctly positioned, and the driver is inside, the pilot may safely release the parking brakes. These brakes, located on the front and rear landing gears, function similarly to those in a car, preventing the aircraft from rolling under slopes or external forces. Without releasing the parking brakes before pushback begins, attempting to push the aircraft could lead to detrimental consequences, such as the towbar snapping or the nose landing gear collapsing (Aviation Learnings, 2020).

To ensure ramp safety, clear communication and precise phraseology between the aircraft pushback crew and the pilot are paramount. It is essential for both parties to use unambiguous language regarding the status of the aircraft brakes. For instance, instead of a vague statement like "Cleared for pushback," specific instructions such as "Ready for pushback. Please release the parking brakes" followed by confirmation from the pilot and acknowledgment from the crew minimize any misunderstanding and ensure a safe pushback operation.

Maintaining uninterrupted communication between the headset man and the pilot is imperative during aircraft pushback operations. Any disruption in this communication, whether due to technical issues or other reasons, warrants an immediate halt to the pushback operation until the problem is resolved. If the issue persists and communication cannot be restored, the headset man must inform the pilot, and a mutual decision must be made regarding the continuation of the operation without audible communication. Some airports also require notification to the control tower in such instances to ensure additional precautions are taken, such as avoiding parallel pushback on adjacent aircraft stands. Clear communication is essential to prevent misunderstandings and ensure that any further communication with ground crew is conducted through hand signals if necessary.

Effective communication during aircraft pushback operations extends beyond the pilot and ground crew to include the control tower. It is essential that any clearance issued by the air traffic controller is unambiguous and unconditional, eliminating any ambiguity or decision-making on the part of the pushback crew and pilot. Additionally, pushback tractor drivers should monitor the control tower frequency to receive instructions and observe any discrepancies in instructions between the controller and the pilot. Encouraging open communication and removing reluctance to challenge decisions from pushback crews contribute to enhancing safety during pushback operations (Aviation Learnings, 2020).

During pushback operations, the headset man plays a crucial role in maintaining visual communication with the pilot. It is essential for the headset man to walk alongside the aircraft, maintaining eye contact with the pilot, rather than riding inside the pushback tractor. This ensures clear visual communication and orientation for the pilot and enhances coordination among the pushback crew. Moreover, wing walkers and tail walkers play a vital role in ensuring the safety of the pushback operation by providing additional visibility and communication regarding the clearance of aircraft wings and tail. Their involvement is particularly critical for wide-body aircraft due to challenges in accurately perceiving distances and clearances. Effective coordination and communication among all members of the pushback crew are essential to prevent accidents and ensure the safe execution of pushback operations.

Several safety precautions must be observed during pushback operations to minimize the risk of injury and accidents. These include ensuring that personnel avoid walking alongside the towbar and refraining from stepping across it to prevent injury from potential towbar failure or stumbling accidents. Additionally, pushback operations should be conducted at a slow pace to maintain control and prevent hazards associated with excessive speed. Engine startup procedures must be carefully coordinated to avoid conflicts between the pushback tractor and aircraft engines, particularly under wet conditions, which may compromise traction and stability. Proper training and adherence to safety protocols are essential to mitigate risks associated with engine startup and ensure the safe execution of pushback operations.

Just as the initial sequence of releasing parking brakes, removing chocks, and connecting the towbar to the pushback tractor is crucial, the sequence at the end of the pushback operation is equally significant for safety. At the conclusion of the pushback operation, it is imperative to apply the aircraft parking brakes before disconnecting the pushback tractor. This sequence is crucial because pilots typically start one of the main jet engines towards the end of the pushback operation. Without applying the parking brakes, disengaging the towbar or pushback tractor could lead to the aircraft instantly moving forward due to the thrust produced by the engine, potentially resulting in an accident.

The final step in the aircraft pushback operation involves the insertion and removal of the bypass pin, a critical safety measure. Initially, the pushback crew inserts the bypass pin into the nose landing gear of the aircraft, effectively disabling the cockpit crew's steering control and granting full steering authority to the pushback crew. This control is necessary for the pushback tractor to steer the aircraft during reverse movement. However, once the pushback operation is complete, it is essential to return steering control to the cockpit.

Forgetting to remove the bypass pin can prevent the cockpit crew from manoeuvring the aircraft, potentially leading to an accident. To mitigate this risk, a standard safety procedure is followed after completing the pushback operation. The pushback crew disconnects all equipment, removes the bypass pin, and stands at a suitable distance from the aircraft, visible to the cockpit crew. The cockpit crew visually confirms that no equipment remains under the nose of the aircraft and observes the pushback crew raising their arm with the bypass pin, indicating its removal. Only after visual confirmation of these steps do they proceed with taxiing for departure. This procedure incorporates human factors to enhance ramp safety during the pushback operation.

Concluding Pushback Tug Operations

Post-operational checks of the tug are vital to ensure its continued functionality and safety. These checks should be conducted in accordance with workplace procedures and manufacturer instructions. The process typically involves a thorough inspection of the tug's various components and systems to identify any faults or malfunctions that may have arisen during operation. This includes examining the engine, transmission, hydraulic system, brakes, lights, and any other relevant equipment.

If any equipment faults or malfunctions are identified during the post-operational checks, they should be rectified promptly or reported in accordance with workplace procedures and regulatory requirements. This may involve performing minor repairs or adjustments on-site, or notifying maintenance personnel for further investigation and repair.

MATERIAL HANDLING EQUIPMENT OPERATION

Prompt action is essential to prevent potential safety hazards and ensure the tug remains in optimal working condition.

Following the completion of checks and any necessary repairs, the tug should be refuelled, and fluid levels topped up as per workplace procedures and manufacturer instructions. This ensures that the tug is ready for its next operation and can perform efficiently without any interruptions due to low fuel or fluid levels. Additionally, proper refuelling and fluid maintenance help prolong the lifespan of the tug's components and prevent premature wear and tear.

Finally, it is essential to complete the equipment log or operational documentation in accordance with workplace procedures, local instructions, and regulatory requirements. This documentation serves as a record of the tug's operational history, including any maintenance or repairs conducted, fuel consumption, fluid top-ups, and any other relevant information. Accurate and thorough documentation is crucial for maintaining compliance with regulatory standards and ensuring accountability for the tug's operation and maintenance activities.

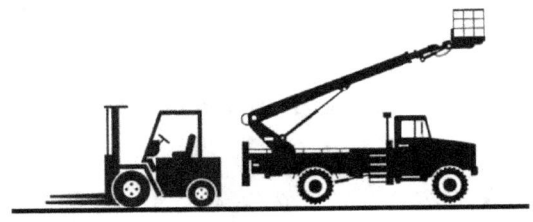

References

Anster. (2024). *What is a container side lifter? – Learn the Design and Specs*. Retrieved 2/3/2024 from

Association Sectorielle Transport Entreposage. (2010). *Order Picking Truck*.

Aviation Learnings. (2020, 2/3/2024). How Aircraft Pushback Tractors Work?

Conger. (2024, 27/2/2024). What Are Order Pickers? [Definition, Types, Pros/Cons, Uses].

Construction Plant-hire Association. (2015). *Safe Use of Telehandlers in Construction*

EP Equipment. (2019). *How to drive a low level order picker*. Retrieved 27/2/2024 from

Hammar. (2017). *Hammar User Manual*.

Hinz, P. (2013, 27/2/2024). Order Pickers - Operating Safely at Height *Logistics & Materials Handling Blog*.

JLG. (2020, 27/2/2024). Order Pickers: Seven Tips for Safer Operation at Your Facility.

Logisnext. (2024). *Anatomy and Parts of a Forklift*. Retrieved 26/2/2024 from

Paul. (2022, 29/8/2024). Popular telehandler types and their benefits.

Sanders, D. (2008). Controlling the Direction of "Walkie" Type Forklifts and Pallet Jacks on Sloping Ground. *Assembly Automation*.

Taylor Machine Works. (2024). Safety Check.

Vector Solutions. (2023, 26/2/2024). How to Operate a Forklift: Pre-Operation, Traveling, Load Handling, and Maintenance.

Index

A

Agriculture, 15–16

Airport operations, 396

Attachment, 17–18, 136–137, 156–157, 172–173, 175, 177–178, 181, 196–200, 204, 212–213, 219, 222–223, 228, 231, 282, 291, 298, 303, 315–317, 320, 327, 340–342, 353–355

Attachment Capacity, 157

Attachments, 15–16, 136–139, 145–147, 149, 157, 169–179, 183, 186, 191, 196–197, 199–201, 204, 212–213, 219–223, 226, 231, 250, 308, 313, 346, 359

B

Boom, 15–16, 18, 136–149, 152–156, 158–161, 163–167, 169, 177–178, 185–186, 191, 194, 196, 200–202, 204–205, 207–209, 212–215, 217, 220, 224, 226, 228, 235, 240–243, 246–247, 256–257, 260–262, 264, 270, 272–275, 277, 279, 282–284, 288–289, 295–297, 301

Braking, 22, 400, 413

Bucket, 15, 143, 175, 235

C

Certification, 10

Construction, 12, 15–16, 235, 243, 246–247, 294

Container handling, 19, 21, 304–305, 308, 348–349

Container spreader, 348, 350, 358

Container terminals, 303

Container yards, 18, 303

Controls, 14, 17, 20, 22, 91–92, 95, 114–115, 121–123, 133, 145–146, 168, 171, 183–192, 196, 203, 205, 207, 210, 219, 233, 240, 247, 267–268, 272–274, 276–278, 285, 288–291, 314, 332, 339, 345–348, 355–356, 359–360, 368–369, 373, 377–378, 386, 391, 401, 415–416, 419

Counterweight, 242

D

Data Plate, 114, 124, 129, 211, 258–259

Diesel, 12, 22, 34, 145, 258, 264, 274, 305–307, 338, 367, 394, 398–399, 405

Dock, 131, 363, 366

E

Electric, 12, 90, 92, 118–119, 134, 243, 258, 277, 279, 286, 304, 306–307, 367, 381

Elevated work area, 242, 245–246, 248

Elevating work platform, 11, 16–17, 235, 239, 241, 245, 253–254, 256, 258, 260, 263–264, 268, 271, 276, 278, 280, 291–292

Emergency lowering, 17, 239, 272–278, 285

Emergency procedures, 258, 278, 287

Equipment, 9–13, 15–19, 21–22, 25, 27, 29, 31, 33, 35, 37, 39, 41, 43, 45, 47, 49, 51, 53, 55, 57, 59, 61, 63, 65, 67, 69, 71, 73, 75, 77, 79, 81, 83, 85, 87, 91, 93, 95, 97, 99, 101, 103, 105, 107, 109, 111, 113, 115, 117, 119, 121, 123, 125, 127, 129, 131, 133, 135, 137, 139, 141, 143, 145, 147, 149, 151, 153, 155, 157, 159, 161, 163, 165, 167, 169, 171, 173, 175, 177, 179, 181, 183, 185, 187, 189, 191, 193, 195, 197, 199, 201, 203, 205, 207, 209, 211, 213, 215, 217, 219, 221,

223, 225, 227, 229, 231, 233, 235, 237, 239, 241, 243, 245, 247, 249–253, 255–261, 263, 265, 267, 269–271, 273–277, 279–281, 283–287, 289, 291, 293, 295–301, 305, 307, 309, 311, 313, 315, 317, 319, 321, 323, 325, 327, 329, 331, 333, 335, 337, 339, 341, 343, 345, 347, 349, 351, 353, 355, 357, 359, 361, 363, 365, 367, 369, 371, 373, 375, 377, 379, 381, 383, 385, 387, 389, 391, 395, 397, 399, 401–403, 405, 407, 409, 411, 413, 415, 417, 419, 421, 423, 425, 427, 429

F

Fall arrest system, 259
Fall protection, 91, 109, 254–255
Forks, 12, 15, 92, 98, 119, 125–127, 129, 133
Fuel, 274, 276, 297, 306, 337–338, 341, 347

G

Ground crew, 421, 424
Guardrails, 14, 17, 239, 242, 254–255, 290, 294

H

Handling, 9–13, 15–19, 21, 25, 27, 29, 31, 33, 35, 37, 39, 41, 43, 45, 47, 49, 51, 53, 55, 57, 59, 61, 63, 65, 67, 69, 71, 73, 75, 77, 79, 81, 83, 85, 87, 90–91, 93, 95, 97, 99, 101, 103, 105, 107, 109, 111, 113, 115, 117, 119, 121, 123, 125, 127, 129, 131, 133, 135, 137, 139, 141, 143, 145, 147, 149, 151, 153, 155, 157, 159, 161, 163, 165, 167, 169, 171, 173, 175, 177, 179, 181, 183, 185, 187, 189, 191, 193, 195, 197, 199, 201, 203, 205, 207, 209, 211, 213, 215, 217, 219, 221, 223, 225, 227, 229, 231, 233, 237, 239, 241, 243, 245, 247, 249, 251, 253, 255, 257, 259, 261, 263, 265–267, 269, 271, 273, 275, 277, 279, 281, 283, 285, 287, 289, 291, 293, 295–297, 299, 301, 303–309, 311–315, 317, 319, 321, 323, 325–327, 329, 331, 333, 335, 337–339, 341, 343, 345, 347–349, 351, 353–355, 357, 359, 361, 363, 365, 367, 369, 371, 373, 375, 377, 379, 381,

383, 385, 387, 389, 391, 393, 395, 397–399, 401, 403, 405–411, 413, 415, 417, 419, 421, 423, 425, 427, 429

Handling equipment, 9–13, 15, 17–19, 21, 25, 27, 29, 31, 33, 35, 37, 39, 41, 43, 45, 47, 49, 51, 53, 55, 57, 59, 61, 63, 65, 67, 69, 71, 73, 75, 77, 79, 81, 83, 85, 87, 91, 93, 95, 97, 99, 101, 103, 105, 107, 109, 111, 113, 115, 117, 119, 121, 123, 125, 127, 129, 131, 133, 135, 137, 139, 141, 143, 145, 147, 149, 151, 153, 155, 157, 159, 161, 163, 165, 167, 169, 171, 173, 175, 177, 179, 181, 183, 185, 187, 189, 191, 193, 195, 197, 199, 201, 203, 205, 207, 209, 211, 213, 215, 217, 219, 221, 223, 225, 227, 229, 231, 233, 237, 239, 241, 243, 245, 247, 249, 251, 253, 255, 257, 259, 261, 263, 265, 267, 269, 271, 273, 275, 277, 279, 281, 283, 285, 287, 289, 291, 293, 295, 297, 299, 301, 305, 307, 309, 311, 313, 315, 317, 319, 321, 323, 325, 327, 329, 331, 333, 335, 337, 339, 341, 343, 345, 347, 349, 351, 353, 355, 357, 359, 361, 363, 365, 367, 369, 371, 373, 375, 377, 379, 381, 383, 385, 387, 389, 391, 395, 397, 399, 401, 403, 405, 407, 409, 411, 413, 415, 417, 419, 421, 423, 425, 427, 429

Hydraulic system, 15, 18, 22, 242–243, 245–246, 248, 255, 257, 272, 295, 299, 312, 345–346, 354

Hydraulics, 339, 343, 359

I

Industrial, 11–13, 15, 243, 247, 305, 352

Inspection, 105–106, 108, 115–119, 124, 135, 164, 184, 189, 192, 200, 203–204, 213, 218, 221–222, 227, 229–230, 248, 252, 255–257, 259, 266, 268, 275, 277, 282, 287, 295, 298, 323, 328–331, 339–340, 342, 345, 356, 408, 411–412, 417, 421, 426

Intermodal operations, 307

L

Load, 10–13, 15–16, 19, 39, 90–91, 95–96, 98–99, 101, 104–105, 109, 111, 114–115, 120, 123, 125–132, 136–140, 142–146, 148–150, 152–167, 169, 171–172, 174, 177–178, 182, 193–194, 196–201, 204–218, 227, 248–249,

253–254, 256–258, 260–261, 265, 278, 292, 294, 304–305, 307–308, 311–313, 315–322, 326–328, 333, 346, 350–353, 355–360, 367–370, 372–374, 378–380, 382–384, 429

Load capacity, 91, 95–96, 98, 104, 115, 123, 160, 212, 249, 254, 257–258, 260, 265, 320, 326

Load Chart, 10, 138, 155, 158–164, 172, 198–200, 211, 213, 218, 256–257, 261

Loading and unloading, 11, 313

Logistics, 11–12, 19, 21, 303–304, 308

M

Maintenance, 16, 155, 169–170, 175, 181–182, 184–185, 192–193, 195, 200, 221–223, 229–231, 233, 235, 243, 246–247, 256–259, 266, 268, 274, 290, 295, 301, 328, 337–340, 356

Manoeuvring, 21, 249, 303, 326, 349, 357

Material handling, 9, 11–13, 15, 17–19, 21, 25, 27, 29, 31, 33, 35, 37, 39, 41, 43, 45, 47, 49, 51, 53, 55, 57, 59, 61, 63, 65, 67, 69, 71, 73, 75, 77, 79, 81, 83, 85, 87, 90–91, 93, 95, 97, 99, 101, 103, 105, 107, 109, 111, 113, 115, 117, 119, 121, 123, 125, 127, 129, 131, 133, 135, 137, 139, 141, 143, 145, 147, 149, 151, 153, 155, 157, 159, 161, 163, 165, 167, 169, 171, 173, 175, 177, 179, 181, 183, 185, 187, 189, 191, 193, 195, 197, 199, 201, 203, 205, 207, 209, 211, 213, 215, 217, 219, 221, 223, 225, 227, 229, 231, 233, 237, 239, 241, 243, 245, 247, 249, 251, 253, 255, 257, 259, 261, 263, 265, 267, 269, 271, 273, 275, 277, 279, 281, 283, 285, 287, 289, 291, 293, 295, 297, 299, 301, 303–305, 307, 309, 311–315, 317, 319, 321, 323, 325, 327, 329, 331, 333, 335, 337, 339, 341, 343, 345, 347, 349, 351, 353, 355, 357, 359, 361, 363, 365, 367, 369, 371, 373, 375, 377, 379, 381, 383, 385, 387, 389, 391, 395, 397, 399, 401, 403, 405, 407, 409, 411, 413, 415, 417, 419, 421, 423, 425, 427, 429

O

Operating manual, 253, 290

Operator, 9–10, 12–15, 17, 19–20, 22, 89–96, 98–99, 104, 106–114, 117, 120, 122, 125–126, 128, 138, 140, 145–148, 157–158, 163, 166–172, 185–187, 192–194, 196, 200–203, 205, 210–211, 213, 218–219, 228–229, 231, 233, 242–243, 246–248, 254–257, 259–262, 266–267, 270, 275, 278–279, 281, 286, 289–292, 298, 300–301, 313, 316–317, 320–321, 326–328, 330–331, 333, 336–341, 343, 345, 347–348, 352–355, 357–360, 400–401, 415–421

Overhead clearance, 356

P

Pallet, 11, 13, 16, 96–97, 109, 114, 122, 131, 140–141, 146, 169

Pedestrians, 109–110, 148, 166, 169–171, 201, 220, 284, 324, 329, 344, 352, 355–356

Personal protective equipment (PPE), 249, 252, 255, 267, 270, 274, 280, 298, 402

Platform, 9, 11, 13–17, 92, 176, 235–236, 238–243, 245–247, 252–258, 260, 263–264, 267–268, 271–272, 274–278, 280–284, 286–294, 297–298

Productivity, 11–12, 15, 19, 312

Propane, 12

Pushback tug, 393, 399–401, 415–416, 418, 426

R

Ramp, 224–225, 283, 289, 352, 355

Rated Capacity, 10, 129, 155, 157, 256–257, 317, 320, 353

Reach, 9, 11, 13, 15–16, 18–19, 136–137, 140, 142, 144–145, 157–158, 163, 166, 177–180, 186, 194, 212, 236, 240–241, 243, 246, 260, 262, 303–308, 311–350, 352–361, 401, 416

Repairs, 17, 117, 135, 183, 246, 256, 413, 426–427

Rescue equipment, 291

Rescue plan, 277–278, 292

Risk assessment, 168, 170, 197, 217, 253, 280, 290
Rotating, 19, 141, 148, 162, 243, 339
Rough terrain, 235, 305

S

Safety, 9–14, 17, 19, 90–93, 95–96, 100–101, 103, 107–111, 113–118, 121, 124, 126, 129–132, 187, 191, 235, 239, 242, 245, 248, 250, 252, 254–259, 261, 263, 265, 267–272, 275, 278–283, 286, 288–290, 292, 295–301, 308, 311, 313–314, 317, 321, 323–325, 328–331, 333–334, 338, 340, 343–345, 348–349, 351, 355–356, 358–359

Side loader, 9, 19–21, 362–366, 373, 376–378, 381–383, 385–391

Speed, 21, 91, 110, 118, 130, 152–153, 160, 162, 167, 171, 185, 200–201, 203–204, 210, 215, 218, 257, 269, 282–285, 289–290, 292–293, 335, 343, 346, 350, 398, 400, 404, 415, 417, 420, 425

Stability, 16–17, 19, 151–152, 154, 239, 241–243, 246–248, 253–254, 257, 265–267, 280, 282–283, 285, 291–294, 332

Stability Triangle, 152

Stack, 12, 18, 206–207, 212, 217, 351, 355

Stacking, 16, 18, 178, 206, 304–307, 320, 357

Steering, 13–14, 20, 22, 144, 185, 284, 303, 312–314, 332, 342, 344–346, 348, 350–351, 400–402, 411, 413, 415, 422, 425–426

T

Telehandler, 15–16, 136–175, 177–179, 181–223, 225–231, 233

Telescopic, 15–16, 18, 20, 136–137, 139–140, 142–143, 145, 166, 176, 178, 186, 191, 205, 236, 240, 243, 313

Tilt, 128, 153, 186, 191, 194, 205, 207–209, 242, 259, 288, 320–321, 346, 370

Tip-over, 278, 326

Towing, 22, 395–396, 398–400, 405, 407–410, 416

Training, 12, 17, 19, 239, 252, 255, 296, 329–330, 339, 418, 425

Truck trailer, 9, 19–21, 362, 364

V

Visibility, 191, 287

W

Warehouse, 12–13, 15, 17, 235, 293
Work at height, 276, 287

www.ingramcontent.com/pod-product-compliance
Lightning Source LLC
Chambersburg PA
CBHW072144070526
44585CB00015B/996